Oxford *Living* GRAMMAR

elementary

Ken Paterson

OXFORD
UNIVERSITY PRESS

OXFORD
UNIVERSITY PRESS

Great Clarendon Street, Oxford OX2 6DP

Oxford University Press is a department of the University of Oxford.
It furthers the University's objective of excellence in research, scholarship,
and education by publishing worldwide in

Oxford New York

Auckland Cape Town Dar es Salaam Hong Kong Karachi
Kuala Lumpur Madrid Melbourne Mexico City Nairobi
New Delhi Shanghai Taipei Toronto

With offices in

Argentina Austria Brazil Chile Czech Republic France Greece
Guatemala Hungary Italy Japan Poland Portugal Singapore
South Korea Switzerland Thailand Turkey Ukraine Vietnam

OXFORD and OXFORD ENGLISH are registered trade marks of
Oxford University Press in the UK and in certain other countries

ISBN: 978 0 19 455703 0 Student's Book
ISBN: 978 0 19 455704 7 Student's CD-ROM Pack

Printed in China

ACKNOWLEDGEMENTS

Illustrations by: Tim Bradford/www.illustrationweb.com pp 16 (Paris), 16
(theatre), 20, 22, 28, 34, 34, 38, (weather and walking the dog), 42, 44 (boat),
(sandwiches), 46, 48, 50 (computers), 50 (window), 52, 52, 54 (car), 54 (dog), 54
(swimmer), 56 (waiter), 58, 58, 60 (party planning), 62, 62, 64 (car), 64 (hotel),
66, 66, 66, 68 (directions), 68 (plates), 68 (umbrella), 70, 70, 72, 72, 72, 76, 76,
78, 78, 80, 80, 82, 82, 84 (grandparents' belongings), 86, 88, 88, 90 (elephant),
90 (lecture), 92, 92, 94, 100, 100, 102, 102, 106 (desk), 106 (bowl), 108, 108,
110, 110, 111 (Paul/Rubberball Productions), 112, 114, 116, 118, 118, 120;
Frances Castle/www.arenaworks.com pp 19, 21, 44 (car), 50 (snooker etc), 53,
59, 60 (wardrobe etc), 68 (black dog), 69, 81, 89, 95, 97, 97, 103, 113, 121; Ned
Jolliffe pp 16 (instruments), 17, 39, (street in Bristol), 47, 54 (polite requests),
56 (lamp etc), 63, 64 (waiter), 73, 83, 84 (food shop), 85, 90 (garden), 98, 99,
101, 106 (computer), 107, 109, 115, 115, 117

*We would also like to thank the following for permission to reproduce the following
photographs*: Alamy p 104 (ImageState); Getty Images pp (Ling Wang/
Imagemore), 9 (restaurant/Antonio Mo), 67 (woman/UpperCut Images), 67
(pool/AAGAMIA), 111 (Paul/Rubberball Productions); Photolibrary.com pp 87,
111 (Toronto/Chromorange)

Images sourced by: SuzanneWilliams/Pictureresearch.co.uk

Introduction

What is Oxford Living Grammar?

Oxford Living Grammar is a series of three books which explain and practise grammar in **everyday contexts**. They show how grammar is used in **real-life situations** that learners themselves will experience. The books can be used for self-study, for homework, and in class.

Elementary: CEF level A1+ (towards KET level)
Pre-intermediate: CEF level B1 (KET and towards PET level)
Intermediate: CEF level B2 (PET and towards FCE level)

How are the books organized?

The books are divided into four-page units, each of which deals with an important grammar topic. Units are divided into two two-page parts. Each unit begins with an explanation of the grammar point, and includes a unique **Grammar in action** section which shows how the grammar is used in typical everyday situations. It explains **when** to use the grammar point. This is followed by a number of **contextualized exercises** for learners to practise the grammar they have read about. The second part of each unit introduces additional explanation of the topic, more Grammar in action, and more contextualized exercises. The last exercise in every unit provides practice of a variety of the points and contexts introduced across the four pages.

The intention is that the fully contextualized explanations and exercises will show real English in real situations, which learners can recognize and apply to their own experience.

Word focus boxes highlight unfamiliar words or expressions and enable learners to widen their vocabulary.

The **Over to you** section at the back of the book provides a **comprehensive bank of review exercises**. Learners are encouraged to complete freer practice exercises and more creative tasks about themselves. The sample answers to these tasks provide a bank of texts for extra reading practice.

There is an *Oxford Living Grammar* **Context-Plus CD-ROM** at each level with further grammar practice and Word focus exercises. Learners can also build longer texts, and build and take part in dialogues; learners can record and listen to their own voice to improve pronunciation. There are six grammar tests at each level so learners can see if there are any areas they would like to study again.

What grammar is included?

At Elementary level, you will study much of the grammar necessary for Cambridge KET. The choice of contexts in the exercises has been informed by the Common European Framework of Reference and the framework of the Association of Language Testers in Europe at A1+.

How can students use Oxford Living Grammar on their own?

You can work through the book from beginning to end. All the units will present and practise the grammar in typical everyday situations. When you have finished the exercises, you can go to the Over to you task for that topic at the back of the book for extra practice, and then check your answers.

When you have a particular grammar problem, you might want to study that topic first. You can look up the topic you need in the Contents at the front of the book, or in the Index at the back.

How can teachers use the material in the classroom?

Oxford Living Grammar enables your students to learn and practise English grammar in context. The contexts themselves are typical everyday situations that your students will experience, such as talking about their own experiences, having conversations with people they have met, talking about other people, and discussing common topics.

The syllabus is divided into 30 four-page units, which we hope will make the book ideal for study over an academic year. Units can be studied in any order, or you and your students can work through the book from beginning to end. The Over to you tasks provide freer practice and more creative review tasks.

Contents

01 *Be*: Present simple
I am; I'm not

1 Some examples of **be** in the **present simple**.

*This **is** my brother. He's ten years old.*
*I'm eighteen and a student; these **are** my books.*
*My parents **aren't** at home; they're at work.*

2 Here are the **present simple** forms of **be**:

POSITIVE	Full form	Short form
Singular	I **am**	I'**m**
	you **are**	you'**re**
	he/she/it **is**	he/she/it'**s**
Plural	we **are**	we'**re**
	you **are**	you'**re**
	they **are**	they'**re**

NEGATIVE	Full form	Short form
Singular	I **am not**	I'**m not**
	you **are not**	you'**re not** *or* you **aren't**
	he/she/it **is not**	he/she/it'**s not** *or* he/she/it **isn't**
Plural	we **are not**	we'**re not** *or* we **aren't**
	you **are not**	you'**re not** *or* you **aren't**
	they **are not**	they'**re not** *or* they **aren't**

> **TIP**
> We usually use the short forms in speech.
> *She's my sister. He's my brother.*
> *I'm from Germany. They're students.*

→ For information on **question forms**, see p. 4.

3 We use **be** to talk about the family, jobs, saying who we are, talking about the weather or a location and talking about age.

Grammar in action

1 We use **be** when we introduce ourselves and our families:

These are my sisters and this is my brother.
I'm Steve; this is my partner, Ruth.
She's 30 years old but I'm younger.

2 We use **be** when we talk about our jobs:

I am a doctor and they are nurses.

3 We use **be** when we say where we're from:

I'm from Brazil; my aunt is Portuguese.
I'm not from England. I'm from Wales.

4 We use **be** when we talk about the weather:

It's a beautiful day but it's cold.
It's not very warm today and it's very windy.

5 We use **be** when we talk about location:

Milan is in the north but it isn't near Venice.

> **TIP**
> We also use **be** to form continuous tenses.
> → For more information on the **present continuous**, see p. 10.

A Introductions

(i) Add the correct forms of *be*. Use the short form where possible.

I ___'m___ ⁰ 20 and I _____¹ a student. My father _____² from Brazil. My mother _____³ (not) from Brazil. She _____⁴ Irish. Her parents _____⁵ from Dublin. Paul and Simon _____⁶ my brothers. They _____⁷ both teachers. Simon _____⁸ 23 and Paul _____⁹ 25, so I _____¹⁰ (not) the oldest.

(ii) Which use of *be* in (i) matches these contexts? Choose one example.

0 Age ___I'm 20.___
1 Job _____
2 Nationality _____
3 Family _____

B   Home, nationality and jobs

We're meeting people at a party. What are they saying? Add the correct forms of *be*.
Use the short form where possible.

Paola and Federico _____ *are* _____ ⁰
from Naples. Naples _____ ¹
in the south of Italy. Paola
_____ ² a photographer and
Federico _____ ³ a dentist.

We _____ ⁴ artists.
We _____ ⁵ English.
We _____ ⁶ from London.

I _____ ⁷ a teacher.
This is my husband, Tom.
We _____ ⁸ from Scotland.

C   The weather and location

It's the first day of a new class. Four students are talking about
their countries. Add the correct forms of *be* or one of the words in
the box. Use the pictures to help you.

sunny	sea	near	south	north	cold

KUMIKO   Hello. I'm Kumiko. I'm from Tomakomai. It *'s* _____ ⁰ in the
north ⁰ of Japan.
It*'s* _____ ⁰ cold in the winter, and it _____ ¹ hot
in the summer. Tomakomai _____ ² a small town
_____ ³ Sapporo.

GALINA   Hi, I'm Galina. I'm from St. Petersburg. It _____ ⁴ in the
west of Russia. It _____ ⁵ (not) very hot! In fact, it's very
_____ ⁶ in the winter. But sometimes it _____ ⁷
sunny! St. Petersburg _____ ⁸ (not) the capital of Russia,
of course, but it's a very big city.

ABBAS   I'm Abbas, and this is my cousin, Sulama. We're from
Oman. It _____ ⁹ a hot country and it's very _____ ¹⁰.

SULAMA   We're from two small towns in the _____ ¹¹, Salalah
and Mirbat. They _____ ¹² by the _____ ¹³. They
_____ ¹⁴ (not) near Muscat, the capital city. Muscat
_____ ¹⁵ a thousand kilometres away.

4 To make questions with **be**, we put the verb before the subject:

QUESTIONS			
Singular	**Am** I?	Plural	**Are** we?
	Are you?		**Are** you?
	Is he/she/it?		**Are** they?

5 These questions can be answered with *yes* or *no*:

> **Are** you here on holiday? ~ *Yes, I am.*
> **Is** your son a student? ~ *No, he's not.*

The answers are short: *Yes, I am.*
NOT ~~Yes, I am on holiday.~~

→ For more information on **yes/no questions** and **short answers** see unit 12.

6 We can use question words to make questions with **be**, too:

> **What's** your job?
> **Where are** your friends?
> **How old is** your brother?

→ For more information on **question words**, see unit 12.

Grammar in action

6 We use **be + adjective** to describe how we feel. We might talk about a journey:

> *Are you unhappy? ~ No, but I'm cold and tired. ~ I'm sorry. It's a long journey.*

7 We use **be + noun** and **be + adjective** to describe things. Here, we're describing a house in our village:

> *It's a lovely old house and the garden's very large, but it's so expensive!*

€5,000,000

> We can use **there + be** to talk about where things are or when things happen.
> → For more information, see p. 82.

TIP

D Asking and answering questions

Ming is a student from Shanghai. This is her first day in London. People ask her questions at the airport and at her new college. First put the words in the right order to make the questions on the left of the page.

0 *Is this your suitcase?* (your suitcase/this/is) *Yes, it is.*

1 .... (a student/you/are) ....

2 .... ('s/your name/what) ....

3 .... (you/are/how old) ....

4 .... (are/from Hong Kong/you) ....

5 .... (your ID card, please/is/where) ....

6 .... (what/your address in the UK/'s)

Now write these answers in the correct spaces next to the questions above:

> Here it is.   I'm 22.   Yes, I am.   ~~Yes, it is.~~   No, I'm from Shanghai.
> It's The Hyde Park Hotel, Queensway, London W2 3BJ.   It's Ming Yifeng.

Finally, use a form of *be* to make the questions that Ming asks at her college and hotel.

0 *Is this my new timetable?* (this my new timetable)

0 What time *is our first class?* (our first class)

7 .... (this your first day here, too)

8 Where .... (you from)

9 .... (I in the correct classroom)

10 .... (this the bus to Queensway)

11 Where .... (the Hyde Park Hotel, please)

12 What time .... (breakfast tomorrow morning)

E A holiday conversation

Sally is on holiday in Greece. She meets Liga in a café. Add the word(s) in brackets and a form of *be* to their conversation. Use capital letters where necessary.

SALLY   Hi, _____I'm_____ 0 (I) Sally.

LIGA   Pleased to meet you. I'm Liga. .... 1 (you) here on holiday?

SALLY   Yes. .... 2 (it) a beautiful town, and it's so sunny here! But .... 3 (I) sad because it's my last day.

LIGA   Oh, I'm sorry. Where .... 4 (you) from, Sally?

SALLY   Athenry. .... 5 (it) a nice little town in Ireland, but .... 6 (it/not) very sunny. And you?

LIGA   I'm from Riga. It's the capital of Latvia. I'm here with my boyfriend, and .... 7 (this) our first day, so .... 8 (we) happy!

SALLY   .... 9 (you) lucky!

WAITER   Good morning, ladies. Would you like something to eat?

SALLY   .... 10 (I/not) hungry, thanks, but I'd like an orange juice, please.

LIGA   .... 11 (I) thirsty, too. A lemonade, please.

SALLY   Well, ... 12 (it) good to meet you, Liga, if only for a day!

F At a bus stop

Katie and Asif meet Dieter at a bus stop. After the example, add twenty more positive and two more negative forms of *be*. Use capital letters where necessary.

ASIF   Look at the time. It's two in the morning. Where we?

KATIE   On Burley Street, I think. you hungry, Asif?

ASIF   No, I hungry, but I tired. Where the bus stop?

KATIE   Look, it there! Come on!

(At the bus stop they meet Dieter.)

ASIF   Excuse me. this the bus stop for Rayne's Park?

DIETER   Yes, I hope so. It a cold night.

KATIE   Hi. I Katie and this my friend Asif.

DIETER   Pleased to meet you. I Dieter. you students?

KATIE   No, we students. We doctors. And you?

DIETER   I a waiter at the Hamburger restaurant on Park Street.

ASIF   Where you from? you German?

DIETER   No, I Austrian, but I in Leicester for six months. It an interesting city.

KATIE   Look, the bus here! I hope it warm inside. After you, Dieter. Come on, Asif.

OVER TO YOU Now go to page 122.

02 Present simple
I work; he studies

1 Some examples of the **present simple**:
> I **come** from France, but I **speak** English.
> She usually **phones** me at the weekend.
> We **live** in the centre of Beijing.

2 The positive form of the **present simple** only changes after *he/she/it*:

POSITIVE			
Singular	I **stop**	Plural	we **stop**
	you **stop**		you **stop**
	he/she/it **stops**		they **stop**

3 The changes after **he/she/it**:

For most verbs, we add **-s**:

> I eat → she eat**s**   they pay → he pay**s**

But for verbs ending in **-o**, **-ch**, **-sh**, **-ss** and **-x**, we add **e** before **-s**:

> I go → it go**es**   I wash → she wash**es**
> you fix → she fix**es**   they miss → he miss**es**
> we watch → he watch**es**

And for verbs ending in a consonant (b, c, d, etc.) + **y**, we change the **y** to **ie**, and then add **-s**:

> I carry → he carr**ies**   you study → she stud**ies**

For the verb **have**, we say 'he/she/it **has**…':

> These spelling rules work for nouns too:
>   potato → potato**es**   match → match**es**
>   box → box**es**   baby → bab**ies**
> TIP

4 We use the **present simple** to talk about ourselves, where we live, and where we work, to talk about our hobbies and timetables, to talk about things we don't like and to talk about things we don't know.

→ For information on **present simple negative**, see p. 8.

Grammar in action

1 We use the **present simple** to talk about facts. Here, we're talking about where we live, and where we work:
> My parents live in Scotland.
> My mum comes from Australia.
> My dad works for an American company.

2 We use the **present simple** to talk about our hobbies, timetables, and things we do regularly:
> I sometimes play football on Sunday mornings.
> They never go on holiday.
> Megan comes to a French class with me on Mondays.

We often put a frequency adverb (*usually, sometimes, never*, etc.) before the verb, or we give a time, day or period (*at 9.30, in the morning, on Tuesdays, at the weekend, in the summer*, etc.) after the verb.

TIP

→ For information on **frequency adverbs**, see p. 16.

A   Talking about where we live and where we work

Joe and his friends share a big house in London. Jean-Paul is going to stay with them. Add the correct form of the verbs in brackets to this letter.

Hi Jean-Paul!

Here's some information about our house. Sally and I ___live___ ⁰ (live) on the first floor. Sally ___works___ ⁰ (work) for a travel company and I _____ ¹ (drive) a taxi. Paul _____ ² (have) a room on our floor, too. He _____ ³ (fix) cars. Mario _____ ⁴ (live) on the second floor with his wife, Lucia. They _____ ⁵ (come) from Italy. Lucia _____ ⁶ (speak) a little French, I think. They both _____ ⁷ (make) great pasta! Finally, Greg _____ ⁸ (sleep) on the top floor. He _____ ⁹ (teach) maths in a local school.

See you soon!

Joe

B Things we do regularly

(i) Here is an interview with Anisha Chetty, the managing director of the supermarket company, Bisco's. Add the correct verb, changing the form if necessary.

INTERVIEWER   When do you start your day?

ANISHA   My husband _sleeps_ ⁰ (sleep/stay) until 8 a.m., but I always _get_ ⁰ (start/get) up at 6.30 a.m. I usually ....¹ (leave/go) to the gym first. Then I ....² (have/sit) breakfast at the London office at 7.30 a.m. I ....³ (start/stop) work at 8 a.m.

INTERVIEWER   Wow! That's early. Are you the first person to arrive at the office?

ANISHA   No, actually. My Personal Assistant, Philip, ...⁴ (get/arrive) at 7.45 a.m., but he ....⁵ (finish/lose) work at 3 p.m. to pick up his children from school.

INTERVIEWER   Do you have meetings all day long?

ANISHA   No, not all day. On Wednesdays I ....⁶ (fly/catch) to Glasgow to visit the Scottish manager, Derek. He ....⁷ (give/make) me information every week on the eleven Bisco supermarkets in Scotland.

INTERVIEWER   Do you have any time to relax?

ANISHA   Sure. You have to relax. I ....⁸ (make/do) yoga on Tuesday afternoons. And I ....⁹ (try/come) to get home early on Friday afternoons.

(ii) Check your answers to (i), and then add the verb in the correct form to these sentences about Anisha.

0   She always ...._gets_.... up at 6.30 a.m.

1   She usually .... to the gym first.

2   Then she .... breakfast at the London office.

3   She .... work at 8 a.m.

4   On Wednesdays she .... to Glasgow.

5   She .... yoga on Tuesday afternoons.

6   And she .... to get home early on Friday afternoons.

C Facts and regular activities

Gill is showing a family photo to her friend. Cross out the wrong verb forms in the sentences in the first half (1-4), and add them to the sentences in the second half (5-8).

0   My mother ~~make~~/makes TV programmes.

1   My father *work/works* in a travel agency.

2   My parents *spends/spend* two months every year in California.

3   My grandfather *speaks/speak* five languages.

4   He *plays/play* jazz piano at the weekends.

5   My brothers .... for a South American bank.

6   They both .... Spanish as well as English.

0   They ...._make_.... a lot of money.

7   My older brother, Matt, ... all his money on cars.

8   They both .... tennis together on Sundays.

02 Present simple
We don't know; he doesn't remember

5 Some examples of the **present simple negative**:
*I **don't like** music in shops.*
*She **doesn't eat** meat.*
*We **do not know** the answer.*
*This train **does not stop** at York.*

6 We make the negative form by using **do not/don't** or **does not/doesn't** before the **infinitive**:

NEGATIVE		
	Full form	Short form
Singular	I **do not stop**	I **don't stop**
	you **do not stop**	you **don't stop**
	he/she/it **does not stop**	he/she/it **doesn't stop**
Plural	we **do not stop**	we **don't stop**
	you **do not stop**	you **don't stop**
	they **do not stop**	they **don't stop**

TIP

1 Note that we don't add -s after **he/she/it** in the negative form: *He doesn't stops.*

2 In speech and informal writing, we usually use short forms.

Grammar in action

3 We use the **present simple** to talk about things we like or don't like:
I love sunny days!
I like most classical music.
Mike doesn't like golf.
We want an ice cream!
My dad hates motorbikes.
I don't want another book for my birthday!

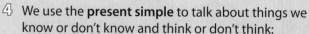

4 We use the **present simple** to talk about things we know or don't know and think or don't think:
I don't know her name. Do you?
Jeremy knows the way to the hotel.
I'm sorry, but I don't understand.
I think it's time to go home.
Jo doesn't think this restaurant is very good.
I understand a few words in French.

→ For information on **present simple questions**, see p. 18.

D Sightseeing in Edinburgh

Bob and Jess and their kids, Sam and Mel, are visiting Edinburgh. Add the correct verb in the correct form.

BOB   I <u>don't know</u> [0] (not think/not know) where we are, Jess. Mel <u>thinks</u> [0] (think/want) we're on Princes Street - the street with all the shops - but I'm not sure.

SAM   I _____ [1] (hate/love) shops! They're boring. I want to go to the zoo.

JESS   I _____ [2] (not think/not understand) the zoo is in the city centre, Sam. And Mel _____ [3] (not hate/not like) zoos anyway.

BOB   Listen. I'm going to ask this man where we are. Excuse me, sir, what is the name of this street?

JESS   Bob! He _____ [4] (not understand/not think) you. I don't think he's British.

BOB   OK. Sorry, sir. Look, Jess. What's that?

JESS   I _____ [5] (not know/not understand), Bob.

MEL   But I _____ [6] (think/know) what it is! It's the Scott Monument. I read about it at school.

BOB   Thanks, Mel. This is Princes Street, then. So now I know the way to the Tourist Information Office.

JESS   Great! We can ask for directions to the National Gallery of Scotland. I _____ [7] (love/hate) paintings!

SAM   Well, I _____ [8] (not hate/not like) paintings. They're boring. I'm thirsty. I _____ [9] (want/love) a drink.

JESS   We can have a drink at the café in the National Gallery, Sam. We may see some paintings of lions or tigers there. That will be nice, won't it?

E A day in the life of Ling Wang

(i) We use the present simple for facts and regular activities; things we like and don't like; and things we know and don't know. In the first part of this magazine article, tick (✓) the verb forms if they're correct. If they're wrong, cross them out and write the correct forms. This informal magazine uses short forms of the present simple negative.

Ling Wang ~~read~~ *reads* ⁰ the evening news on a Beijing TV channel. She lives ___✓___ ⁰ in a beautiful apartment in the centre of the city. She don't _____ ¹ get up early. She likes _____ ² to sleep late, until 10 or 11 a.m. She have _____ ³ three cups of green tea for breakfast. At 11.30 a.m. she go _____ ⁴ for a swim in a pool in her apartment block. Then she relaxes _____ ⁵ until lunchtime.

"Sometimes I meets _____ ⁶ a friend for lunch," she says. "We talk _____ ⁷ about our jobs, and music and films and things. I know _____ ⁸ a lovely restaurant near my apartment…"

(ii) In the second part, add the verb forms from the box.

> understand   takes   think   don't eat   don't speak
> studies   ~~arrive~~   don't meet   love

"…We normally *arrive* ⁰ there at 1 p.m. I'm a vegetarian, so I _____ ⁹ meat or fish, but I _____ ¹⁰ fresh fruit and vegetables. I _____ ¹¹ it's important to look after your body."

After lunch, Ling always _____ ¹² her language books for an hour. She speaks English and Japanese as well as Chinese. "I _____ ¹³ one or two words in Spanish, too, but I _____ ¹⁴ it," she says. "I _____ ¹⁵ many Spanish people in Beijing!" At 4 p.m. a taxi _____ ¹⁶ her to the TV studio.

OVER TO YOU   Now go to page 122.

03 Present continuous
I am waiting; he's making

1 Some examples of the **present continuous**:

*Hurry up! Sara and Tom **are waiting** for us!*
*I'm sorry, Matt**'s shopping** at the moment. Do you want to leave a message for him?*
*I don't like my boss – I**'m looking** for a new job.*

2 Here is the positive form of the **present continuous**:

POSITIVE		
	Full form	Short form
Singular	I **am waiting**	I**'m waiting**
	you **are waiting**	you**'re waiting**
	he/she/it **is waiting**	he/she/it**'s waiting**
Plural	we **are waiting**	we**'re waiting**
	you **are waiting**	you**'re waiting**
	they **are waiting**	they**'re waiting**

> **TIP**
> In speech and informal writing, we usually use the short forms after pronouns. We can use the short form with singular nouns, too:
> *He**'s eating**.   The dog**'s**/dog **is eating**.*

3 To make the **-ing form**:

For most verbs, we add **-ing**:

sleep → sleep**ing**	work → work**ing**

But for verbs ending in **-e**, we take away the **-e** first:

live → liv**ing**	make → mak**ing**

And for these common verbs, we double the final consonant:

begi**nn**ing	ge**tt**ing	ru**nn**ing
sho**pp**ing	si**tt**ing	swi**mm**ing
trave**ll**ing	wi**nn**ing	

→ For more information on the **-ing form**, see p. 128.

4 We use the **present continuous** to talk about things that are happening right now and things that are happening around now, but perhaps not at the exact moment of speaking.

→ For information on the **present continuous negative**, see p. 12.

Grammar in action

1 We use the **present continuous** to describe things that are happening <u>now</u>. This is often in an email, on the telephone, or in a radio or TV report:

I'm sitting at my desk and it's snowing outside. (in a letter)
Bob's watching TV, and Jo's reading. (in an email)
Steve Jordan is running towards the goal now! (in a report on the radio)

2 We use the **present continuous** to tell people about things that are happening now so that they do or say something in response:

That big dog is running towards us! Let's go!
I'm listening to the radio. Be quiet!
It's getting late. Shall we go home?
That man is looking at you. Do you know him?

A   A telephone conversation – things that are happening now

WORD FOCUS
Two water verbs
To splash is to make someone wet by making water fall on them.
To sink is to go below the surface or towards the bottom of water.

Patrick is at home with his son Pete, who is sick. His wife, Simona, is on holiday with their daughters, Ally and Becca. Add the verbs to their phone conversation in the present continuous form. Use short forms if possible.

PATRICK   Everything is fine, thanks. Pete *'s sleeping* ⁰ (sleep) and I .... ¹ (sit) in his bedroom. The sun .... ² (shine) in the garden. What about you? I hope you .... ³ (enjoy) the holiday.

SIMONA   Well, I .... ⁴ (think) about Pete and you, of course. But we .... ⁵ (have) fun. Becca .... ⁶ (swim) in the pool and .... ⁷ (splash) her new friend, and Ally .... ⁸ (run) around. She .... ⁹ (play) football with some Spanish kids.

B Responses to things that are happening now (1)

Add these verbs in the present continuous to the pictures on the right.
Use short forms if possible.

> try   sink   splash   stand   shout   walk

0 I 'm trying............... to read my newspaper! Be quiet!
1 You .... too fast! Please slow down!
2 That boat .... ! We should help!
3 She .... me! Tell her to stop!
4 That man .... at us! What does he want?
5 You .... on my foot! Please can you move?

C A television report – things that are happening now

In this news report, add the correct verb form in the present
continuous. Use short forms if possible.

'This is Francesca Martin for 'Liverpool Newstime'. I ....'m standing.... 0
(stand/stay) outside the new Ship Museum. I can see a car. Yes, the Queen
.................................¹ (land/arrive). Her car ....² (stop/start)
near a group of local people. Now Her Majesty ....³
(get out/get up) of her car. She ....⁴ (wait/wear) a blue
coat and a blue and white hat. Someone ....⁵ (have/give)
her some flowers. She ....⁶ (smile/say) now, and she
.................................⁷ (take/talk) to a man and woman at the front of the
group. The director of the museum, Pandit Desai, ...⁸
(become/come) to meet her. In a moment, the new Liverpool Ship Museum
will be open. And now, back to the studio.'

D Responses to things that are happening now (2)

Jan and Dave are on holiday. Add these sentences to the dialogue:

> My husband and I are having a cup of coffee on the deck.
> I'm taking photos of that yacht.   Yes. She's walking towards us now.
> Dave, I think the owner is looking at you.   It's getting late.

JAN   Are you taking a photo of me?
DAVE   No. I'm taking a photo of that yacht. 0 Can you move to the
          left, please?
JAN   ....¹ Perhaps you should stop.
DAVE   Are you sure?
JAN   ....² Put your camera in your bag.
DAVE   Oh dear. I don't think she's happy.
OWNER   It's a nice yacht, isn't it? ....³ Would you like to
          join us?
JAN   That's very kind of you, but ....⁴ We should go
          back to our hotel.
OWNER   Well, come again tomorrow afternoon. We can show you our yacht.

5 Some examples of the **present continuous negative**:
*Look! It **isn't raining** any more.*
*They**'re not playing** very well at the moment.*
*He **isn't working** on the computer, he's sleeping.*

6 Here is the negative form of the **present continuous**:

NEGATIVE	Full form	Short form
Singular	I **am not working**	I'm **not working**
	you **are not working**	you**'re not** / **aren't working**
	he/she/	he/she/it**'s not**/
	it **is not working**	**isn't working**
Plural	we **are not working**	we**'re not** / **aren't working**
	you **are not working**	you**'re not** / **aren't working**
	they **are not working**	they**'re not** / **aren't working**

7 We often use these expressions with the present continuous:

> at the moment   these days   this week/month/year

*She isn't working very hard **at the moment**.*
*You're watching a lot of TV **this week**.*

8 We **don't** normally use these verbs in the present continuous:

> like   love   hate   want   know   understand

I don't like musicals. (NOT ~~I'm not liking musicals.~~)
She knows London. (NOT ~~She's knowing London.~~)

→ For on **present continuous questions**, see p. 20.

Grammar in action

3 We can use the **present continuous** to talk about things that are happening around now (but perhaps not at the exact moment of speaking). Often we are giving news about friends and family:
My parents are driving across America at the moment.
Marsha is learning German at evening class.

4 Sometimes we use the **present continuous** to talk about how life is slowly changing:
The world is getting warmer.
We're all working longer hours these days.

E   News about friends and family

Dimitri is visiting a museum in London. Put the verbs in the positive or negative form of the present continuous. Use short forms if possible.

DIMITRI Hazel! I don't believe it! How are you? How nice to see you! Is Joe with you?

HAZEL Dimitri! I'm fine, thanks. No, *Joe is working* ⁰ (Joe/work) in Paris this month. What about Galina?

DIMITRI She's fine. ....¹ (She/not stay) in London with me, because ....² (her sister/move) house this week, and ....³ (Galina/help) her. Anyway, how is life at the BBC?

HAZEL Actually, ...⁴ (I/not work) in television these days. ....⁵ (I/learn) Russian.

DIMITRI ....⁶ (You/learn) my language! That's wonderful. But why?

HAZEL ....⁷ (I/write) a book about Moscow. Perhaps you can help me!

DIMITRI Of course. ....⁸ (We/not live) in Moscow at the moment, but we have many friends there.

HAZEL And what about your children? Are they still enjoying their music?

DIMITRI Yes, but ....⁹ (they/not play) together these days. ....¹⁰ (Alexander/study) in Germany now, and ....¹¹ (Fedor/teach) the piano at home. Anyway, Hazel, here's my email address.

HAZEL Thanks, Dimitri. We must keep in touch.

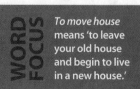
WORD FOCUS
To move house means 'to leave your old house and begin to live in a new house.'

F   Life in modern Britain

Finish the *-ing* forms of the verbs in the first part of this article on modern Britain.

Life is changing in the UK, but is it getting better? For example, we have wonderful computers at work, but we're wo_rking_.⁰ harder. We aren't enj_____¹ ourselves more. We're g_____² up earlier and we're sta_____³ longer at the office. At the supermarket, we're b_____⁴ more interesting food. But often, we're e _____⁵ it on our own in front of the TV. Of course, we're l_____⁶ longer. But we aren't ha_____⁷ as many children, so who will look after us when we're old? Dr Brian Dixon, Professor of Sociology at the University of Yorkshire, has some of the answers. He says …

G   A phone call to a friend

We use the present continuous for things that are happening right now; and for things that are happening around now. Add the words from the boxes in the present continuous form to this conversation. Use short forms if possible.

Twins are two children who were born at the same time. If they look the same, we call them identical *twins*.

WORD FOCUS

| eat   eat   look   play   spend   visit   wash   watch |

MANDY Sally? It's Mandy here. What are you doing?
SALLY   I _'m washing_ ⁰ the dishes at the moment. What about you?
MANDY I _____¹ TV. My parents _____² the weekend in Mallorca, so I _____³ after the twins. Ben _____⁴ ice cream, and Joe _____⁵ with his trains. What about you? Is Clare in?
SALLY   No, she _____⁶ Mum and her new husband. It's just me and dad.
MANDY Ben! You _____⁷ too quickly! You'll be sick. So Sally, how is your dad, anyway?

| drive   get   meet   play   not spend   think   work |

SALLY   Better, thanks. He _____⁸ so much time on his own in his room – he _____⁹ people, and he _____¹⁰ tennis again.
MANDY Joe! You _____¹¹ that train too fast! Sorry, Sally.
SALLY   That's OK. I'm going to do some homework in a minute.
MANDY You _____¹² very hard at the moment.
SALLY   I know. I want to go to university next year. What about you?
MANDY I'm still not sure. I _____¹³ about it. Anyway, I'd better go and put the twins to bed. They _____¹⁴ very tired.
SALLY   OK. See you tomorrow!

OVER TO YOU   **Now go to page 122.**

PRESENT SIMPLE	PRESENT CONTINUOUS
Long-term	**Temporary**
We use the **present simple** for facts: *Sally **speaks** French and German.* *I **don't drive** a car – I **have** a bicycle.*	We use the **present continuous** for things that are happening now, to describe things: *Jack **is speaking** to his dad on the phone.*
and to talk about our hobbies, timetables and things we do regularly: *We **study** maths on Monday mornings.* *I often **go** swimming.*	and to tell people about things so that they do something in response: *You**'re driving** too fast! Slow down!*
We usually use the **present simple** *with like, love, hate, want, know, think, understand.* MIKE *Do you like the film?* (NOT *Are you liking the film*) NIKKI *Yes, but I don't understand the story!* (NOT *I'm not understanding the story*)	We use the **present continuous** for things that are happening around now, but not perhaps at the exact moment of speaking – such as study courses: *Marsha **is studying** Japanese at university.* and how life is slowly changing: *Children **are living** at home longer these days.*
Facts and regular activites are **long-term** (true for a long time).	Things that are happening right now and around now are **temporary** (true for a shorter time).
Use with: *often, sometimes, etc. on Tuesdays, at 9.30, etc.*	Use with: *at the moment, these days, this week/month/year*

Grammar in action

1 We normally use the **present simple** for things that are long-term and the **present continuous** for things that are temporary or different from our normal lives.

    Look at this information about John:
    John lives in London. (LONG-TERM)
    He works for 'The Times'. (LONG-TERM)

Every week, he writes about football. (LONG-TERM)
At the moment, he's writing a book on 'Great American Golfers', too. (TEMPORARY)
In fact, he often plays golf with his son, Luke. (LONG-TERM)
But Luke is skiing in Colorado this week, (TEMPORARY)
so today John is working at home in his garden instead. (TEMPORARY)

A Long-term and temporary activities (1)

Luis is describing his business trip to London. Circle the correct options.

My name is Luis. *I'm coming / I come*[0] from Mexico. *I normally work / I'm normally working*[1] in Mexico City. But this week *I'm visiting / I visit*[2] our offices in London. In Mexico City, *I live / I'm living*[3] with my wife and two children in a large house with a garden. At the moment, though, *I stay / I'm staying*[4] in a very small apartment in central London. *I usually drive / I'm usually driving*[5] to work in Mexico City. But this week, *I walk / I'm walking*[6] everywhere! It's very good for me. And *my English improves / my English is improving*[7] – a little!

B Long-term and temporary activities (2)

(i) Three international exchange students are waiting for a college bus at a university in Madrid. Put the verbs in the present simple or continuous. Use short forms if possible.

XU   Hi! Do you guys speak English? I'm Xu, and I'm from Beijing.

UWE Hi! _____I come_____ 0 (I/come) from Germany, but _____ 1 (I/speak) English. My name is Uwe.

KHAN I'm Khan. I'm from Liverpool. _____ 2 (I/study) music. What about you two?

XU _____ 3 (I/do) computer studies.

UWE Really? _____ 4 (My dad/work) for a computer company in Berlin. But _____ 5 (I/study) art.

KHAN Do you guys know if they have a football team here? _____ 6 (I/play) every week in England.

XU I'm not sure. Do you play outside or inside? _____ 7 (It/rain) a lot in England, doesn't it?

KHAN Yes, but it's OK. _____ 8 (We/have) a nice hot shower after every game. What about you, Uwe? Do you play any sports?

UWE Actually, _____ 9 (I/learn) to play tennis at the moment. I'm not very good.

XU Really? _____ 10 (My mum/teach) tennis at school. But she's in China, so she can't help you!

KHAN Look, _____ 11 (that man/shout) at us!

UWE It's OK. He's the bus driver. He wants us to get on board.

(ii) A month later, Xu is emailing his English friend, Sharon. Again, put the verbs in the present simple or continuous. Use short forms if possible.

How are you? At the moment, _____I'm sitting_____ 0 (I/sit) next to the window in one of the university's excellent computer rooms. _____ 1 (The sun/shine). I've got my timetable now. Basically, _____ 2 (I/go to) classes in the morning, and _____ 3 (I/do) sports in the afternoon! And I've got two new friends, Khan and Uwe. _____ 4 (Khan/come) from Liverpool, and _____ 5 (he/study) music. _____ 6 (He/spend) a couple of days in England at the moment. I think his sister is getting married. Uwe is German. _____ 7 (He/do) art. In fact, _____ 8 (he/paint) a picture of me this week. I'll show it to you one day! _____ 9 (He/speak) really good English. Of course, _____ 10 (my Spanish/get) better all the time. 'Es hora de ir' - that's Spanish for 'it's time to go' - I think.

See you!

C   Long-term and temporary activities (3)

Gail is talking on the phone to her sister about her son. Add the verbs in brackets in the present simple or continuous. Use short forms if possible.

TINA What's he doing now?

GAIL He _____'s opening_____ 0 (open) the back door and he _____ 1 (walk) into the garden.

TINA So what?

GAIL Well, he _____ 2 (wear) his pyjamas and he _____ 3 (sing) something. And it's midnight.

TINA Oh dear, he _____ 4 (fall) in love again, isn't he?

GAIL I think so. Normally he _____ 5 (come) back from work, and he _____ 6 (have) his dinner. Then he _____ 7 (watch) TV, and he _____ 8 (go) to bed at 10 p.m.

TINA And now?

GAIL He _____ 9 (not eat) at all. And look, he _____ 10 (dance)!

3 When we use the **present simple** for regular activities, we often put a frequency adverb (**usually**, **sometimes**, **never**, etc.) before the verb, or we give a time, day or period (**at 9.30**, **in the morning**, **on Tuesdays**, **at the weekend**, **in the summer**, etc.) after the verb:

*Carla **often visits** her grandmother.*
*I **eat** lots of ice cream **in the summer**.*

And when we use the **present continuous** for things that are happening around now, we sometimes use expressions like **at the moment**, **these days**, **this week/month/year**:

*We're **buying** a new house **at the moment**.*
*You're **not eating** very much **these days**.*

4 We use the **present simple** (and not normally the present continuous) when we talk about things we like or don't like, using the verbs **like, love, hate, want**:

*Dave **likes** jazz.* (NOT ~~Dave is liking jazz.~~)
*I **want** a cold drink.* (NOT ~~I'm wanting a cold drink.~~)

and also when we talk about things we know or don't know, using the verbs **know** and **understand**:

*Jo **knows** London.* (NOT ~~Jo's knowing London.~~)

With the verb **think**, we can use the present simple or continuous, but the meaning changes:

*I **think** it's nice.* (= In my opinion, it's nice.)
*I'm **thinking** about her.* (= She's in my mind/thoughts now.)

Grammar in action

2 We use the **present simple** to say how often or when we do things in our daily lives. Here we're talking about our friends' routines:

Mike sometimes cycles to work.
Heather goes to a French class on Mondays.

We use the **present continuous** to say how our lives are different from normal:

I'm working in our Paris office at the moment (but I normally work in Manchester).
Stella is walking to work this week (but she normally goes on the bus).

3 We use the **present simple** to tell friends how we feel about something:

DAVE *I love musicals like 'Phantom of the Opera'.*
MEG *Do you? I like plays by Shakespeare.*
DAVE *Really? I don't understand Shakespeare at all.*

D   A conversation at a music college

A music student introduces herself to Julie. Put a number where the missing word should be.

DIANA (the = 0) Hello, my name's Diana. I'm studying here at *0* moment.

JULIE (every = 1) Hi! I'm Julie. I come to these concerts week. What instrument do you play?

DIANA (this = 2) Well, I normally play the violin, but I'm learning to play the trumpet year, too.

JULIE I love violin music. But the trumpet is a difficult instrument, isn't it?

DIANA (on = 3) Yes! I have a class Tuesdays. It isn't easy. What about you? Do you play anything?

JULIE (is = 4) Not really. My husband teaching me the piano at the moment. He plays every day.

DIANA It's not easy to find the time, is it?

JULIE (these = 5) We're all working very hard days. Too hard. But these concerts after work are great.

DIANA (have = 6) Good. We sometimes concerts at lunchtime, too.

JULIE Lunchtime! What's that?

DIANA (at = 7) Oh dear! You're working much too hard the moment!

E   A public notice

Look at this public notice in Watford. Tick (✓) the verb forms if they're correct. If they're wrong, cross them out and write the correct forms. Use short forms if possible.

We ~~are knowing~~ ......*know*...... ⁰ that people like ......✓...... ⁰ to see beautiful things in their town centres. Some people want .... ¹ fountains. Other people are liking .... ² statues. But most people love .... ³ parks! In Watford, we build .... ⁴ a new park for you this year. We are thinking .... ⁵ you will like it. We understand .... ⁶ that you are wanting .... ⁷ the best, and we work .... ⁸ very hard these days - but the best things take time!

We don't know .... ⁹ exactly when your new park will be open, but we make .... ¹⁰ a special park web page at the moment, so go to www.watford.gov.uk/newpark after 5 May for more information!

F   Meeting old and new friends in a restaurant

We use the present simple for long-term things and with verbs such as *like* and *know*, and we use the present continuous for temporary activities. In this conversation, Sam is introducing Michiko to his brother, Chris and Chris' wife, Rachel, at a local restaurant. Use the correct verb forms. Use short forms if possible.

SAM   Chris, Rachel! Hi! Have a seat. This is Michiko. ....*She comes*.... ⁰ (she/come) from Tokyo.

RACHEL   Hi, Michiko! Welcome to Edinburgh, and to Mario's. I hope .... ¹ (you/like) Italian food.

MICHIKO .... ² (I/not know) Italian food well, but .... ³ (I/love) pizzas.

CHRIS   Good to meet you. Sam says .... ⁴ (you/study) at the university.

MICHIKO That's right. .... ⁵ (I/learn) about international business systems.

CHRIS   .... ⁶ (The waiter/come) I'll get some cola, shall I?

SAM   .... ⁷ (Michiko/not like) cola. Can you order some water, too? Anyway, what's new, Rachel?

RACHEL   .... ⁸ (We/look) for a bigger house, Sam. But they're very expensive. .... ⁹ (Chris and I/teach) French at a local school, Michiko, so we're not well-off!

MICHIKO .... ¹⁰ (I/not understand). What does 'well-off' mean?

CHRIS   'Rich'. We're not rich. But we're OK. What about you, Sam? Anything new?

SAM   Nothing, apart from Michiko! .... ¹¹ (I/get up), ... ¹² (I/go) to work, ... ¹³ (I/play) football on Saturdays!

RACHEL   .... ¹⁴ (The waiter/bring) our drinks. Shall we look at the menu?

OVER TO YOU Now go to page 122.

05 Present simple and present continuous questions
Do you understand?; When does the library open?

1 Look at these **present simple questions**:
Do you want a sandwich?
Do they remember me?
Where does he live?

2 To make **present simple questions** we put **do/does** before **I/you/he/we/they**:

> **do/does + subject + verb**

You speak English. → *Do you speak English?*
He comes from London. → *Does he come from London?*
They have an English dictionary. → *Do they have an English dictionary?*

We form **present simple questions** like this:

QUESTIONS		
Do	I/you	
Does	he/she/it	} **want** (a drink)?
Do	we/you/they	

> **TIP**
> Note that the verb after **do/does** doesn't change: *Does he go to the gym?*
> (NOT *Does he goes to the gym?*)

3 We sometimes put the question words **what**, **when**, **where**, and **how much** before **do/does**:
Where does Michael work?
What do you want?
How much does it cost?
When does the next train leave?

→ For more information on **question words** and **short answers**, see p. 48.

Grammar in action

1 We use **present simple questions** to get useful information. At a tourist information office we might ask about travel timetables, ticket prices or opening times:
Do these buses go to the stadium?
How much does a ticket cost?
Does Windsor Castle open on Sundays?

2 We use **present simple questions** to ask our friends what they want:
Do you want an ice cream?
Does Dave want a newspaper?
What do you want?

A Getting information (1)

Daniel, from France, is going to spend six months at a college in Madrid. Put the words in brackets in the right order, and write out the questions that he asks his new American flatmate, Greg, on his first day in Madrid.

0 *Do you speak French?* (speak/French/you/do) ~ No, I'm afraid I don't.

1 .... (the local shops/you/do/like) ~ Yes, the best are on Calle Gracia.

2 .... (you/do/sports in Madrid/play) ~ Yes, I play tennis.

3 .... (a map of Madrid/do/have/you) ~ Sure. There's one in the kitchen.

4 .... (do/a lot of money/metro tickets/cost) ~ No, they're really cheap.

5 .... (start/does/college/when) ~ On 14 January.

Now, use the words in brackets to form questions.

0 *Do you go to college every day?* (go/to college every day/you) ~ No, I don't go on Fridays.

6 .... (cook/Spanish food/you) ~ Well, I sometimes make paella.

7 .... (at the weekend/open/the college library) ~ Yes, I think so.

8 .... (change/money/the local bank) ~ Yes, it sells euros.

9 .... (traditional food/cook/the local restaurants) ~ Yes, the food's delicious.

10 .... (cost/the cinema/how much) ~ It's about six euros for a film.

B   Getting information (2)

Faroukh and Aisha are in the Tourist Information Office in Dublin. Use the words in brackets to form questions. Use capital letters where necessary.

ASSISTANT   Hello. Can I help you?

AISHA   Yes, please. We're spending the weekend in Dublin.
Do you have a map of the city centre? **0** (of the city centre/have/ a map/you)

ASSISTANT   Of course. Here you are. What do you want to see during your visit?

FAROUKH   Everything! Dublin Castle, for example. .... **1** (how/Dublin Castle/we/find)

ASSISTANT   It's here on Dame Street. A long time ago, there was a small lake in the castle, called the 'Black Pool', and that's what Dublin means - 'black pool'.

FAROUKH   That's interesting. We also want to see Trinity College.
.... **2** (it/Sundays/on/open)

ASSISTANT   Yes. From 9 a.m. to 5 p.m.

AISHA   Thanks. And .... **3** (open/the National Gallery/when)

ASSISTANT   Every day, from 10 a.m. to 7 p.m. It's a great place. Do you have any more questions?

AISHA   Yes. One more. .... **4** (Dublin Bay/to/the train/go)

ASSISTANT   Sure. I'll give you a timetable.

FAROUKH   Thanks. .... **5** (the train/much/how/cost)

ASSISTANT   Oh, it's not very expensive. It's £5 for a return ticket.

C   Asking friends what they want

Sal, Kit and Kit's baby son, Max, are in a restaurant. Use the words in brackets to form questions with *want*.

SAL   That fish was good. *Do you want a dessert?* **2** (you/a dessert?) This chocolate fudge cake looks good.

KIT   No, I don't. The food was great, but I'm really full.
.... **1** (you/some more water?)

SAL   Yes, please. I'm thirsty today. But what about some apple pie with cream, Kit? That's just fruit, really. Or
.... **2** (you/some cheescake?)

KIT   No, I'm OK, thanks.

SAL   What about Max? .... **3** (he/a banana split?)

KIT   No, I don't think so, Sal. He looks tired.

SAL   OK. .... **4** (we/coffee afterwards?) They say the cappuccino here is very good.

KIT   Sure. Are you OK, Max? .... **5** (you/some more orange juice?)

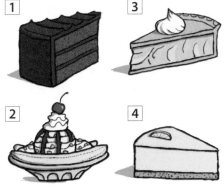

1   3

2   4

Present simple and present continuous questions
Is it snowing?; What are they doing?

4 Look at these questions:
Are you waiting for me?
Is Mike working upstairs?
What are you doing?

5 To make **present continuous questions**, we put the form of the verb **be** before **I/you/he/we/they**:

> **am/is/are + subject + -ing form**

You are sleeping. → *Are you sleeping?*
It's raining. → *Is it raining?*

We form **present continuous questions** like this:

QUESTIONS		
Am	I	
Are	you	
Is	she/he/it	leaving?
Are	we/you/they	

6 We sometimes put the question words **what** and **where** before **am/is/are**:
Where are you going? What is she watching?

→ For more information on **question words** and **short answers**, see p. 48.

Grammar in action

3 We use **present continuous questions** to ask about people's actions at the present moment:
What are you watching?
Are you enjoying that pizza?
What's your mum doing?

4 We use **present simple** and **present continuous questions** to ask people about their lives. On your first day at school you might ask a new friend:
Do you live near here?
Are you studying French?

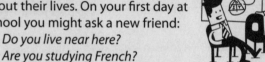

D **Getting ready to go out in New York**

Juan and Cova are staying with friends in New York. Use the words in brackets to form present continuous questions.

DIANE Are you enjoying that CD, Juan? ⁰ (that CD, Juan/you/enjoy)
JUAN Yes, I am. It's a great band. Are they American?
DIANE No, they're Canadian. Is Cova OK? _____ ¹ (she/what/do)
JUAN She's resting, Diane. What about Joe? _____ ² (he/in the kitchen/cook)
DIANE No, he's doing something on the computer upstairs. But it's time to go. Joe!
JOE (*Coming downstairs*) Hi, Juan. Diane. _____ ³ (listen to/you/what)
DIANE It's that 'Paper Dog' CD. _____ ⁴ (leave now, Joe/we)
JOE Yes, darling. _____ ⁵ (rest/upstairs/Cova)
JUAN Yes. Cova! _____ ⁶ (downstairs/come/you)

E **At the opening of an art gallery**

(i) Here are eight questions you can ask people you meet. We often use *sort of* in questions: it means 'type of'. Question 2 is for a visitor or a tourist. Complete the words.

Basic information: Do you l̲i̲v̲e̲ ⁰ near here?
Are you sta_____ ¹ near here?   Where do you c_____ ² from?

Work/study: Do you w_____ ³ near here?
What sort of j_____ ⁴ do you do?   Are you stu_____ ⁵ anything?

Free time: What sort of things do you d_____ ⁶ in your free time?
What sort of food do you l_____ ⁷ ?

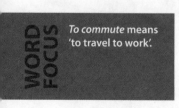

To commute means 'to travel to work'.

WORD FOCUS

(ii) A group of people are going to look at some paintings in a new gallery in a small town. Add seven more of these eight questions in the right place.

0 _Are you staying near here?_

Yes, we've got a room in a hotel on Oak Street.

1 ....

I play tennis sometimes, but I don't have much free time!

2 ....

I'm a doctor.

3 ....

We really love Indian food. There's a great restaurant near here.

4 ....

I'm from Portugal, actually. What about you?

5 ....

Yes, we've got a flat in the town centre.

6 ....

No, not really. I commute every day to London.

7 ....

Yes, I'm trying to learn Chinese

F   A conversation at a bus station in New Delhi

We use questions to get information; to ask people what they want; to ask what people are doing at the present moment; and about their lives. Make present simple or continuous questions in this conversation.

ALLY   Excuse me, please. _Does this bus stop at Mumbai?_ **0** (this bus stop/ at Mumbai?)

DRIVER Yes it does, Madam. .... **1** (you/want/a ticket?)

ALLY   I think so. .... **2** (the bus/leave soon?)

DRIVER No it doesn't, I'm afraid. But you can wait on these seats.

ALLY   Thank you. .... **3** (When/it/go?)

DRIVER In an hour.

ALLY   Thank you. (*Ally sits down next to a man.*) Excuse me. .... **4** (you/wait/for the bus to Mumbai?)

ROD   Yes, I am.

ALLY   Me too. .... **5** (you/stay/in New Delhi at the moment?)

ROD   No, I work in Mumbai.

ALLY   Really? .... **6** (What sort of work/you/do/there?)

ROD   I'm a doctor. And you? .... **7** (you travel/around India?)

ALLY   Yes, it's my first visit. It's very hot, isn't it?

ROD   Of course! We aren't in London, you know! .... **9** (you/want/a cold drink?)

ALLY   Sure. (*Rod stands up*) .... **10** (where/you/go?)

ROD   To a nice hotel near here. We'll have some cold lemonade.

OVER TO YOU   **Now go to page 122.**

06 Past simple
I played; he made

1 Two examples of the **past simple**:
*I **went** to London with two friends last summer.*
*We **stayed** in a hotel near Hyde Park.*

2 To make the positive form of the **past simple** we add **-ed** to **regular verbs**:

POSITIVE
I/you he/she/it   }   asked we/you/they

➜ For **-ed** spelling changes (e.g. try/tried), see p. 128.

3 But many common verbs have **irregular past simple** forms. Look at these examples:

break/broke	buy/bought	catch/caught
come/came	do/did	drink/drank
eat/ate	find/found	forget/forgot
go/went	have/had	know/knew
leave/left	lose/lost	make/made
meet/met	pay/paid	run/ran
read/read	see/saw	sell/sold
send/sent	speak/spoke	spend/spent
take/took	win/won	write/wrote

The verb **be** has two past forms: **was** and **were**.

BE: POSITIVE
Singular I/he/she/it **was** **Plural** we/you/they **were**

*Chris and I **were** in Scotland at the weekend, and it **was** very cold!*

➜ For a full list of irregular past participles, see p. 129.

4 We use the **past simple** for finished past actions:
*Liz **lived** in Madrid for two years. She **had** a fantastic time there.* (Liz doesn't live in Madrid now.)

*When Mike **was** a child, he **spent** every summer holiday in Cornwall.* (Mike isn't a child now.)

5 We often use **expressions for a finished time** with the past simple to talk about when things happened in the past:
*I lost my watch **last week**, but I found it in the bathroom **this morning**.*
*Josie phoned about **ten minutes ago**.*

6 We use the **past simple** to talk about recent actions in finished time periods, to talk about our past, to tell stories and to talk about history.

➜ For **past simple negatives** and **questions**, see p. 24.

Grammar in action

1 We use the **past simple** to talk about recent actions in finished time periods – things we did last week, at the weekend, yesterday or this morning:
I went to Brighton last Sunday with Katie. We had a picnic on the beach. It was really nice.

2 We use the **past simple** to tell people about our lives in the past:
I studied music at college, and we started a band. We played at parties.

We often describe holidays and trips:
My brother travelled by bus from Brazil to Chile when he was a student. He spent a month in Santiago and met a lot of interesting people.

3 We use the **past simple** to tell true stories (lists of past actions) about ourselves, our families and friends:
I heard a loud noise, so I went downstairs, and I saw a big black dog in the kitchen.

We also tell fictional stories (children's stories and novels):
A long time ago, an old man lived with his beautiful young daughter in a small house.

A Talking about things we did last week

Tim and Greta meet at the photocopier at work. Make forms of the past simple.

GRETA   Did you have a good weekend, Tim?

TIM   Not bad, thanks. <u>My brother and his wife arrived</u> ⁰ (My brother and his wife/arrive) from Scotland on Friday evening, and .... ¹ (they/stay) with us until Sunday lunchtime.

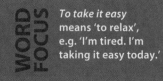

WORD FOCUS
To take it easy means 'to relax', e.g. 'I'm tired. I'm taking it easy today.'

GRETA Really? What did you do?

TIM Not much. ....² (We/talk) a lot, of course, and ....³ (we/see) a film on Saturday night. Then ....⁴ (we/eat) at that French restaurant, 'Serge's'. What about you? Did you have a good weekend?

GRETA Yes, ...⁵ (it/be) OK, thanks. ....⁶ (I/go) into town on Saturday morning and ....⁷ (I/meet) Dave, and ....⁸ (we/do) some shopping. Then ....⁹ (we/watch) United in the afternoon. ....¹⁰ (They/lose) again, of course. And on Sunday, ...¹¹ (I/take) it easy.

TIM Well, you need a rest now and again.

B Telling people about a holiday

In this email message, choose the right verb, and make forms of the past simple.

Hi Ed,

Thanks for your message. I think you're working too hard. You need a long holiday. Last year, Barry, the kids and I _spent_ ⁰ (spend/live) four weeks in Cornwall. It ....¹ (have/be) great! We ....² (find/stay) a really nice little house near the sea. We ....³ (go/get) for walks, and we ....⁴ (buy/make) food from the local farms. We ....⁵ (cook/clean) dinner at home most nights, we ....⁶ (read/look) books instead of watching TV, and the kids ....⁷ (run/play) games in the garden. It rained sometimes, of course, but we ....⁸ (spend/enjoy) every day. I ....⁹ (take/watch) a few photos the day before we ....¹⁰ (leave/miss). I'll send you them, and give you the address of the house!

Best wishes, Stephanie

C Telling true stories about our family

Graham is writing about his Italian grandfather. Add these verbs in the past simple form:

wake stay wear lose tell go marry come
sell spend catch become drink

Before you begin, make sure you know the meaning of these three business words: *to borrow, a profit,* and *a factory*.

WORD FOCUS

My grandfather, Alfredo, borrowed £70 and _went_ ⁰ to Egypt when he was twenty. He wanted to make money. He studied Arabic. He ....¹ Arabic clothes. He spoke to the old men in the markets. He ....² tea with them. When he was hungry, he ....³ fish. Sometimes he washed dishes in restaurants. Then one day an old man ....⁴ him to buy coffee. He travelled about, and bought all the coffee he could find from farmers. He ....⁵ about £50. Then he waited. The following year, 1947, the price of coffee increased by 200%. So he ....⁶ his coffee and made his first profit. After that, he worked hard. He ....⁷ every morning at 6 a.m. He bought things when they were cheap, and he sold them if they ....⁸ expensive! Sometimes he ....⁹ money, of course, but in the end he became very rich. In 1955, he ....¹⁰ my grandmother, the daughter of an Egyptian farmer. He ....¹¹ in Egypt for another 15 years. Then he returned to Italy with my grandmother and a baby son, my father. He built a factory in Naples. But his son, Davide, ...¹² to England, where I was born.

06 Past simple
We didn't go; did they see?

7 Look at this dialogue:

Did you **see** Stella yesterday? ~ No, she **didn't come** to college.

8 We make the **negative form** of the **past simple** like this:

> **subject + did not/didn't + verb**

> I **didn't go** to the game.

NEGATIVE	
I/you he/she/it we/you/they	**did not/didn't wait**

9 We normally make the question form of the **past simple** like this:

YES/NO QUESTIONS
Did + subject + verb

Did I/you/he/she/it/we/you/they **write** to Tim?

QUESTIONS WITH QUESTION WORDS
Question word + did + subject + verb

When did I/you/he/she/it/we/you/they **arrive**?

When did Shakespeare **die**? *(The answer is 1616.)*

> **TIP**
> We must use **did/didn't/Did...?** with the verb **do** too:
> **Did** they **do** their homework? ~ Yes, but they **didn't do** the dishes.

10 With **be**, we don't use **did not/didn't** or **Did...?**:

BE: NEGATIVE	
Singular	*I/you/he/she/it* **was not/wasn't** *in the garden.*
Plural	*You/we/they* **were not/weren't** *at home.*

BE: QUESTIONS	
Singular	**Was** *I/you/he/she/it late?*
Plural	**Were you**/*we/they right?*

Grammar in action

4 We use the **past simple** to talk about national and world history:

Tony Blair was the British Prime Minister from 1997 to 2007. He won three general elections in 1997, 2001 and 2005.

D Sunday evening

Maggie, Dave and Pete are students. Maggie is returning to their flat on Sunday evening. Use the words in brackets to make questions or negative forms.

MAGGIE I'm back! Hi Dave. ....Did you finish your essay.... **0**? (you/finish your essay)

DAVE No, I'm tired today. .... **1** (I/not do anything) this afternoon. .... **2**? (you see Jenny)

MAGGIE No, ... **3**. (she/not be at home) But I met Joanna, the new American student, in town.

PETE Oh. .... **4**? (she/be OK)

MAGGIE I think so, but .... **5** (she/not talk very much).

DAVE .... **6** (you/invite her to our party) next weekend?

MAGGIE Yes. I'm sure she'll come. .... **7** (What/you do all afternoon,) Pete? .... **8** (you/make a wonderful dinner) for us?

PETE No I didn't, I'm afraid. But my parents arrived at two o'clock with a fantastic new TV for the flat.

MAGGIE Well, that's kind of them. .... **9** (When/they leave?)

PETE About an hour ago. Do you want a cup of coffee, Maggie?

DAVE Oh. .... **10** (I/not get any milk this morning,) Pete.

MAGGIE Black coffee is fine. What's on TV?

E Going on holiday

John and Liz are driving to the airport for a two-week holiday. Put the words in brackets in the right order to make questions and negative forms of the past simple. Use capital letters to start your answers.

JOHN   *Did you lock the front door, Liz* ⁰ (lock/you/the front door, Liz/did)?

LIZ   Yes, definitely. But *I didn't make any sandwiches* ⁰ (make/I/any sandwiches/didn't).

JOHN   .... ¹ (forget/you/did)?

LIZ   No, ... ² (didn't/I/time/have). We'll get something at the airport. .... ³ (your passport/under the bed/was)?

JOHN   Yes. *(Later)* .... ⁴ (you/email Sally/did)?

LIZ   Yes, last night. She's going to feed the cat every day.
.... ⁵ (a key/did/you/give her)?

JOHN   Of course. But I forgot one thing. .... ⁶
(didn't/the windows upstairs/check/I). Oh dear.
.... ⁷ (open/were/they)?

LIZ   No, I closed them. *(Later)* Are you going to work on holiday this time?

JOHN   .... ⁸ (my laptop/pack/no,/didn't/I).

LIZ   Good. We both need a break.

WORD FOCUS

Put the correct verb next to the definitions:
to check   *to feed*
to lock

A to close with a key
....

B to give food to an animal or a baby
....

C to look at something to see if it's OK
....

F An accident in the mountains of Iran

Julie is telling Brad about her trip to Iran with two friends. Add these words to the conversation:

broke	stayed	walk	~~have~~	carried	was	were
didn't	made	arrived	what	fixed	put	

BRAD   Hi Julie! Did you ...*have*... ⁰ a good trip? What's wrong with your leg?

JULIE   I'll tell you. We .... ¹ in Esfahan by train, but we .... ² want to spend all our time in the city.

BRAD   So .... ³ did you do?

JULIE   We took a taxi one afternoon to the village of Hafeshjan in the Zagros mountains. The local people .... ⁴ very friendly. We found a small hotel, and we .... ⁵ the night there.

BRAD   And .... ⁶ hotel comfortable?

JULIE   Yes, the hotel wasn't the problem. Next morning we started our walk in a forest outside the village. We didn't .... ⁷ fast, because it was already hot. Soon we saw some rocks and a cave. Then I .... ⁸ a big mistake. I went into the cave. I couldn't see anything, and I .... ⁹ my foot on a wet rock. I fell and .... ¹⁰ my leg. Jim and Daniel .... ¹¹ me back to the village. When we got to the hotel, they phoned for a taxi, and they .... ¹² my leg in the hospital in Esfahan!

OVER TO YOU Now go to page 123.

07 Past continuous
I was sitting; we weren't watching; was he eating?

1 Two examples of the **past continuous**:

I phoned you at nine, but you weren't there.
~ Oh, I was driving to work.
Did you have a good time in Bristol?
~ Not really. I was cooking meals all weekend.

2 We form the **past continuous** like this:

POSITIVE		
I/he/she/it	**was**	eating
you/we/they	**were**	

NEGATIVE		
I/he/she/it	**was**	eating
you/we/they	**were**	

QUESTIONS		
Was I/he/she/it		eating?
Were you/we/they		

→ For rules on the spelling of **-ing** forms, see p. 128.

3 We use the **past continuous** to talk about actions in progress <u>around</u> a particular moment in the past:

I knocked on your door this morning. ~ Oh, I'm sorry.
I didn't hear you. I was sitting in the garden. (NOT ~~I sat in the garden.~~)

knocked (exact moment)
9 a.m.————————|————————11 a.m.
← *was sitting* (background action) →

(= I was sitting in the garden before and after you knocked.)

Here is another example:

*John **was working** at 12 o' clock last night!* (= John was working before (and probably after) 12.)

> We **don't** normally use the past continuous with the verbs **like**, **love**, **hate**, **want**, **know**, **understand**.
>
> TIP

Grammar in action

1 We use the **past continuous** to describe everyday background actions: to tell or ask people what was happening <u>around</u> a particular moment:

What was Paul doing in the library yesterday morning? ~ He was checking his emails.
We were watching TV at about 9 o'clock, and Mike brought us some sandwiches.

A policeman can ask:
What were you doing at 9 o'clock last night?

2 We use the **past continuous** to describe the background of a story. We can talk about the weather or what people were doing before the story starts:

It was snowing! The boys were happily building a snowman and their mum was looking out of the kitchen window. Then Oliver found some old money…

A   Actions around a particular moment in the past (1)

Phil is sending an email from the airport. Add the verbs in the past continuous.

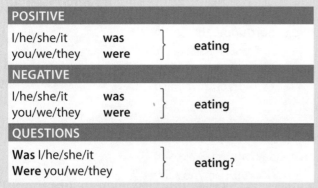

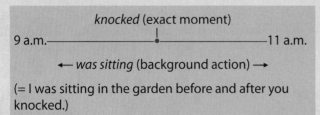

Hi Diana

I'm at the airport. I took a taxi from the flat at midnight. All your old friends were there. When I left, Patti _____was having_____ [0] (have) a little party in the living room. Lourdes and Tom _____ [1] (dance). Nick _____ [2] (eat) fish and chips as usual. Patti _____ [3] (not play) the music loud, though, because Giovanni _____ [4] (work) in his room and Jill _____ [5] (sleep). Anyway, they all send their best wishes to you.

See you soon in Berlin!

Phil

B Actions around a particular moment in the past (2)

Boris tells Ron about a visit from an old friend. Look at the phrases in the box. Put the verbs in the past continuous form, and then add the phrases to the conversation.

> Lorna/sleep.   What/Svetlana/do/in London?   No,/she/not work.
> We/meet/an old friend.   I think/she/joke.   Where/you/go?
> But/she/not ring/from Moscow.   ~~I/walk/past the station.~~

RON   Hello, Boris. How are you? I saw you on Saturday at about 11 o'clock, but I don't think you saw me.

BORIS   Really? Where were you?

RON   *I was walking past the station.* ⁰ You and Lorna were at the ticket office.
.... ¹

BORIS   We weren't travelling anywhere, actually. .... ²
It's quite funny really. I was making some tea at about 9 o'clock and
.... ³ Suddenly the phone rang. It
was my Russian friend, Svetlana. .... ⁴
She was spending a few days in London.

RON   Really? .... ⁵ She's a businesswoman,
isn't she? Was she meeting people?

BORIS   .... ⁶. She was looking for a flat to buy!

RON   Wow! She must have lots of money. Did she find anything?

BORIS   Yes. She said that she bought the first flat she saw in Kensington, because it was raining and she didn't have an umbrella. .... ⁷

C Telling a story

Bill and Maria are in Bill's garden. Use the words in brackets to make past continuous question forms for Maria, and past continuous negative forms for Bill.

BILL   I saw a man in the woods last night.

MARIA   *What were you doing in the woods?* ⁰ (What/you/do/in the
woods?) .... ¹ (you/walk/home?)

BILL   No, ... ² (I/not/go/home.) It was almost
midnight. It was raining, and I was looking for Ben, my cat. Then I saw a man.

MARIA   Really? .... ³ (What/he/do?)
.... ⁴ (he/jog?)

BILL   No, ... ⁵ (he/not/run.)

MARIA   Well, ... ⁶ (he/walk?) Did he have a dog with him?

BILL   No, he didn't have a dog, and .... ⁷ (he/not/
walk.) He was sitting under a tree.

MARIA   Really? .... ⁸ (he/sleep?)

BILL   No, he was watching me. His eyes were open. .... ⁹
(He/not/sleep.)

MARIA   Was he an old man or a young man? .... ¹⁰
(What/he/wear?)

BILL   He was young. He was wearing a very big black hat and he was holding Ben!

MARIA   No! What did you do?

BILL   I ran home and phoned the police. But he wasn't there when they arrived. And my cat came home about an hour later.

Past continuous
Past simple and past continuous

4 We sometimes use the **past continuous** and the **past simple** together in one sentence:

> Barry **phoned** three times while I **was working**.

The past continuous (**was working**) describes background events, and the past simple (**phoned**) describes interruptions (complete actions that happened during the background event.)

5 When we use the **past continuous** and the **past simple** together like this, we often use **while** or **when**:

> **While** I was living in Spain, I ate at 9 or 10 o'clock in the evening.
> It was snowing **when** I woke up this morning.

While and **when** mean the same, but we don't use **while** for very short actions:

> I was walking to work when ~~while~~ I saw Roger in his car.

> If you're writing, and you begin a sentence with **when** or **while**, put a comma (,) at the end of the first part:
>
> **While** you were talking to Max, I got an email from Sue.

TIP

Grammar in action

3 We often use the **past continuous** and the **past simple** together to describe interruptions at home or at work:

> While I was cleaning the house, Kay and Peter came round for a coffee.
> I was doing my emails when my boss phoned.

4 We also use the **past continuous** and the **past simple** together to describe the background and the main actions when we tell our friends about interesting events or news:

> I was driving home when I saw a beautiful rainbow in the sky.
> I met Nicole while I was shopping this morning.

D   Interruptions; interesting events and news

Look at these two email messages. When you see a word in brackets at the end of a sentence, put a number where the missing word should be.

Hi Sean,
I hope you've had a better day than me! It○raining hard when I got up, so I didn't go jogging (was = 0). Then, I was having breakfast, my boss phoned (while = 1). He wants me to work tomorrow - Sunday! After breakfast I went upstairs to start my essay for college. I was writing the first sentence when Mike on my door, and said he was feeling really ill (knocked = 2). So I downstairs again and phoned for the doctor, and while we were for her, Mum arrived and said, 'If you're not doing anything this weekend, you can help me paint the kitchen.' (went = 3, waiting = 4).
Sharon

Hi Sharon,
Thanks for your message. I'm sorry about your weekend. Things are going better for me. I buying a new CD in town I saw a really good TV for £150, so I bought it for the flat (was = 5, when = 6). Then I did some shopping and went for a coffee in that new café by the library. While I waiting for my cappuccino, I Julie and she invited me to her party tonight (was = 7, met = 8)! Do you want to come? Charlie will be there. Julie said he had some good news. He looking for a flat, when his brother got a job in America (was = 9). So now he can live in his brother's flat - it's really nice. Anyway, perhaps I'll see you tonight.
Sean

E Working with elephants in Africa

We use the past continuous for past activities around a particular moment; and, with the past simple, to describe interruptions or news and interesting events. Lucy is going to Africa for six months. Add these verbs in the past continuous form to the conversation:

> do   travel   not enjoy   help   look for   ~~work~~   get off

ABIGAIL   Jay says you're going to Africa in September.

LUCY   I know, Abigail. I __was working__ ⁰ very hard last month at the office, as usual, but I _____¹ my job.

ABIGAIL   Oh dear. Perhaps you need a change.

LUCY   That's right. Anyway, last Friday, while I _____² to work on the bus, I saw a poster on the street with some pictures of elephants. People _____³ the bus, so I had time to read it.

ABIGAIL   What did it say?

LUCY   Well, they _____⁴ people to work in East Africa for six months.

ABIGAIL   It's called 'Elephant Projects', isn't it? I _____⁵ the washing-up a few days ago, and I heard an interview with the director.

LUCY   Really? Yes, you're right. The director _____⁶ a sick elephant one day, and he had the idea of starting 'Elephant Projects'. People go to Africa for six months, and they work on small projects.

ABIGAIL   It's a great idea, Lucy. I'm sure you'll enjoy it.

F Breakfast, a hot afternoon and a small accident

Jack, Olivia and Marcia are describing what they did yesterday. In each text, you need to change two verbs from the past simple to the past continuous. Cross out the verbs, and rewrite them at the end.

Jack: morning   I got up at 7 a.m. as usual. The sun shone. My dad was having a shower. I got dressed and went downstairs to have some breakfast. When I ate, the phone rang. It was Benjamin on his mobile. He ran along Green Street. He said, 'I'll be at your house in ten minutes.' I normally go to school with Benjamin. While I was waiting for him, my sister came downstairs and put the radio on.

__was shining__ ⁰   _____¹   _____²

Olivia: afternoon   I was working hard all morning, so I went for a walk after lunch. I walked through the park when I met Megan. She sat on the grass. We went to the library together, but it was very busy. Some students were reading, and others were working on the computers. It was very hot, too, so we didn't stay.

_____³   _____⁴

Marcia: evening   I drove home from work at about 6.30 p.m., when I saw a small accident on the other side of the road. A car stopped quickly and another car hit it. It rained hard at the time. When I got home at about 7 p.m., my husband Oliver was making dinner in the kitchen. I told him about the accident. We had dinner and watched TV until bedtime.

_____⁵   _____⁶

OVER TO YOU   Now go to page 123.

08 Present perfect
I have finished; they've left

1 Two examples of the **present perfect**:
*Felicity **has worked** here for ten years.*
*I'm sorry. I**'ve broken** this cup. ~ Don't worry.*

2 We make the **present perfect positive** like this:

> **subject + have/has + past participle**

*Sheila **has paid** the bill.*

POSITIVE		
Full form	**Short form**	
I/you **have arrived**	I**'ve**	
he/she/it **has arrived**	he**'s**	arrived
we/you/they **have arrived**	we**'ve**	

Note that in speech and informal writing, we usually use the short form.

3 **Regular past participles** end in -ed:

walk → walk**ed**	play → play**ed**
finish → finish**ed**	

→ For **-ed** spelling changes (e.g. **try/tried**), see p. 128.

But many common verbs have **irregular past participles**. Look at these examples:

do → **done**	make → **made**
eat → **eaten**	find → **found**
read → **read**	speak → **spoken**

→ For a full list of irregular past participles, see p. 129.

4 We normally use the **present perfect** when we think about the past and present together. We use it for past actions that are linked to the present (the result is important now). Look at these examples:
*I**'ve lived** in this house for 20 years.*
This means 'I started to live in this house 20 years ago (past action), and I'm still here **now**.' (present moment)

*Tom**'s lost** his watch.*
This means 'Tom lost his watch recently (past action) and he still can't find it **now**.' (present moment)

> With actions that happened a very short time ago, we often use **just**:
> *I've **just** made some coffee. Do you want a cup?*
>
> **TIP**

5 We use the **present perfect** to describe recent past actions that are linked to the present moment, to describe our lives up to now, to talk about personal news and about local, national, or international news.

→ For **present perfect negatives** and **questions**, see p. 32.

Grammar in action

1 We use the **present perfect** to describe our lives from any time in the past up to now. Here two people are talking about past holidays:
I've been to Portugal and Spain. ~ Greg's visited Seville twice and he says it's wonderful.

2 We use the **present perfect** when we tell someone about recent past actions that are linked to the present moment. A student can talk about his progress in class:
I've finished this exercise, and Jack and I have just discussed our answers.

3 We use the **present perfect** to talk about personal news. Here, we're telling a friend about our family:
Serena's bought a holiday flat in Spain, Mike's moved to Scotland and I've got a new job in London!

A **Describing our lives**

This is Lewis' first day at work for a small charity in South Africa. Lisa, his boss, is introducing Lewis to his new colleagues. Choose the right verb, and make short forms of the present perfect.

LISA   Good morning, everyone! This is Lewis, our new worker. Lewis, this is our small but fantastic team! First, here's Kate. She *'s worked* ⁰ (spend/work) here for two years. She _____ ¹ (send/have) thousands of emails for us, and she speaks French, Spanish and Dutch. Very useful.

KATE   Hi, Lewis. I'm sure you'll enjoy it here. I _____ ² (live/know) all over the world, but South Africa is the best!

LISA And this is Tony. He ....³ (visit/spend) a lot of time in Zimbabwe
and Kenya. He ....⁴ (travel/see) in Liberia and Sierra Leone,
too. If you have any questions about Africa, ask Tony. And Kate and Tony
........................⁵ (talk/meet) Nelson Mandela!

TONY He's a great guy, Lewis. He ....⁶ (go/do) so many amazing things.

LISA And the final member of the team is Anya. She ....⁷ (be/come)
to New York and London several times to talk to other charities. And she
........................⁸ (make/speak) at least a million telephone calls for us in the
last three years!

ANYA And I've just made some coffee, too. Would you like some, Lewis?

B Things that have happened today

Vincent and Brian are at the zoo with Vincent's son Sam, and Brian's daughters, Josie
and Stella. Sophie, Brian's wife, rings from home. **Make short forms of the present
perfect from the words in the brackets.**

BRIAN Hi, Sophie. We're at the zoo now. _We've just had_ ⁰ (We/just/have) coffee and
cakes. ....¹ (The kids/see) the giraffes, the crocodiles and
the elephants.

SOPHIE Are they enjoying themselves?

BRIAN Oh yes. Stella's using her new camera. ....² (She/take)
lots of photos. Josie is OK, but ....³ (she/lose)
her blue teddy bear. We may find it later. Oh, and Sam ate too much cake.
........................⁴ (He/just/be) sick. What about you?

SOPHIE Me? I'm all right. ....⁵ (I/do) quite a lot of work.
........................⁶ (I/write) six or seven pages of my report, and
........................⁷ (I/speak) to Phil at the office. Things are going OK.

BRIAN Good. Well, ...⁸ (Vincent/just/pay) the bill,
and ....⁹ (Josie and Stella/run) out of the café,
so I think it's time to see the monkeys. Bye!

C Personal news

Baz is spending a month in Thailand, and Bart is emailing him news about their
flatmates. **Add the following verbs in the present perfect form:**

buy   write   have   win   go   start   break   leave

How are you? I hope things are going well in Bangkok. I've got some
bad news, I'm afraid. Christine _'s had_ ⁰ an accident on her bike.
She ....¹ her leg. Scott ....² the flat and he
........................³ to New Zealand. So we need a new flatmate. But Susie
is fine. She's doing well at work, and she ....⁴ a new car - a
red sports car, this time. Omar ....⁵ £1000 for a photo of his
sister's baby! Finally, I ....⁶ my new evening course at college,
and I ....⁷ my first essay. Studying after work is not very nice!

All the best, Bart

6 Look at these examples:
> *I **haven't done** any work today.*
> ***Have** you **seen** Clare this morning?*

7 We make the **present perfect negative** like this:

NEGATIVE	
Full form	**Short form**
I/you **have not seen**	I **haven't** ⎫
he/she/it **has not seen**	he **hasn't** ⎬ seen
we/you/they **have not seen**	we **haven't** ⎭

8 We make **present perfect questions** like this:

QUESTIONS		
Have	I/you	⎫
Has	he/she/it	⎬ eaten?
Have	we/you/they	⎭

9 Ever and **never**
We often use **ever** when we're asking questions about people's lives:
> *Have you **ever** been to Australia?*

We sometimes use **never** instead of the negative form to make the meaning stronger:
> *I've **never** played golf in my life.*

We put **ever** and **never** before the past participle.

10 Gone and **been**
When we say 'Joanna's **been** to London,' we mean 'she was in London, but now she is back at home.'

When we say 'Joanna's **gone** to London,' we mean 'she is in London now.'

Grammar in action

④ We use the **present perfect** to talk about local, national and international news:
> *Catherine Ndereba has won the gold medal for Kenya for the third time and has run 1500m in a new world-record time!*

⑤ We can use the **present perfect** when we tell someone what we haven't done or what hasn't happened in the time up to now.
> *The rain hasn't stopped today, so I haven't been to the shops and Dad hasn't done the gardening.*

We can also ask questions about events in the time up to now. Here, we're asking a friend about their week:
> *Have you been to the gym this week? Has Steve phoned? Have your parents emailed you?*

D A holiday in Greece

We use the present perfect to talk and ask about things in the time up to now. Make questions and negative forms in this telephone conversation.

MINA Hi Gill. *Has Anne phoned you?* ⁰ (Anne/phone/you?)

GILL No. I'm bored, actually. *Anne hasn't phoned me* ⁰ (Anne/not phone/me), and .... ¹ (Steve/not email/his new photos) and, of course, ... ² (I/not do/my homework.)

MINA Oh dear. .... ³ (you/eat?)

GILL Yes. I had a horrible sandwich. What about you? .... ⁴ (you/talk/to Luke?)

MINA No. .... ⁵ (He/not/finish work.) And there's nothing on TV except a film called *Cold Days In Stockholm.* .... ⁶ (you/ever/see/it?)

GILL No, but there is some good news, actually. .... ⁷ (Steve/speak/to you about a holiday in Greece?) His parents have bought a house there.

MINA Wow! .... ⁸ (I/never/be/to Greece.) I'm sure it's lovely. .... ⁹ (you/see/any photos of the house?)

GILL No. His parents bought it six months ago, and .... ¹⁰ (Steve/not be/there.)

MINA Well, a holiday in Greece is a great idea. Talk to you tomorrow, Gill.

E   The news from East Cumbria

Look at the website for East Cumbria Radio News. Match the beginnings and endings of local news stories.

East Cumbria Radio News | HOME | PHOTOS | OLD NEWS | FAQ | CONTACT US |

Today's news...

The old library at Lofton... _____e_____ **0**

Milford United have... _____ **1**

A local woman has found... _____ **2**

Two large pigs called Rosie and Millie... _____ **3**

A local restaurant has made... _____ **4**

Lord Milchett's son... _____ **5**

a ...have escaped from Hill Farm. (CLICK FOR MORE)

b ...a five-metre pizza for charity. (CLICK FOR MORE)

c ...has sold a bottle of wine for £10,000. (CLICK FOR MORE)

d ...won their first match of this season. (CLICK FOR MORE)

e ...has closed after seventy five years. (CLICK FOR MORE)

f ...six gold coins on the beach. (CLICK FOR MORE)

F   Returning from a business trip

We use the present perfect to talk about recent actions, our lives and news linked to the present. Toby has just come back from Thailand, and is making phone calls to a restaurant and to his wife's sister.

(i) Add the following words to his telephone messages. Note that there is one extra word:

| returned   have   gone   been   just   made   ever   never |

(1) Hello. It's Toby Daw here. I've ___just___ **0** seen the name of your restaurant on my bank statement, but I've _____ **1** eaten at the Country Kitchen. I've _____ **2** to my bank this morning. They told me to phone you. Have you _____ **3** a mistake? The date of the meal was 17 December and the price was £64. Please ring me back on 960123.

(2) Hi Karen. It's Toby here. I've just _____ **4** from Thailand. Have you _____ **5** been to Bangkok? It's a really interesting city. Anyway, _____ **6** you seen Diana? She isn't work or at home. Bye for now!

While Toby is out, the restaurant and Karen both phone back.

(ii) Find four more mistakes in their messages, and rewrite them correctly at the end.

(3) Hi Toby. Karen here. I've just listen to your message. Diana isn't at home because she's been to London. Mum is ill, I'm afraid. We tried to phone you lots of times. Has you lost your mobile again? Ring me back.

(4) Good afternoon, Mr Daw. This is Brian Hart from the Country Kitchen. We haven't make a mistake, I'm afraid. Someone used your card and your name on 17 December. I am just spoken to our manager, Greg Turner. He says you must contact your bank again.

listened **0**   _____ **1**   _____ **2**   _____ **3**   _____ **4**

OVER TO YOU   **Now go to page 123.**

A *bank statement* is printed information from your bank about how much money you've spent.

WORD FOCUS

We use the past simple:	We use the present perfect:
1 for recent actions in finished time periods: *Susie **phoned** for a taxi and **left** the party at 10 p.m. yesterday.*	1 for recent actions with a present focus: *Paul **hasn't phoned**, and Susie **has** just **left**.*
2 to tell people about our lives in the past: *I **went** to Florida in 2007. The sun **shone** all the time.*	2 to describe our lives up to now: ***Have** you ever **been** to America?*
3 to tell stories about the past: *Sal **met** Joe at college, but then she **moved** to China, and Joe **didn't hear** from her again until 2006.*	3 to talk about recent personal news: ***Have** you **heard** about Sal? She's **moved** house and she's **had** a baby.*
4 to talk about history: *The Queen's father, George VI, **died** in 1952.*	4 to report local, national and international news: *The actor Michael Stage **has died**.*
Use with: **yesterday, two years ago, in 1976, at school**	Use with: **just, ever, never**

Grammar in action

1 We use the **past simple** to talk about the things we did recently in **finished time periods** – last week, at the weekend, or yesterday:
Steve went shopping yesterday. He bought ten new CDs and two pairs of trainers! (we're giving information about a past event.)

We can use the **present perfect** to tell people about things we've done recently too, but all these things have a **present focus**: we're thinking about the past and the present together.
The Queen has gone to Canada. (= the Queen is in Canada now.) I've just finished my college project. I've bought a DVD to celebrate!

2 We use the **past simple** to talk about things we did **in the past**. This might be when we were young, or at work, or on holiday:
My parents lived in Australia for ten years. I didn't see Joshua at the office. Did you play football at school?

We use the **present perfect** to describe and ask about our lives **up to now**. We can talk about the places we've visited, our jobs, and free time activities:
Henry has lived here since May. Have you ever seen a tiger? I've played tennis all my life. I love it!

3 We often use the **present perfect** and then the **past simple**. We use the **past simple** when we give more details or information:
Have you ever been to India? ~ Yes, I have. I visited Goa last November. I've lost my glasses. I put them on the table ten minutes ago. James has passed his exam. He got 80%.

A Actions in finished periods, and actions with a present focus

Sara and Aisha, on a business trip, are meeting for breakfast in their hotel. Circle the correct verb phrases.

SARA Hi Aisha. How are you? *I've started breakfast. / I started breakfast.*[0] I hope that's OK. *I've phoned Clare / I phoned Clare*[1] five minutes ago, but she's still in her bedroom. *She's lost / She lost*[2] her new watch.

AISHA Oh no. I hope she finds it. *Her husband has given / Her husband gave*[3] it to her for her birthday last month, didn't he?

SARA That's right. Anyway, *what have you done / what did you do*[4] yesterday evening?

AISHA *I have met / I met*[5] Karl and Franco, and we had a pizza together. What about you?

SARA *I have gone / I went*[6] to bed early. I was a bit tired. Are you hungry? *I've just asked / I just asked*[7] the waiter for some eggs. What about you?

AISHA   No, thanks. I'll just have coffee and toast. *Have you spoken / Did you speak* [8] to Joe today?

SARA   Yes. *I have seen / I saw* [9] him on the stairs half an hour ago. Why?

AISHA   *He's bought / He bought* [10] another phone, and I don't have his new number.

SARA   We'll see him later. Here are my eggs, anyway, and there's Clare, by the door.

B   Talking about the past, and describing our lives (1)

Read Keiko's letter, and put the verbs in the past simple or present perfect form.
Use short forms if possible.

Dear Sir/Madam,

I *'ve seen* [0] (see) your advertisement in 'Metro'. Please would you send me an application form for the Saturday job in the Oxfam shop on Parsons Lane?

I _____ [1] (work) in shops before. Last year, for example, I _____ [2] (spend) two months in my uncle's shoe shop in Kyoto, and when I _____ [3] (be) at school, I _____ [4] (sell) fruit and vegetables on a Saturday market. I _____ [5] (live) in London for six months now. I _____ [6] (start) a short course in Business at a local college, and I'll be in UK until September.

I _____ [7] (pass) all my English exams at university last year in Japan, and I _____ [8] (use) PCs all my life. I also like talking to people and helping them. I look forward to hearing from you.

Yours faithfully,

Keiko Tachibana

C   Talking about the past, and describing our lives (2)

David works for an international bank in London. He's meeting his boss. Put the verb phrases in the past simple or present perfect forms. Use short forms if possible. Make questions when you see a question mark (?).

ALISON Hello, David. Have a seat. *You've worked* [0] (you/work) for us for three years now, and you're doing a good job, but my secretary says you want to go to the Boston office. _____ [1] (you/spend) much time abroad, David?

DAVID   _____ [2] (I/live) in Australia for a few years when I was a child. _____ [3] (My parents/return) to England in 1990. But _____ [4] (I/not/work) abroad. I'd really like to.

ALISON And _____ [5] (you/visit) America on holiday?

DAVID   Oh yes. _____ [6] (I/be) there twice. _____ [7] (I/go) to Florida on a school trip in 1995, and _____ [8] (I/travel) in New England in 2000 when I was at college. I loved it.

ALISON _____ [9] (you/go) to Boston on that New England trip, David?

DAVID   Yes, _____ [10] (we/stay) there for a couple of days. It's a great city.

ALISON And _____ [11] (you/talk) to your wife about going to Boston?

DAVID   Yes. Fay is a writer, so she can do her work anywhere. She'd like to spend some time in Boston.

ALISON OK, David. I'll talk to the Boston manager tomorrow morning.

1 We often use expressions for a finished time with the **past simple**:

> last month   last year   last Thursday etc.
> ten minutes ago   a few days ago   a year ago etc.
> in October   in the summer   in 2002 etc.
> at the weekend   at Christmas   at Easter etc.

or place expressions:

> on the street   in town   in Manchester   in a café
> at college   at the station   at Greg's house etc.

> *I had a meal with my uncle **a month ago**.*
> *Francesca met me **at the station**.*

> **TIP**
> With this morning, today, this month, etc., we normally use the **present perfect** if the period is not finished. At 11 a.m., for example, we say, *'**Have** you **worked** hard this morning?'* but at 3 p.m., we say *'**Did** you **work** hard this morning?'*

2 Just, **ever** and **never**

When we use the **present perfect** for recent activities, we often use **just** (= a moment ago):
> *I'm sorry, Henry's **just** left. Can I help you?*

When we're talking about our lives, we sometimes use **ever** (= at any time) or **never** (= not at any time):
> *Have you **ever** worked in America?*
> *I've **never** eaten rabbit or snake.*

We put **just**, **ever** and **never** between **have/has** and the past participle.

Grammar in action

4 We use the **past simple** to talk about lists of past events:
> *Martin left his job, sold his house and travelled across India for six months!*

We use the **present perfect** to talk about recent personal news:
> *Chrissie has left her job at the bank. She wants to do something different.*

5 We use the **past simple** to talk about national and world history:
> *Explorers found the Titanic in 1985.*
> *The Beatles sang their first songs at the Cavern Club in Liverpool.*

We use the **present perfect** to talk about local, national and international news:
> *A woman from Liverpool has found £100,000 in her garden!*
> *U2 have played at Wembley.*

D   A village website

We use the past simple for stories and history, and we use the present perfect for personal, local and national news. Cross out six wrong verb forms in this village website and rewrite them.

> ## 🌐 Poire Village Website
> Home   Village News   Business   Photo gallery   Contact us   Links
> Home page highlights . . . news and history . . . click for the full story . . .
>
> • Exactly a hundred years ago, Jean Marais ~~has travelled~~ from Poire to Paris, and, a year later,   *travelled*⁰
>
>   he opened his first cigar shop. Between 1910 and 1940, he has sold a million cigars to Parisians!   1
> • 90 year-old Colette Duboeuf bought a car, and she has just had her first lesson!   2
> • The French President sang a song with local schoolchildren when he has visited Poire in 1962.   3
> • Mme Chamot's son returned from Africa, and he has brought his new wife, Adela. Her son, ... 4
>
>   Christophe, left the village two years ago, and has gone to Kenya.   5
> • In 1975, the American actor Hal Brown has bought a house in Poire. He lived here for ten years.   6

E A holiday friend

Michael is emailing Holly about his holiday in France. Fill the spaces with these words:

> ago   ever   in   in   just   last   ~~last~~   never

Hi Holly,

I saw this great film _last_ ⁰ week about Peru. Have you .... ¹ been to South America? I'd love to go there. We've .... ² been to France again, but I really want to travel to Asia or Africa or Brazil. I've .... ³ been outside Europe! We met a guy (Abdou) from Senegal on the campsite .... ⁴ France. He left his country two years .... ⁵ to find work. His father became sick .... ⁶ 2005, so now Abdou sends money home. He found work .... ⁷ month in the campsite restaurant. I've got his email address, so we'll keep in touch. Hope you're well, Holly.

Regards,

Michael

F Lunch in a Yorkshire garden

Ai-Li, from China, is staying with an English family (Susi and Chris, and their daughter, Keira). It's Sunday, and they're finishing lunch in the garden. Put the verbs in the past simple or the present perfect. Use short forms if possible.

CHRIS   I _I've just made_ ⁰ (just/make) some tea, Ai-Li. Would you like a cup?

AI-LI   No, thanks. I .... ¹ (have) four cups today. Can I have some water, please?

SUSI   Of course you can. We drink too much tea in this house, Ai-Li. .... ² (you/have) a good day yesterday? I'm sorry I .... ³ (not-be) here. I'm so busy at work at the moment.

AI-LI   Great, thanks. Keira .... ⁴ (show) me the shops in Harrogate in the morning.

KEIRA   And in the afternoon, Dad .... ⁵ (drive) us to the Scarecrow Festival in Kettlewell.

AI-LI   It was amazing! I .... ⁶ (never/see) so many scarecrows.

SUSI   My father lived in Kettlewell, Ai-Li. He .... ⁷ (work) on a farm there when he was a young man.

KEIRA   We .... ⁸ (not/see) him for a long time, Mum. Is he OK?

SUSI   Yes, he's fine. He .... ⁹ (just/buy) a new car, so I'm sure he'll visit us more often now. Do you see your grandparents sometimes, Ai-Li?

AI-LI   Every week. They live close by. .... ¹⁰ (you/ever/be) to China, Mrs Bell?

SUSI   Call me Susi, Ai-Li. Yes, I .... ¹¹ (go) to Hong Kong on business in 2002. But I .... ¹² (not-be) to Beijing or Shanghai or the rest of China.

KETTLEWELL SCARECROW FESTIVAL

OVER TO YOU Now go to page 123.

10 The future with *going to*
Things we have decided to do

1 Some examples of the future with **going to** (**be going to** + verb):

> I**'m going to buy** a new TV.
> Look out! You**'re going to burn** that toast!
> Where **are we going to meet** tonight?
> She **isn't going to win** this time.

2 To form the future with **going to** we use:

present continuous form of go + to + verb

> They **are going to win**.

POSITIVE	
I am/**'m going** he/she/it **is/'s going** you/we/they **are/'re going**	**to** see

NEGATIVE	
I am not/**'m not going** he/she/it **is not/'s not/isn't going** you/we/they **are not/'re not/** **aren't going**	**to** see

QUESTIONS	
am I **going** **is** she/he/it **going** **are** you/we/they **going**	**to** see?

3 We normally use the short forms of **be**:

> I**'m going to phone** Penny.
> They**'re going drive** to Manchester.

4 We use the future with **going to** to talk about our plans or intentions. If, for example, a friend says *'I'm going to find a new job,'* then she's decided that she wants a new job, but she probably hasn't started looking yet.

> We sometimes use **going to** with the verb **go**:
> *I'm going to go home soon and then I'm going to go to the cinema this evening.*

Grammar in action

1 We can use the future with **going to** to talk about things we've decided to do in our free time:

> *We're going to have a picnic in the park this afternoon. Would you like to come?*

2 We can use the future with **going to** to talk about things we've decided to do around the house:

> *I'm going to paint my bedroom this weekend. What are you going to cook tonight?*

3 We can use the future with **going to** to talk about our plans at college or at work:

> *I'm going to do a project on whales. We're going to open a new shop in Leeds.*

A   Talking about things we've decided to do in our free time

Lily and Ethan are on holiday with their friends, Jamie and Ella. Put the words in the right order to form the future with *going to*. Use capital letters where necessary.

LILY ....What are you going to do.... [0] (you/to/are/what/going/do) today, guys?

JAMIE .... [1] (to/a swim/going/have/I'm) before breakfast. What about you, Ethan?

ETHAN .... [2] (get/I'm/to/going) an English newspaper.

LILY .... [3] (an English paper/to/going/buy/aren't/you) every day, are you Ethan? We're in Italy now!

ELLA .... [4] (are/spend/Jamie and I/the morning/to/going) on the beach, Lily. We need a rest.

LILY That's fine. .... [5] (some shopping/do/to/Lily and I/going/are) before lunch. We want to get some presents for our families.

JAMIE .... [6] (cycling/going/I'm/go/to) in the afternoon, Ethan. There's a little fishing village about twenty kilometres away. Do you want to come?

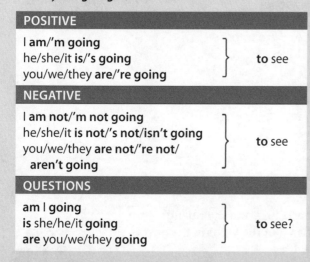

ETHAN   Perhaps. _____ ⁷ (going/what/do/
            are/you/to) in the afternoon, Lily?

LILY   _____ ⁸ (to/not/cycling/I'm/going/go)
            with you. I'll probably read my book.

B Talking about the things we've decided to do around the house

Ryan is emailing Daisy. Look at the picture on the right, and then add these phrases
to his message, using short forms of the future with *going to*:

> I/vacuum the carpet   I/clean the windows   I/cut the grass
> I/do some work around the house   I/wash the bath
> I/put some old suitcases   I/tidy my clothes

Thanks for your message. Yes, I can come to dinner on Sunday evening.
I'm looking forward to it, because *I'm going to do some work around*
the house ⁰ today and tomorrow. First _____
_____ ¹ in the attic. Then _____ ²
in the bedroom. Next _____ ³ in the
bathroom. Then _____ ⁴ outside. After lunch,
_____ ⁵ in the living room. Finally, on Sunday
morning, _____ ⁶ in the garden. So I'll be ready
to relax on Sunday evening!
Love, Ryan

C Talking about our plans after leaving college

Harry and Jessica are having a coffee at college. They're taking their final exams
this month. Use positive, negative and question forms of the future with *going to* to
complete their conversation. Use short forms if possible.

JESSICA   *Are you going to study* ⁰ (you/study) all weekend, Harry?

HARRY   No. _____ ¹ (I/not work) on Sunday. I need some fresh air.
             _____ ² (I/go) to the seaside with Abigail. Do you want to come?

JESSICA   I can't. I've got an exam on Monday morning. But _____ ³ (I/
             spend) two or three weeks in Spain in the summer. What about you?
             _____ ⁴ (you/have) a holiday?

HARRY   No, I haven't got any money. _____ ⁵ (Abigail and I/find) summer jobs.

JESSICA   And _____ ⁶ (what/you/do) after that?

HARRY   Well, I've got a job in London, but _____ ⁷ (Abigail/stay) in America
             with her mother's family for six months. What about you?

JESSICA   _____ ⁸ (I/not look) for work in the UK immediately. Amy and I want
             to go abroad. _____ ⁹ (We/teach) English in Shanghai for a year.

HARRY   That's a good idea. I'm sure it's a really interesting place to see.

10 The future with *going to*
Predictions

5 We use **going to** when something that we can see <u>now</u> makes us think that an event is sure to happen:
Look at the time! You're going to miss your train.
(When we look at the clock, the time helps us to predict that we're going to be too late for the train.)

If the car park near town is almost full, we can say:
It's going to be busy in town today.

Or, if our team is playing badly, we can say:
We're going to lose the match.

6 We use the negative form to talk about things which probably aren't going to happen:
It's 8 o'clock. We aren't going to find a present for her now.

7 And we can ask questions about the future:
Is it going to be windy today?

Grammar in action

4 We use **going to** to predict the future using information that we can see around us now. We can make predictions about the weather or the actions of other people:
Look at the clouds! It's going to rain.
She's going to sleep well tonight!
That dog looks really angry. It's going to attack her!

D What's going to happen?

This is a street in Bristol. Make sentences using forms of *going to*.

> She/break/her leg!   Careful! The traffic lights/change.
> The old man/win/again.   It/be/a hot afternoon.
> ~~They/make/a mess.~~   you/have/an ice cream?

They're going to make a mess **0**   **3**
                              1   **4**
                              2   **5**

E Talking to a friend in the park

We use *going to* to talk about our plans, and to predict the future. Ruby and Emma are sitting on a park bench. Add the words in brackets and the *going to* form of one of these verbs:

> say   do   ~~do~~   spend   go   work   cook   meet   get up

RUBY   What _are you going to do_ ⁰ (you) at the weekend?

EMMA   I'm quite busy, really. .... ¹ (I) on the computer on Saturday morning. Then on Saturday evening .... ² (I) Daniel's sister for the first time. Normally she lives in New Zealand, but she's staying in England for a couple of weeks. What about you, Ruby?

RUBY   I'm a bit tired, so .... ³ (I, not) anything on Saturday. But on Sunday morning, ... ⁴ (I) early, if I can. I want to go to the market.

EMMA   .... ⁵ (you) with Grace and Lucy?

RUBY   No, only Grace. .... ⁶ (We) dinner on Sunday evening for Grace's mum, so we'll try to get something good to eat at the market. .... ⁷ (Lucy) the weekend with one of her friends in Brighton or Cambridge.

EMMA   That's nice. Ruby, do you see that man? What's he doing?

RUBY   He's coming towards us. I think .... ⁸ (he) something.

MAN   Excuse me, I've lost my dog. She's small and black. Have you seen her anywhere?

F New Year blog

Nathan writes a blog every week about his family and friends. This is the beginning of his first blog in January. To make the text correct, add the following words:

> are   be   you   ~~going~~   not   to   do   is

> going
> ˅
> My brother Luke and I have got plans, of course, for the New Year. First, we're both to learn Chinese, because China is now the most important country in the world. In fact, I'm going to fly to Beijing, if I can find the money. Luke is going visit Mr Xu at our local Chinese restaurant, Hot Wok, to get some information about China. Next, we're going to paint our bedroom. The walls going to be green and red, and the ceiling is going to dark blue with stars, like the sky at night. Luke going to talk to Dad about this. Finally, I'm going to better at school. I'm going to work harder, because I work hard enough already - I'm going to use a new system, called the 'System of Seven': I'm going to learn seven new things every day, and write them down in a special book. Are going to do anything interesting this year? Send me an email.

OVER TO YOU   Now go to page 123.

11 The future with *will* and *shall*
Will: predictions, decisions, and offers

1 Some examples of the future with **will** and **shall**:
Where's Jo? ~ I don't know. I'll give her a ring.
Do you think it will rain this evening?
Shall we wait for them, or shall we go in?

2 To form the future with **will** we use:

> **will/'ll + verb**

We will help them.

POSITIVE	
I/he/she/it/we/you/they	**will/'ll talk** to Sam.
NEGATIVE	
I/he/she/it etc.	**will not/ won't talk** to Sam.
QUESTIONS	
Will I/he/she/it etc.	**talk** to Sam.

We can put a question word before **will**:
When will you talk to Sam?

3 We use **will** to talk about the future in general. Normally we say what we <u>think</u> will happen:
She'll do very well in her exam tomorrow.
That's a very big pizza. You won't finish it!
Will they stay in London all week?

Sometimes we say what we <u>know</u> will happen:
Ben will be eighteen next month.

4 We use **will** to make quick decisions and offers:
What would you like? ~ I'll have a tea, please.
I'm just going to the shops. ~ OK, Tom will drive you.

5 We sometimes use **I think/don't think** with **will**:
I think she'll ring tonight.
I don't think they'll win today.

And when we want someone's opinion, the question form with **you** is very common:
Do you think it will rain?
Do you think Adam will come with us?

We also use **I'm sure** with **will** or **won't**:
I'm sure they won't stay long.

> Another way of saying 'goodbye' informally is *I'll see you later* or *See you later.* **TIP**

Grammar in action

1 We use **will** to say what we think or know about future events in our personal and work lives:
I'll be busy at work this week.
The tickets won't arrive today.
Will Molly take a taxi to the station?

2 We use **will** to make quick decisions and offers in social situations:
You look tired. I'll make you a cup of coffee.
Is that the phone? ~ I'll answer it.
We'll help you with the washing-up.

A   Saying what we think or know about the future

Lauren has a job interview later this morning. Her friend James phones her. Add short forms of *will* to make positive and negative sentences and questions.

JAMES   When will the interview finish? **0** (When/the interview/finish?)
Perhaps I can meet you for lunch.

LAUREN   I don't know. .... **1** (I think/it/last/about an hour.)

JAMES   Good. .... **2** (You/finish/at twelve.)
We could meet at 'Alonso's'. **3**
(It/not be/busy/at that time, Lauren.) Their fish is really fresh.

LAUREN   That's fine.

JAMES   Are you feeling OK about the interview?

LAUREN   I'm not sure. .... **4** (Do you think/
they/ask me/about my year in Africa?)

JAMES   Yes, I think so. Don't worry. **5**
(I'm sure/you/do/well.)

LAUREN   I hope so.
JAMES   .... ⁶ (When/you/get the result?)
LAUREN   .... ⁷ (They/tell/me/at the end of
         the interview.)
JAMES   OK. Good luck, then, Lauren. I'll see you later.

B   Quick decisions and offers in social situations

Adam and Emily are meeting Carmen, a Spanish friend, at a restaurant. Add these phrases to their conversation:

| Adam will fix it   I'll open   I'll have a glass   we'll have a bottle |
| I'll take   we'll drive   I'll order   I'll bring |

WORD FOCUS

Restaurant words
1 You can order *still water* (without gas) or *sparkling water* (with gas).
2 A first course is called a *starter* and a second course is called a *main course*.

ADAM   Here we are. .... I'll take .... ⁰ your jacket, Emily. Can you see Carmen?
EMILY   Yes. She's here by the window. Hi, Carmen! How are you?
CARMEN   Fine thanks, Emily, though it's a bit hot in here.
EMILY   .... ¹ this window. Is that better?
ADAM   Did you find the restaurant easily?
CARMEN   Actually, I got lost, Adam. It's a long way by bus.
EMILY   Don't worry, ... ² you home afterwards.
WAITER   Good evening. Welcome to 'Mildred's'. Would you like some drinks?
CARMEN   .... ³ of still water, please.
EMILY   And .... ⁴ of white wine.
WAITER   Of course. .... ⁵ the wine list.
ADAM   So, Carmen, how's life?
CARMEN   Not bad, thanks. My flat is OK, but my car won't start. That's why I came by bus.
EMILY   Don't worry. .... ⁶ for you. You love fixing cars, don't you, darling?
ADAM   .... ⁷ some starters. What would you both like?

C   Future events, and making offers

Read this email from Veronica to her friend Mary. Put '/' in the seven places where the word *will* is missing.

Hi Mary

I'm so sorry to hear about the flood in Gloucester, and to see the photo of your house. They say the weather / get better on Thursday and Friday. I hope so, but life be difficult for you in the next few days. I saw the Prime Minister on TV in Gloucester yesterday, but you get any help from the government? They need to spend more money. I'm sure we see more floods in the UK in the future. Anyway, I listened to the news this morning. The roads near you be OK at the weekend, so Tom and I come over on Saturday morning. We help you to clean your floors, and Tom buy us all some fish and chips on Saturday night!

Love and best wishes,

Veronica

6 We normally use **shall** in questions:
Shall we take a taxi?
Where shall I put my coat?
Shall I get you a glass of water?

7 We form questions with **shall** like this:

(question word) + shall + I/we + verb

Shall we see a film?
When shall I meet you?

8 We use **shall I/shall we** to make suggestions, and to find out what people think about them:
Shall we have a cup of coffee? ~ That's a good idea.
You look tired. Shall I drive?

9 We use **Shall I** to make polite offers:
Shall I take your bag?
It's quite cold outside today. Shall I get you a jumper?

Grammar in action

3 We often use questions with **shall I/shall we** to make suggestions when we're at home or going out with friends or family:
Shall we take a boat on the lake?
Shall I book a table at 'Franco's'?
Which film shall we see?

4 We often use **Shall I** to make polite offers when we're at home with guests:
Shall I make some sandwiches?
Shall I get you some ice?
Shall I call a taxi for you?

D Suggestions in town; polite offers at home

Hannah and Anton are meeting Colette and Vincent at the station. Use *shall* and these words to complete the conversation:

I/drive   we/have   ~~I/put~~

ANTON   Colette, Vincent! Good to see you! ___Shall I put___ **0** your suitcases in the car?
COLETTE   Thanks very much. How are you both? We haven't seen you for such a long time!
HANNAH   We're fine, thanks. Are you hungry? _____ **1** a meal in town?
VINCENT   That would be great. We didn't have any lunch.
ANTON   Excellent! _____ **2** us to that restaurant by the river, Hannah?
HANNAH   The Italian place? Why not? It's very friendly there.
(*Later, in the car.*)

we/get   we/park

VINCENT   This is a new car, Anton. It's very nice.
ANTON   Thanks, Vincent. I bought it last month.
HANNAH   _____ **3** here, darling? We can walk along the river.
ANTON   I know it's cold, but _____ **4** some fresh air for ten minutes?
COLETTE   That's a good idea.
(*Later, at Hannah and Anton's house, after the restaurant.*)

I/take   I/make

HANNAH   Come in and have a seat. _____ **5** your coats?
COLETTE   Thanks. It's nice and warm in here.
ANTON   _____ **6** you both some coffee?
VINCENT   Tea for me, please. I never sleep after coffee.
COLETTE   Coffee is fine for me, Vincent. I'm sure I'll sleep tonight. We've had a long day.

E Returning from South Africa

We use *will* to say what we think or know about the future, and to make quick decisions and offers. We use *shall* for suggestions and polite offers. David and Linda's daughter, Beth, is coming home to Scotland after eighteen months in South Africa. Add *'ll*, *will* or *shall* to the conversation.

LINDA	Do you think Beth .... *will* .... [0] look for a job in Scotland?
DAVID	I don't know. She didn't say very much to me on the phone. I think she .... [1] do nothing for a couple of weeks. Life in Scotland .... [2] be a big change for her.
LINDA	Yes, I suppose you're right. .... [3] I make some dinner for her?
DAVID	.... [4] she want dinner? It's almost 10 o'clock. I .... [5] make her a sandwich, if she's hungry.
LINDA	OK. .... [6] we listen to some music? Her train may be late.
DAVID	She .... [7] phone if it's very late.
LINDA	.... [8] she get a taxi from the station? (*Someone knocks on the door.*) That's her. I .... [9] go.
BETH	Hi Mum, Dad!
LINDA	Beth! How are you, love? .... [10] I take your bags?
BETH	Thanks, Mum, but I .... [11] carry the big one. It's very heavy.
DAVID	It's great to see you, Beth. You look well. .... [12] we have a cup of tea?

F Deciding what to do on a night out by email

Read Mia's email and Alfie's reply. Use the verbs in brackets to form phrases with *will* or *shall*.

Hi Alfie

Shall we go [0] (we/go) out tomorrow night? Do you want to go to the pub or .... [1] (we/do) something different? .... [2] (I/be) busy until 7 p.m., but I could meet you in town afterwards, if you like. .... [3] (you/see) Santiago tomorrow at college? It would be nice to meet him again. .... [4] (I/ask) Katie too? I'm sure .... [5] (I/see) her some time during the day.

Hi Mia

Thanks for your message. .... [6] (we/see) a film? I think .... [7] ('CIA Blues'/be) good. It's a sort of comedy. .... [8] (Santiago/not be) in college tomorrow. He's got an interview in London. .... [9] (I/call) him in the afternoon, but I'm sure .... [10] (he/stay) in London with his father for a couple of days. Yes, it would be good to see Katie. By the way, thanks very much for the book. It was great. I finished it yesterday. .... [11] (I/bring) it with me tomorrow?

WORD FOCUS

If we are speaking or writing and we want to *change the subject* (say something different), we can use the phrase *by the way* - there's a good example in Mia's message to Alfie.

OVER TO YOU Now go to page 123.

1 There are two types of question:

- *Yes/No* questions, where the answer is *Yes* or *No*:
  Do you eat meat? ~ **Yes**, I do.
  Have you seen Holly? ~ **No**, I haven't.

- Questions with question words (**what**, **when** etc.),
  where many answers are possible:
  ***Where** are you from?* ~ *Cuba/Japan/France etc.*

2 We make questions with with **be**, **have** and **modal
verbs** (e.g. *will*, *shall*, *can*) like this:

> **(question word) + be/have/modal + subject**

Was Dave at home?   *Why has she left?*
Where shall we meet?

We make questions with all the other verbs like this:

> **(question word) + do + subject + verb**

Did you enjoy the meal?   *When does Tom get up?*
Who did you talk to?

3 Question words (1)

- We use **where** to ask about places:
  ***Where** are you going?* ~ *To Morocco.*

- We use **when** to ask about times and dates:
  ***When** did you finish work today?*

- We use **why** to ask about reasons/motives:
  ***Why** was Joan crying?* ~ *I'm not sure.*

- We use **how** to ask 'in what way?':
  ***How** are you going to get to Paris?* ~ *By train.*

- We also use **how + an adjective/adverb** to ask for
  exact information:
  ***How old** is your daughter?* ~ *She's seven.*
  ***How often** have you been to the USA?* ~ *Twice.*

***How far** did you walk this morning?*
***How many** brothers and sisters have you got?*
***How much** will it cost?* ~ *Twenty pounds.*

→ For more on **question words**, see p. 48.

Grammar in action

1 We use **why** to get extra information about people:
Why did you stay at home yesterday? (= I know you
were at home, but I'd like more information.)

We use **how** to get extra information about the way
people do things:
How did you get home so quickly? (= I know you got
home, but I'd like more information.)

2 We use **where** and **when** to get
information on places, times and
dates. We can use **where** when we
meet people for the first time, or
arrive in new places:
Where do you live? ~ *Sydney.*
Where shall we eat tonight?

We can use **when** to talk about train and plane times.
We can also use it to talk about the start of an event or
people's routines:
When did your plane arrive? ~ *At 8.30 p.m.*
When do you usually go to bed? ~ *About eleven.*
When are you going to start college?

3 We use **how + an adjective/adverb** to get exact
information about people's families, and about prices
and distances:
How often do you see your grandparents?
How much was that blue jumper in the window?

A   Getting extra information

Mike and John are on holiday. Mike stops their car, and they get out. Add *How* or *Why*
and one more word to the beginning of the questions.

JOHN   <u>Why have</u> ⁰ we stopped, Mike?

MIKE   Because I ate a fantastic meal at a restaurant near here three years ago. Come on!

JOHN   All right. ....¹ you walking so fast?

MIKE   The restaurant closes at 3 p.m.

JOHN   ....² we going to find it, Mike? We haven't got a map.

MIKE   (*Fifteen minutes later.*) Look, there's a river. We're almost there.

JOHN   ....³ you know?

MIKE   I remember the river.

JOHN   ....⁴ you cross the river three years ago?

MIKE   There was a bridge. ....⁵ you asking so many questions?

JOHN   Because we're lost. (*He sees a man.*) Excuse me, but ....⁶ we get to the 'Hungry Bear' restaurant?

MAN   ....⁷ you want to go there? The restaurant closed two years ago.

B   Arriving in a new place; asking about times and routines

Ingrid is arriving at a yoga centre in Scotland. Put the words in brackets in the right order to make questions, adding *where*, *when* or nothing (for Yes/No questions).

INGRID   Hi. I'm Ingrid. I'm looking for Mrs Miller.

CLARE   Oh. She'll be here soon. *Where have you come from, Ingrid?* ⁰ (come from, Ingrid/you/have)

INGRID   Israel. I took a plane today, and then I drove here.
....¹ (do/begin in the morning/the classes)

CLARE   Seven o'clock. Oh dear. You look tired. ....² (get up this morning/you/did)

INGRID   Five o'clock, so I'm looking forward to my bed.
....³ (I/sleep/going to/am)

CLARE   In that brown tepee by the river. It's very comfortable.
....⁴ (in a tepee before/slept/you/have)

INGRID   No, I haven't. And ....⁵ (the bathroom/is)

CLARE   In the cottage. ....⁶ (bring/did/a towel with you/you)

INGRID   Yes, I've got two in my bag. ....⁷ (will/the other students/meet/I)

CLARE   Tomorrow morning. I think they've gone to sleep.
....⁸ (you/did/leave your bag)

INGRID   In the car. ....⁹ (I/go/shall/to my tepee now)
I can see Mrs Miller tomorrow.

CLARE   Yes, that's a good idea.

C   Getting exact information

Katerina is emailing Susi. After the example, add the following words to the message. There is one word that you don't need to use. Use capital letters where necessary.

much	old	far	many	is	are	did	going

Hi Susi

......*Did*...... ⁰ you have a good time at the shops? ....¹ you at home now? How ....² new CDs ....³ you get? Jess says you're going to go jogging later. That sounds good, but how ....⁴ are you ....⁵ to run? I'll come with you, if you're only going to run a couple of miles. By the way, how ....⁶ is your laptop? It's quite new, isn't it? My laptop is OK, but my brother thinks you need to buy a new one every year! How ....⁷ did you pay for yours? Anyway, it's time to go. I've got some French homework to do.

Love, Katerina

4 Question words (2)

We normally use **what** to ask about things:
What's his mobile phone number?

But we prefer to use **which**, if there is only a small number of possible answers:
which pizza do you want - the big or the little one?
~ The little one. I'm not very hungry.

We normally use **who** to ask about people:
who was Jon speaking to? ~ His sister, I think.

And we use **whose** to ask who something belongs to:
whose coat is this? ~ It's Pete's.

5 Short answers

When we reply to *yes/no* questions, it's polite to use **short answers:**
*Do you live near college? ~ **Yes, I do.***

We form short answers by only using the first part of the verb in our reply:
Did you go to the bank? ~ Yes, I did ~~go to the bank~~.
Does he speak Greek? ~ No, he doesn't ~~speak Greek~~.
Have you finished? ~ Yes, I have ~~finished~~.
Will they win? ~ No, they won't ~~win~~.
Are you hungry? ~ Yes, I am ~~hungry~~.
Were your exams OK? ~ No, they weren't ~~OK~~.
Is she leaving? ~ Yes, she is ~~leaving~~.

Grammar in action

④ We can use **what** and **which** to get information on the things we see around us, in shops, in the street, or in restaurants:
What is he going to sell? ~ Watches, I think.

⑤ We can use **what** and **which** to get information about friends and the people we meet:
Which flat will she buy? ~ The one on the top floor.

⑥ We normally use **who** and **whose** to get more information about people and their possessions:
Whose bag is this?
Who did you know at the party? ~ No one!

D A party in Tokyo

Julie has just started work for an American bank in Tokyo. The bank is having a party, and Julie goes with her husband. Look at the questions people ask her, and give short answers.

0 Do you like Tokyo ~ ....Yes, I do........ (yes/I)

1 Was your flight here comfortable? ~ .... (yes/it)

2 Are you enjoying the party? ~ .... (yes/I)

3 Does your husband speak any Japanese? ~ .... (no/he)

4 Have you visited Mount Fuji yet? ~ .... (no/we)

5 Are you going to visit other parts of Japan? ~ .... (yes/we)

6 Has your husband met your boss yet? ~ .... (yes/he)

7 Will you buy a flat in Tokyo? ~ .... (no/we)

8 Do you like Japanese food? ~ .... (yes/I)

9 Do you have any children? ~ .... (no/we)

E   At a food market

Anne and Gary and their friends, Pierre and Isabelle, are at a food market. Put the words in the right order. Start your questions with *what, which, who, whose* or, for *yes/no* questions, nothing.

ANNE   Is that Gary over there? _Who is he speaking to?_ [0] (speaking to/is/he)

PIERRE   A woman on a stall.

ANNE   Oh. .... [1] (he/buy/to/going/is)

PIERRE   I don't know. .... [2]
         (do/at this market/normally buy/you)

ANNE   Everything! Look at that lovely bread, for example!
         .... [3] (two small loaves/I/get/shall)

PIERRE   Yes, that's a good idea.

MAN   Hello, darling. .... [4]
         (loaves/want/do/you) - the white or the brown ones?

ANNE   The white ones, please. .... [5]
         (have/Isabelle/seen/you), Pierre? Perhaps I'll give her a ring.

PIERRE   I spoke to her five minutes ago.

ANNE   Really? .... [6] (say/did/she)
         Wait a moment, Pierre. There's something on the ground. (*She picks up a phone.*)
         .... [7] (is/phone/this)

PIERRE   Isabelle's. Oh dear.

MAN   Excuse me. .... [8] (you/looking for/are)

ANNE   His girlfriend, Isabelle. She's wearing a long white coat.

MAN   Don't worry. I can see her. She's at the fish stall over there.

F   A car journey to North Wales

Linda and Roger are driving their children, Jessica and Marc, to a holiday cottage in North Wales. Put a circle around the correct question words.

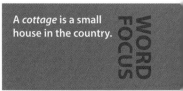
A *cottage* is a small house in the country.

WORD FOCUS

LINDA   Are you OK, Marc? *Which/(What)/When/Why* [0] did Jessica do?

MARC   She ate my chocolate. *Where/When/Why/How* [1] far is the cottage now?

LINDA   Fifty miles or so. *Who/Why/Whose/How* [2]'s got the map?

ROGER   I have, I think. *Why/What/Where/Who* [3] did you put my glasses, though?

LINDA   *What/Which/Whose/Where* [4] glasses are you looking for, your sunglasses or your reading glasses?

ROGER   My reading glasses, of course, for the map!

LINDA   I think they're in the pocket of your jacket, dear.

ROGER   Thanks. *When/Which/What/Whose* [5] shall we stop for some lunch, Linda?

LINDA   In half an hour? *Where/Who/Why/How* [6] were you shouting, Marc?

MARC   Jessica took my ball.

ROGER   Are you sure? *When/Who/How/Whose* [7] is that ball by the window?

MARC   Oh, yes. It's mine. But I'm hungry. *Which/What/When/Whose* [8] time is it, Dad?

ROGER   Half past eleven.

MARC   Are we nearly there?

OVER TO YOU   **Now go to page 123.**

13 *Can*
Ability and possibility

1 Here are some examples of **can**:
*She **can speak** French and Arabic.*
*I **can't come** with you tonight, I'm afraid.*
***Can** I **have** a small black coffee, please?*

2 We form sentences with **can** like this:

> **can + verb**

*I **can see** Tom's car.*

POSITIVE		
I/he/she/it/we/you/they	**can**	help.
NEGATIVE		
I/he/she/it/you etc.	**cannot/can't**	help.
QUESTIONS		
Can I/he/she/it/you etc.	**use** your phone, please?	

> We write the negative form **cannot** as one word, but we use **can't** when we speak or write informally.
>
> TIP

3 We use **can** to talk about our skills (our general abilities):
*I **can sing**, but I **can't play** the piano.*

4 We sometimes use **can** with **see**, **hear** and **smell** to talk about things we are able to do right now:
***Can** you **see** Milly anywhere?*

5 We use **can** to talk about things that are (not) possible:
*We **can call** a taxi, or we **can get** a bus.*

> If something very unusual happens, we sometimes say, 'I can't believe it!'
> *I can't believe it. I've just won a holiday!*
>
> TIP

Grammar in action

1 We use **can** to talk about our skills. Here we're thinking about people's abilities at work:
*I know she **can do** anything on the computer, but **can** she **work** with other people?*
*He **can't type** quickly, but he would like to learn.*

2 We use **can** to talk about the things we see, hear or smell right now. We might write a postcard describing our experiences on holiday:
*I **can hear** the sea from my balcony.*
*I **can see** the beach from my room.*
*The food at the local market looks delicious, but I've got a cold - I **can't smell** anything.*

3 We use **can** to talk about the things that are possible or not possible in our daily lives. Here, we're thinking about our plans for the week:
***Can** you **finish** work early tomorrow?*
*I **can go** to the gym with you on Sunday, but I **can't come** to the cinema on Wednesday.*

WORD FOCUS

First, put these words under the correct pictures of sports:
snooker ....
basketball ....
baseball ....
iceskating ....

A Talking about our skills

Alida from Hungary is spending a month in America with Grace, Ryan and their five-year old son, Mickey. Add *can* in positive, negative or question form to the words in brackets, and complete the conversation.

GRACE   Ryan is going to make some special hamburgers for us tonight.
<u>Can you cook</u> ⁰ (you/cook), Alida?

ALIDA   ....¹ (I/make) a nice salad, but ....² (I/not/do) any interesting Hungarian dishes, I'm afraid. They're too difficult.

MICKEY   ....³ (you/play) basketball or baseball, Alida?

GRACE   Say 'no', Alida, or you'll spend every day in the garden with Mickey.

ALIDA   ....⁴ (I/not/play) basketball or baseball, Mickey, but ....⁵ (I/skate).

MICKEY   On ice? That's fantastic! ....⁶ (you/play) snooker too, Alida? We've got a new snooker table!

ALIDA   No, I can't, I'm afraid.

GRACE   Alida can skate, Mickey, and .... ⁷ (she/play) the piano, too. That's
         pretty good.
MICKEY   And .... ⁸ (she/speak) Hungarian and English!

B   Talking about the things we can see, hear and smell

Amelia and Karen are going to look after Harry's house by the sea while he is
in hospital. Put the words in brackets in the right order, and add them to the
conversation. Use capital letters where necessary.

In the kitchen, we use
a *kettle* to heat water
for tea or coffee.

WORD FOCUS

KAREN   It's dark in here. _I can't see anything_ ⁰ (anything/I/see/can't). Can you put
         the light on?
AMELIA   OK. It's very quiet. Listen. .... ¹ (the sea/hear/can/you)?
KAREN   The kitchen's not very clean, is it? .... ² (see/you/a kettle/can)
         anywhere? I'd like a cup of tea.
AMELIA   Shall we have some orange juice? .... ³ (a lot of/can/
         old newspapers/see/I), but .... ⁴ (any cups/can't/I/see) or a kettle
         at the moment.
KAREN   OK, but are you sure we're the only people here? .... ⁵ (hear/
         a noise/can/I) in the next room.
AMELIA   .... ⁶ (I/anything/hear/can't). Perhaps you're tired.
KAREN   No, I'm not. And .... ⁷ (you/fish/smell/can)? I'm going to have a look.
AMELIA   Well, ... ⁸ (you/anything/see/can)?
KAREN   Yes, there's a small black cat here, and it's eating fish from a plate!

C   Talking about the things that are (not) possible in our daily lives

Sue is emailing Max on Friday evening. Add the words *can* or *can't* to these two
messages. You will need to add three words to each message.

(i)

Hi Max,

                                                                                              can
I tried to speak to you at work today, but you were busy. I know you're working hard right now, but /

we meet on Monday evening, perhaps? We could have something to eat. I see you at the weekend,

because I'm going to visit my dad in Wales. He's ninety now. He get to the shops every day, so he

always has enough to eat, but he do all the jobs around the house. Anyway, email or ring me!

Sue

(ii)

Hi Sue,

Thanks for your message. I see you on Monday evening, because I'm flying to Sweden on business on

Monday morning, but thanks for asking me. I do something with you next weekend, though. Do you

want to see a film or go for a walk? I know I'm working too hard at the moment, but I stop because

this is my first big project, and my boss is watching me! I hope your weekend with your dad is OK.

Max

6 We use **can** to ask for things (make requests):
Can I borrow your pen, please?

and to offer to do things:
Can I take you to the station?

> **We don't use please with offers:**
> *I can meet you at the airport, ~~please~~.*
> *Can I help you, ~~please~~?*
>
> TIP

7 We use **can** to talk about permission and rules (things we must or must not do):
Can we play football here?
You can't eat inside.

Grammar in action

4 We use **can** to make simple requests with friends and family. Here a father is talking to his daughter:
Can you speak to your mother before you leave?
Can you ring me when you get to Paris?

5 We use **can** to offer to do things for friends and family. At the end of a meal, you might say:
Can I help you? I can wash up, if you like.

6 We use **can** in public places like shops, cafés, stations and hotels to make requests and offers:
Can we check our email here, please?
I can give you a table by the window, Madam.

7 We use **can** to talk about permission and rules. Here is a traveller on a train:
Can I use this ticket at any time?
~ No, you can't, I'm afraid. It's for today only.

D   Making requests and offers at a friend's house

James is staying in Hanoi with Tam and Minh. Add these phrases to their conversation:

Can you take some books	I can make some food	~~Can you pass me~~
Can I give them	I can take you	Can I do anything	can you bring	Can I help

JAMES   ___Can you pass me___ ⁰ the rice, please?

TAM   Sure. You need to eat before your journey. _____ ¹ to the station on my bike in the morning.

JAMES   That's very kind of you, Tam.

MINH   And _____ ² for you to take. The food on the train is terrible!

JAMES   Thank you very much. _____ ³ for you while I'm in Ho Chi Minh city?

TAM   Actually, there is something, James. _____ ⁴ for my sister? I could post them, but it takes a long time.

JAMES   No problem.

TAM   Thanks. _____ ⁵ to you now? I'll forget in the morning!

JAMES   Of course! _____ ⁶ with anything else?

TAM   Well, if you're sure it's no trouble, _____ ⁷ my blue suitcase back from my sister's house? She borrowed it when she moved.

JAMES   It's not a problem. I'm pleased to be able to help.

E Making requests and offers at a hotel

James is talking to a member of staff, Tran, in a business hotel in Ho Chi Minh city. Look at the example, and then cross out six more wrong words in the conversation.

TRANG Good evening, sir. Can I ~~can~~ help you?

JAMES Yes, I hope so. Can ~~you~~ I have a single room for two nights, please?

TRANG Of course, sir. I can ~~have~~ give you a room on the top floor, if you like. You'll have a great view!

JAMES That's fine, thanks.

TRANG Can you fill in this form, please?

JAMES Sure. Can I ~~buy~~ pay by credit card?

TRANG Of course, sir. No problem. Can ~~you~~ I see your card now, please?

JAMES Here it is. By the way, is it possible to use the internet here?

TRANG Certainly, sir. The business lounge is on the seventeenth floor. You can check your email there at any time, but you can't send faxes after 10 p.m. Now, can I ~~show~~ see your passport, please?

F In a sports clothes shop in Manchester

We use *can* to talk about our skills; the things we see and hear; the things that are and aren't possible in our daily lives; and to make requests and offers at home and in public places. Hideo and Lily are talking to an assistant, Adam, in a sports clothes shop in Manchester. Add the following phrases, using capital letters where necessary:

> I can   I can't   can I (x 2)   can you (x 3)   you can't

ADAM   Hi, ...*can I*.... ⁰ help you?

HIDEO Yes, please. .... ¹ try these trainers on? I'm size forty-three or forty-four.

ADAM   Certainly. .... ² bring both sizes if you like. I'll be back in a couple of minutes.

HIDEO Thanks. Have you found anything, Lily?

LILY   Perhaps. .... ³ see those ski jackets in the corner? The red ones?

HIDEO Sure, but .... ⁴ ski?

LILY   No, but they look good. .... ⁵ play football, Hideo, but you sometimes wear a Manchester United shirt, don't you?

HIDEO That's true. How much are the jackets?

LILY   A hundred and fifty quid. .... ⁶ buy one at the moment. I don't have enough money. But they're having a sale here after Christmas.

HIDEO .... ⁷ wait?

LILY   I suppose so, but it's a hard life, isn't it?

OVER TO YOU Now go to page 124.

WORD FOCUS

Shop words
1 To *try something on*: if you want to try clothes or shoes before you buy them, to see if they're right, say 'Can I try these shoes / this jacket on, please?'
2 A *sale* is the time when things in a shop are cheaper. In the UK, shops have sales after Christmas and in the summer (and at other times, too.)

1 Some examples of **could**:
*Could you **tell** me the time, please?*
*The car's not working, but we **could take** a taxi.*
*Ellen **couldn't meet** us at lunchtime.*

2 We form sentences with **could** like this:

could + verb

*We **could go** to the cinema.*

POSITIVE		
Could	I/he/she/it/you/we/they	**use** your phone, please?

NEGATIVE		
Could	I/he/she/it/you etc.	**come**.

QUESTIONS		
Could	I/he/she/it/you etc.	**say** something?

3 **Could** is the past form of **can**, but we often use it to make polite requests in present time:
*Could I **have** some water, please? ~ Of course.*
*Could you **shut** the door? I'm cold.*

Grammar in action

1 We use **could** to make polite requests in public places. We might ask for directions on the street, or make a request in a restaurant, hotel or bank:
Could you tell me the way to the town centre, please? ~ Yes, of course. It's straight ahead.

2 We use **could** to make suggestions when we're deciding what to do. Here, we're thinking about the weekend:
What shall we do this weekend? ~ We could go for a walk by the sea. ~ OK. I could make some sandwiches for a picnic.

3 We sometimes use **could** and **couldn't** to talk about our ability to do things a long time ago:
I could swim ten kilometres when I was at school.
People couldn't go to New York for a weekend when I was a child.

A Making polite requests in public places

Lance and Petra are walking along a street in Alice Springs, Australia. **Put the words in the right order, and add polite requests. Use a capital letter at the beginning of the requests, and a question mark at the end.**

PETRA I'm thirsty, Lance. I'm going to get something from this lady.
 <u>Could I have a bottle of water, please?</u> **0** (have/a bottle of water, please/I/could)

LADY Sure. Here you are. That's 75 cents, please. Are you going anywhere nice?

LANCE Yes. We're going to Ayers Rock. **1**
 (tell us/to the bus station, please/could/the way/you) I think we turn left here.

LADY Yes, you do. Walk all the way along Spring Street, and then cross Todd River. Bye!

(*Later, at the travel centre at the bus station.*)

PETRA **2**
 (we/about the trip/some information/have/to Ayers Rock, please/could)

MAN Of course. We have a special offer at the moment – 98 dollars for a return ticket.

LANCE Excellent. **3**
 (a timetable, please/could/us/you/give)

PETRA There's a bus early in the morning, isn't there?

MAN That's right. There's one at seven thirty. Here's the timetable.

LANCE Seven thirty is perfect. **4**
 (have/for tomorrow, please?/we/two return tickets/could)

B Making suggestions with friends and family

Francesca and Sean are going to spend the weekend in Newquay in Cornwall. The word *could* is missing from Francesca's email. After the example, put '/' six more times where *could* is missing.

Hi Sean,

Thanks very much for your message. I'm glad you're free at the weekend. We / drive to Newquay around ten in the morning. It takes about four hours from my house. I bring some sandwiches. We'll be hungry before we get there. In the afternoon we cycle along Watergate Bay, perhaps.

It's beautiful there. You take some fantastic photos with your new camera! Then, in the evening, we eat at 'Mickey's', if you like, the small fish restaurant in Newquay. It's very popular, so I reserve a table before we go. I've booked two rooms at the Sandy Beach Hotel, of course. My friends Dave and Connie stay there every summer. They love it. Then, on Sunday we visit Sheila and Michael. They live in Exeter, on our way home. What do you think?

Best wishes,

Francesca

C Talking about our abilities when we were younger

Bill is having coffee with his grandson, Jake, and his old friend, Lewis. Add the following phrases to their conversation, using capital letters where necessary:

> you couldn't change   some English people could go   I could run
> you could buy   we could only stay   we couldn't travel   ~~I could play all day~~

BILL   How are you, Lewis? You look well.

LEWIS   Really? I played tennis for an hour this morning, and I don't feel well! When I was Jake's age, _I could play all day_ ⁰.

BILL   I know. ....¹ along the road for hours and hours when I was at college. Now I'm tired after a short walk!

LEWIS   Anyway, how are you, Jake? Bill says you're spending your gap year in China and south-east Asia. You're lucky. When we were fifteen or sixteen we left school, and we went to work. ....² across the world.

JAKE   But ....³ to Spain and Greece in those days. I've read books by English writers who travelled in Europe in the 1950s.

BILL   That's true. In fact, I took a train to Italy when I was twenty. But ....⁴ for a week or ten days, not for a year.

LEWIS   Then we started work, and many of us worked for the same company all our lives!

BILL   That's right. ....⁵ jobs easily in those days.

JAKE   But at least ....⁶ a house, Grandad. They're too expensive for young people now.

LEWIS   That's true. Some things are more difficult these days, Bill.

> A *gap year* is the year between school and university, when some students travel around the world, or work on special projects.
>
> WORD FOCUS

Could, was able to, managed to
Couldn't, was able to, managed to: ability in the past

4 Some examples of **couldn't**, **was able to**, and **managed to**:

> I **couldn't go** to Kate's party.
> We **were able to sell** the house quickly.
> Joe **managed to find** a cheap CD player.

5 When we talk about our ability to do something at a particular moment in the past, we can use **couldn't**:

> I **couldn't park** the car anywhere in the centre of town this morning.
> They **couldn't find** a hotel with a sea view.

But we can't normally use **could**:

> ~~We could get two tickets for the concert.~~

Instead, we use **was/were able to** or **managed to**:

> We **were able to get** two tickets for the concert.
> I **managed to speak** to Nancy at the party.

6 We form positive sentences with **was/were able to** like this:

> **was/were able to + verb**

> He **was able to go**.
> They **were able to go**.

And we form sentences with **managed to** like this:

> **managed to + verb**

> We **managed to finish**.

Grammar in action

4 We use **was/were able to**, **managed to** and **couldn't** to talk about our ability at particular moments in the past. Here, we're talking about last weekend:

> We **were able to get** a table at that new French restaurant on Friday, and I **managed to finish** all my college work on Saturday, but we **couldn't go** for a walk on Sunday because it rained all day.

WORD FOCUS

First match these words with the correct pictures:

lamp ....
rug ....
coffee table ....
fan ....
mirror ....

[1] [3] [4] [2] [5]

D Talking about last week

Holly and Eva are having a meal together on Sunday evening in their flat. Add the correct phrases to the conversation.

HOLLY Did you have a good week, Eva?

EVA Not bad, thanks. ___I was able to talk___ ⁰ (I was able talk/I was able to talk) to my boss about my trip to Paris. She's normally so busy. _____¹ (We were able to finish/We able to finish) my schedule of meetings.

HOLLY That's great. When do you leave?

EVA _____² (We were managed to book/We managed to book) a flight for 1 p.m on Tuesday. I'm looking forward to it. What about your week?

HOLLY It was OK. _____³ (I couldn't to sleep/I couldn't sleep) at night at the beginning of the week, because it was so hot.

EVA I know. _____⁴ (I managed to buy/I managed buy) a fan at the shops. You can borrow it when I'm in Paris, if you like. What about your room? Are you comfortable there now?

HOLLY Yes, thanks. _____⁵ (I was able buy/I was able to buy) a beautiful new rug on Saturday, and my sister gave me a lamp. But _____⁶ (I couldn't find/I couldn't to find) a mirror.

EVA Really? Have you tried the market? _____⁷ (George managed to get/George was managed to get) a coffee table there last year.

HOLLY No, I'll have a look there tomorrow.

E Moving flat

We use *could* for polite requests, suggestions, and general ability in the past. We use *was/were able to*, *managed to* and *couldn't* for past ability at particular moments. Add the following phrases to this email:

> managed   could   couldn't   could sleep   managed to
> could put   could eat   ~~you help~~   could you   were able to

Hi Amy

I'm moving flat on Monday. Could ......*you help*...... ⁰ me? On Friday I .... ¹ book a removals van, but I .... ² find any boxes in town. When I was a student, I .... ³ all my things in one box, but now I need ten! Anyway, I phoned my friend Jake yesterday morning, and we .... ⁴ get some boxes from his sister – she moved flat a month ago. And in the afternoon, we .... ⁵ to sell my old bed to Jake's brother for £20! He's going to start university in September. So I need to buy a new bed quickly. I .... ⁶ on the floor for a week or two when I was younger, but not now! Anyway, ... ⁷ help me for an hour or so on Sunday morning? I need some advice in the kitchen: I could take all my old plates, cups and knives and forks to the new flat, or I .... ⁸ throw them away! What do you think? We .... ⁹ a pizza afterwards, if you like. Look forward to hearing from you.

Best Wishes, Fred

F A hospital visit

James and his daughter Kay are visiting Kay's sister, Jo, in hospital. Add the following words or phrases to the conversation:

> managed   able   ~~see~~   have   you   could   couldn't

JAMES Hello. Could we /*see* Jo Corrigan, please?

NURSE I'm sorry, but you can't see her at the moment.

JAMES Really? When my wife was in hospital in January, we were to visit her all the time.

NURSE That's right, but at the moment we don't have enough nurses on the ward.

JAMES I suppose we come back later, Kay.

NURSE Could come back in an hour, perhaps?

KAY But is she OK after the operation?

NURSE Oh yes. She eat her dinner last night, but she to have some breakfast this morning.

JAMES Don't worry, Kay. We could a coffee in the hospital café. Thank you, nurse. We'll come back later.

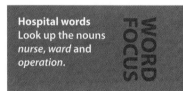

Hospital words
Look up the nouns *nurse*, *ward* and *operation*.

WORD FOCUS

OVER TO YOU Now go to page 124.

15 Should
You should eat more fruit

1 Some examples of **should**:

*You **should learn** some Chinese before you go to Beijing.*
*They **should have** a party in their new house.*
*Dan **shouldn't play** his music so loud.*
***Should** I **buy** a new car?*

2 We form sentences with **should** like this:

> **should + verb**

*You **should have** a holiday.*

POSITIVE		
I/he/she/it/you etc.	**should**	**read** this book.
NEGATIVE		
I/he/she/it/you etc.	**should not/ shouldn't**	**wait**.

Grammar in action

1 We use **should** to say if something is or isn't a good idea. Here, we're talking about travel plans:

You should visit Japan in May or June. It's beautiful. (= It's a good idea for you to visit Japan.)
She shouldn't travel everywhere by taxi.
(= It isn't a good idea for her to travel by taxi.)
They shouldn't go by car. The train is much quicker.

2 We use **You should/shouldn't...** to give practical advice. You might talk to a friend about their work:

You should relax more. You look tired.
You shouldn't stay at the bank if you don't like your job there.
You should take a lunch break every day.

> **TIP**
>
> We sometimes use **I** instead of **You** to give advice:
>
> *My wife and I are going to have dinner in Luigi's on Saturday night. ~ Really? **I should book** a table. It's very busy at the weekend.*

A Saying if something is a good idea

Olivia and her husband Charlie are talking about their twins, Harvey and Emma. Complete their conversation by writing forms of *should* instead of the phrases in brackets.

CHARLIE After their exams Harvey and Emma will be free for eight weeks, before they go to university. They <u>should find jobs.</u> **0** (It's a good idea for them to find jobs.)

OLIVIA I'm not sure, Charlie. It isn't easy to get summer jobs these days, and they've worked so hard! They .... **1** (It's a good idea for them to have a holiday.)

CHARLIE For eight weeks? I don't think so, Olivia. Emma .... **2** (It's a good idea for Emma to talk to Uncle Jim.) Jim could give her a job at his shop. And Harvey could work in a hotel again.

OLIVIA But they .... **3** (But it isn't a good idea for them to work all the time.) It's our last family summer!

CHARLIE Perhaps you're right. We .... **4** (It's a good idea for us all to go to France for a couple of weeks.)

OLIVIA Yes, but we .... **5** (Yes, but it isn't a good idea for us to decide today.) We should talk to them first. They're both eighteen now!

B Giving advice on work, health and relationships

Mike is writing a letter to Rashid, the son of an Indian friend. Rashid is starting a course at a British university. Start the phrase in brackets with *You should* or *You shouldn't*, and then add it to the letter.

Dear Rashid,

I hope you had a good journey. Your father asked me to give you some advice about life at university. Well, first of all, in my opinion, ...you should do a budget...... ⁰ (do a budget), because life can become difficult if you don't have any money! Next, ...¹ (think about food). You can't study if you don't eat well. For example, ...² (eat take-aways) every evening! They're expensive, and they're not very good for you. ....³ (go to your local shops) or the supermarket and buy simple, fresh food. Vegetables and some types of fish are very cheap.

Soon you'll start your course. Your university work is important, but ....⁴ (study) all night! You'll be tired in the morning. Instead, ...⁵ (make a timetable) for yourself, and work regularly. After you've worked for three hours or so, ...⁶ (go for walk) or a swim. It's important to get some fresh air!

It's also important to meet people. ....⁷ (go out every night), because it's expensive, but it's a good idea to make new friends in the first month or two. Friends can help you when life is hard! Finally, if you need any more help or advice, ...⁸ (call me).

Yours truly,

Mike

C Saying something is a good idea and giving advice

Scott is phoning Eve at work. After the example, add *should* and *shouldn't* three more times each, using '/' and writing the correct word at the end of the line.

SCOTT Hi, Eve. It's seven o'clock. Are you still at work?

EVE You / ring me at the office, Scott. I can't talk right now. shouldn't

SCOTT Have you got a headache again?

EVE Yes. It started this afternoon. I get a headache most days.

SCOTT Then you see a doctor.

EVE I know. I'll go next week.

SCOTT Good. Anyway, it's my birthday on Saturday. We have a party. What do you think?

EVE I'm not sure, Scott. I'm so busy at work at the moment.

SCOTT But you work at the weekend! Life is too short.

EVE Perhaps you're right. But if we have a party, we cook anything. I'm too tired.

SCOTT That's fine. We ring Max. He could bring some great cold food from his shop.

EVE OK, but we invite too many people. It's too much work.

SCOTT I understand. Don't worry, we'll have a quiet party!

3 Look at this dialogue:
Should I *wear* a suit tonight?
~ No, but *I don't think you should* wear jeans.

4 We form questions with **should** like this:

> should + I/he/she/it/you etc. + verb

Should we *buy* some food?

Grammar in action

3 We use **Should I...?/Should we...?** to ask for someone's opinion or advice. Here, we're making plans for a party:
Should I invite Sam and Meg, too? ~ *You can, but Sam doesn't like parties.*
Should we cook some food for our guests?
~ *No. Crisps and peanuts will be OK.*
Should I get some new CDs?
~ *That's a good idea. We need some dance music.*

Sometimes we ask **What should I do?**:
Greg wants me to help him with his report, and Sue wants me to go to a meeting at the same time. **What should I do?**

We often use the verb **think** before **should**:
I *think* you *should call* the Police.
I *don't think* you *should eat* another pizza.
Do you *think* I *should* talk to Chris? He looks a bit sad.

WORD FOCUS

First match these words with the correct pictures:
wardrobe ....
armchair ....
chest of drawers ....
sofa ....

1

2

3

4

D Asking for opinions or advice

Lauren and Robert are in a furniture shop, looking for things for their new house. Put the words in brackets in the right order, and add them to the conversation. Use capital letters and question marks where necessary. *Get* sometimes means *buy*.

LAUREN Should we buy a sofa [0] (a sofa/we/buy/should) today, or
.... [1] (buy/should/an armchair/we), Robert?

ROBERT Well, this brown sofa looks nice. .... [2]
(try/we/it/should) (*They sit on the sofa.*)

LAUREN It's very comfortable, isn't it? .... [3]
(get/should/it/we) How much is it?

ROBERT I don't know. .... [4] (ask/I/that assistant/should)

LAUREN I think he's busy at the moment with that couple, but there's some information on the table.

ROBERT I'll have a look. Oh! It's two thousand pounds!
.... [5] (go/to another shop/should/we)

LAUREN I think the prices will be the same.

ROBERT Really? .... [6] (look/I/
on the internet instead/should) It might be cheaper.

LAUREN But we need to get something today, because the house is so empty!

ROBERT Well, ... [7] (a wardrobe/
should/we/buy/do you think) or a chest of drawers for the bedroom, then?

LAUREN Perhaps, or .... [8] (should/a coffee table/get/we)
for the living room?

ROBERT Let's have a look upstairs!

E Making plans for a visit to Britain

We use *should* to say if something is a good idea, to give advice, and to ask for someone's opinion. Bob, from America, is emailing his friend Sally. Add the phrases below to the messages, but there is one phrase you won't need.

> think you   should I   don't think   you should   I visit
> should go   shouldn't try   should you   I fly   should take

---

Hi Sally,

As I said in my last message, I'll arrive in the UK on 4 September, and I can stay for two weeks. I'll spend two days in London with you, but then I'm not sure. Should ___I fly___ ⁰ to Scotland first, and see Edinburgh and the Highlands, or _____ ¹ hire a car and drive to Wales? And I want to see Liverpool too! And what about the old cities like Bath and Oxford and York? Should _____ ² them too? Help me, please!

Hi Bob,

You _____ ³ to do everything! You don't have time! I _____ ⁴ should travel by train, because you can relax and see things as you travel. First, you _____ ⁵ the train from London to York. It only takes two hours, so you can spend the rest of the day looking at the city. I _____ ⁶ to Edinburgh next. It's a nice journey with views of Durham, Newcastle and the sea on the way. There's a lot to see in Edinburgh, but I _____ ⁷ you should stay too long, because I know you want to see the Highlands. So, after a couple of days, _____ ⁸ take the train to Inverness, where you can hire a car and see the mountains! Finally, you can fly down from Inverness to Liverpool in an hour, and then take the train back to London. What do you think?

F Staying in Manchester

Despina has just finished an English summer course in Manchester. She's been living with Rachel and Sean. The word *should* is missing from the conversation. After the example, put '/' five more times where *should* is missing.

RACHEL You know that Despina wants to stay longer in Manchester, don't you, Sean?

SEAN Yes. I think it's a good idea for her. She / look for a room or a small flat.

RACHEL Yes, but she doesn't know the city very well, so we help her? (*Despina arrives home.*)

DESPINA Hi Rachel, Sean! I've found a great photography course at the university, but my mother wants me to return to Greece. What I do?

RACHEL How long is the course, Despina?

DESPINA Six months. Do you think I find a different course in Athens?

RACHEL No, but I think you speak to your mother today or tomorrow.

SEAN You tell her that your course is only six months long, Despina, and that you'll go home for Christmas!

OVER TO YOU Now go to page 124.

16

Must and *have to*
I must or *I have to*

1 Look at these examples of **must** and **have to**:
*I **must get up** earlier. I'm always late for work!*
*We **have to turn** right here for the city centre.*

2 We form positive sentences with **must** like this:

> **must + verb**

*I **must phone** my sister this evening.*

POSITIVE
I/he/she/it/you/we/they **must wash** the car today.

3 We form positive sentences with **have to** like this:

> **has/have to + verb**

*We **have to show** our passports here.*

POSITIVE
I/you/we/they **have to** ⎫
He/she/it **has to** ⎭ **go** now.

4 We use **must** and **have to** to say that something is necessary - or a very good idea - now or in the future:
*You **must visit** India one day! It's fantastic.*
*George **has to go** to New York on business.*

> We use short forms of **have + got to** + verb
> instead of **must** or **have to** in informal English:
> *I**'ve got to go** to the supermarket later.*
>
> TIP

Grammar in action

1 We use **You must…** or **Visitors** etc. **must…** in written rules in public places, on forms or on signs:
All visitors must go to Reception.
Passengers must wear their seatbelts during take-off.
You must bring a passport photo of yourself.

2 We use **must** for things that we decide are necessary. Here, we're talking about our studies:
I must finish my essay tonight.
I don't understand this book. I must talk to my teacher tomorrow.

3 We use **have to** to talk about things that are already arranged, such as the way we do our jobs, regulations in general, and appointments:
We have to wait here for a taxi.
I have to start work at 8 a.m.

4 We often use **have got to** in conversations and in informal writing to talk about things we need to do. We might need to make some changes in our lives:
I've got to get a new flat. It's so noisy where I live! ~ Really? My flat's OK, but I'm so bored at work. I've got to find a new job.

A   Written rules in public places

Daniela is an Italian exchange student at a British university. Match the phrases on the left with a letter to complete the rules she reads on her first day.

0 On arrival, all new students must go… c

1 You must carry… ....
them.

2 Exchange students… ....

3 New students must attend the lecture… ....

4 If you are not sure about your course,… ....

a …at 4 p.m. in the Main Hall.

b …must bring a letter from their home university with

c …to the Campus Office on the first floor.

d …you must talk to a Senior Lecturer today.

e …your new ID cards with you all the time.

B Things we decide are necessary, work and appointments.

In the phone conversation below, use *must* with the words in brackets in all Dave's lines, and *have to* in all Shannon's lines.

DAVE   Hi Shannon, how are you? _We must meet_ ⁰ (we/meet) soon. I haven't seen you for a month at least.

SHANNON   I'm fine, Dave, but I can't see you on Saturday. _I have to do_ ⁰ (I/do) some work for my new boss. What about Sunday lunch?

DAVE   Good idea, but .... ¹ (I/speak) to Mike first. He wants some help in his garden on Sunday.

SHANNON   Really? But .... ² (he/sell) his house because he's going to move to South Africa next month.

DAVE   That's right, but if the garden looks nice, he may get more money! But .... ³ (we/do) something this weekend, Shannon. What about a film on Sunday evening?

SHANNON   I'm afraid not, Dave. .... ⁴ (I/meet) a colleague from our New York office at the airport.

DAVE   OK, but it's my birthday next weekend, so .... ⁵ (we/have) a meal together on Saturday.

SHANNON   Sure. .... ⁶ (I/go) to the dentist's in the morning, but I'm free for the rest of the day.

C Talking about things we need to do

Fran meets Tim, an old friend, in the street. In the lines with numbers at the end, correct or improve the text by writing out a short form of *have got to* and underlining the place where it should go, as in the example.

FRAN   Hi there, Tim! Nice to see you! How's life? Are you still painting?

TIM   Yes, but I <u>find</u> a job this week, because I don't have any money. What about you? Are you OK?
I've got to find ⁰

FRAN   I'm OK, but my mother is ill, so I return to America.
.... ¹

TIM   Oh, I'm sorry. I hope she gets better.

FRAN   I'm sure she will, but she listen to her doctor. She won't stay in bed! .... ²

TIM   If you like, I'll give you one of my paintings to take to her.

FRAN   That's kind, Tim, but you sell your paintings, if you want to make money! .... ³

TIM   I know. Anyway, how are your brother and his wife? I haven't seen them recently.

FRAN   They're fine, thanks. They've just bought a big, new house in the south of London, and now they find some furniture for it. .... ⁴

TIM   Do they want a big painting for their living room?

FRAN   That's a good idea. I'll talk to them. But I go now. I'm going to buy my plane ticket this morning.
.... ⁵

16

Must and have to
I mustn't or I don't have to; Do I have to go?

5 Look at these examples:
*You **mustn't smoke** in the office.*
*You **don't have to cook** tonight, because Steve is going to bring some fish and chips.*
***Do** we **have to leave** the party now?*

6 We form negative sentences with **must** like this:

NEGATIVE	
I/he/she/it/you etc. **must not / mustn't**	be late!

7 We form negative sentences with **have to** like this:

NEGATIVE		
I/you/we/they	**do not/don't have to**	}go.
he/she/it	**does not/doesn't have to**	

*We **don't have to stay** here all night.*
*She **doesn't have to go** to work today.*

8 There is an important difference in meaning between **mustn't** and **don't/doesn't have to**. **Mustn't** means that something is a bad idea, or is wrong:
*You **mustn't use** a dictionary in the exam.*

Don't/doesn't have to means that something is not necessary (i.e. you don't **need** to do it):
*You **don't have to buy** me a birthday present.*

9 We also use **have to** to ask questions:

QUESTIONS			
Do	I/you/we/they	**have to**	get ready now?
Does	he/she/it	**have to**	go to Moscow?

*Do I **have to meet** Sam at the airport?* (= Is it necessary for me to meet Sam at the airport?)

> **Must** is possible for questions, e.g. *Must we finish this today?*, but not as common as **have to**.

Grammar in action

5 We use **mustn't** to say that something is a bad idea, or is wrong. Here, we're going on holiday:
I know we're late, but you mustn't drive so fast. It's dangerous. (on the way to the airport)
I mustn't forget my passport.

6 We use **don't/doesn't have to** to say that something is not necessary. We might be at a party:
We don't have to get a taxi home. Tom's going to take us by car.
Greg doesn't have to sleep on the sofa, because the little bedroom upstairs is free.

7 We use **Do/Does...have to** to ask if something is necessary. Here, we're at a hotel:
Do I have to pay more for a double room?
Do we have to leave before 12 p.m?

D Wrong or unnecessary things at a new job

Luca, Head Waiter at 'Pasta! Pasta!', is talking to Hugo on his first day at work. Add **mustn't** or **don't have to**.

'First of all, you start work at 6 p.m. and you ____mustn't____ ⁰ be late. Never! But you _____¹ take a bus home, because we'll book you a taxi. OK? And you _____² work on Mondays, because the restaurant is closed! You see? We're nice people here! Now, what about clothes? Well, you _____³ wear jeans. They're not very smart, are they? But you _____⁴ wear a black jacket - we will give you a nice white shirt instead every evening. Now, what's next? Oh yes. This will make you happy. You _____⁵ know anything about wine, because we have our own wine waiter, Giuseppe. OK, let's talk about the guests. Sometimes they can be difficult, but rule number one is that you _____⁶ argue with the customers! They are paying for everything here! OK, I think that's everything. You'll meet Mr Locatelli, the boss, tomorrow. He's a nice man, but remember, you _____⁷ talk when the boss is talking. He doesn't like that. Oh, I forgot something nice, Hugo. You _____⁸ cook your own meal in the evening anymore, because we will give you some pasta to take home! Fantastic!'

E What's necessary to travel by train?

Susan is at the Eurostar office at Waterloo station. Write out the questions that Susan asks, using the form *Do/Does…have to…?* and the words in brackets.

SUSAN Hello. My husband and I would like to travel from London to Avignon next month. <u>Do we have to buy a ticket soon?</u> **0** (we/buy a ticket soon), and .... **1** (we/get the ticket at Waterloo)

MAN Well, you can buy tickets here or on the internet, but you should reserve them soon.

SUSAN OK, we'll get two returns tomorrow. .... **2** (we/change in Paris)

MAN No, you can get a train that goes directly to Avignon.

SUSAN Thanks. .... **3** (we/choose our date of return tomorrow)

MAN It's cheaper if you do.

SUSAN OK, I understand. Now, my husband is sixty-one years old. .... **4** (he/pay the full price)

MAN No, it's cheaper for senior citizens. The exact price depends on when you travel.

SUSAN Good. Now, I'm a vegetarian. .... **5** (I/bring my own food) Or is there vegetarian food on the train?

MAN There's one vegetarian meal on the menu every day.

SUSAN OK. One last question. .... **6** (we/arrive early for our train)

MAN You should get here half an hour before it leaves.

SUSAN Thanks. That's great. Oh, I nearly forgot! .... **7** (we/to take our passports)

MAN Yes, Madam. They'll look at your passports in France in the normal way.

F Staying in a friend's house

We use *must* for important things; *mustn't* for things that are a bad idea; *have to* for arrangements; and *don't have to* for things that are not neccesary. Henry is going to live in Sarah's house in the village of Greenleaf, while she goes to France. Read her letter to him, and circle the correct phrase from the brackets.

Dear Henry

Thanks very much for looking after my house. Here are some notes to help you!

- You *mustn't answer/don't have to answer* **0** the telephone for me, because I have an answering machine.
- You *mustn't forget/don't have to forget* **1** to lock the windows when you go out.
- You *have to feed/mustn't feed* **2** the cat twice a day – once in the morning, and again at night.
- You *don't have to eat /must eat* **3** the food in the fridge, or it will go bad. There's some nice fish.
- You *don't have to water/mustn't water* **4** the plants in the garden, because it rains all the time!
- You *have to take/don't have to take* **5** a bus to Haslemere, if you want to shop at a supermarket. There are only three small shops in Greenleaf.
- You *don't have to use/mustn't use* **6** the washing machine, I'm afraid. It's broken and dangerous!
- Finally, you *must ring/don't have to ring* **7** me if you have any problems. I'll be happy to help!

With very best wishes,

Sarah

OVER TO YOU Now go to page 124.

17 The imperative
Come in!; Enjoy your holiday!

1 We use the **infinitive without** *to* (~~to~~ *enjoy*) to form **the imperative**:

> *Enjoy your holiday!* *Text me when you arrive.*
> *Show me your new jumper.*
> *Pass the milk, please.*

2 The **imperative can** be one word only:

> *Help!*

but normally we use it with other words:

> *Wait for me! I'm coming.*
> *Be careful! That case is very heavy.*
> *Follow me, please. I know the way to the museum.*
> *Come in, please.*

2 We use **the imperative** to make offers and suggestions. Here, we're talking to guests:

> *Have another biscuit!*
> *Help yourself to more coffee.*
> *Sit down and relax. Dinner will be ready in half an hour.*

3 We use **the imperative** to finish conversations:

> *Call me when you get there!*
> *Have a nice weekend!*
> *Take care!*

Grammar in action

1 We use **the imperative** to ask or invite people to do things. Here, we're making plans for the evening:

> *Look at the sky. It's going to rain.*
> *I don't want to go out.*
> *Give me a ring later, Janet. I think we're staying in tonight.*
> *Pass me the newspaper, please. I'll see what's on TV.*

> **TIP**
>
> Remember that in some situations (restaurants, for example) **the imperative** (with or without **please**) is **not** a polite way to talk to people - because it sounds like an order!:
> *Could you get me a glass of water, please?*
> (NOT ~~Get me a glass of water, please.~~)

A Asking and inviting people to do things

Mike is visiting Sue and Bill. Complete the dialogue, by rewriting the words in brackets. Use capital letters when you need to.

SUE   Mike! <u>Come in and get warm.</u> **0** (in/and get warm/come) How are you?

MIKE   I'm fine thanks, Sue. It's a cold day, isn't it?

SUE   Freezing. But it's warm in here. .... **1** (coat and gloves/me your/give) Where's Jan?

MIKE   She's not very well, I'm afraid, so I've come on my own.

SUE   Oh dear. Well, ... **2** (give/my best wishes/her) I hope she's better soon. .... **3** (by the fire/have a/seat). Bill will be down in a minute. I've just made some coffee, Mike. Would you like a cup?

MIKE   Thanks very much. You're right - it's nice and warm in here.

SUE   Here you are. .... **4** (yourself/to sugar and milk/help)

MIKE   Thanks. .... **5** (outside at/look/the weather). It's just started to snow!

SUE   Oh dear. It's good to be inside on a day like this. .... **6** (try/with your coffee/my fruitcake)

MIKE   Thanks. It looks delicious. What have you been doing then, Sue? .... **7** (all your news/me/tell)

B Finishing conversations

We often say goodbye with imperative sentences. Match beginnings with the endings to make some common examples.

0 Don't work...	4 Enjoy your...	...to your parents.	...you get there.
1 Give my love...	5 Don't forget...	...after yourself.	...too hard!
2 Give me a ring when...	6 Look...	...holiday!	...carefully.
3 Have...	7 Drive...	...a good journey!	...to email me.

0 *Don't work too hard.*   4 ....

1 ....   5 ....

2 ....   6 ....

3 ....   7 ....

C Making suggestions and offers

Look at this advertisement for a hotel. Complete it by using these phrases:

enjoy it   relax in   turn right at   see the famous   don't forget
have a swim   eat all   spend a couple   forget our   make yourself

WORD FOCUS

If you say to a visitor, *'Make yourself at home!'*, you want them to be as comfortable with you as they are in their own house.

Travelling to the office again?

Well, ___don't forget___ [0] that Friday will be here soon. Do you have any plans for the weekend? No? Don't worry! We have. Come and .... [1] of days at the Northwick Spa Hotel. (Just drive up the M1 and .... [2] Junction 8.)

Start your weekend with a delicious meal on Friday night in our top-class restaurant, 'Bellamy's'. Or .... [3] the food you can in our Chinese buffet restaurant, 'The Great Wall'! And on Saturday and Sunday, ... [4] at home in the hotel and gardens, or walk into the village of Norton and .... [5] castle.

But don't .... [6] wonderful spa! Before you go back, ... [7] in our beautiful, warm pool or just .... [8] the jacuzzi or sauna. It's your weekend, so .... [9]! (Because Monday will soon be here again.)

The imperative
Don't forget!

3 We put **don't** in front of the imperative to form the negative:
> **Don't touch** that plate! It's very hot.
> **Don't be** late home. We're going out tonight.
> **Don't forget** your camera!
> **Don't wait** for me. I'll meet you at the restaurant.

4 We only use **do not** in formal situations:
> **Do not leave** the room before the end of the exam, please.

At the zoo, you may see signs such as:
> **Do not feed** the animals.

Grammar in action

4 We use **the imperative** to give instructions. We might tell someone how to find our house:
> Turn right at the Post Office, and walk along Dean Road for about 100 metres. Don't cross the road. My house is number 24.

5 We use **the imperative** to give warnings. Here, we're in town:
> Be careful! Those plates look very expensive.
> Don't cross now. There's a car coming!
> Look out! That bus isn't going to stop!

6 We use **the imperative** to give advice. We might talk about the weather:
> Take an umbrella with you - I'm sure it's going to rain. ~ Don't listen to Tom. He's always wrong. It's going to be a beautiful day.

D   Giving directions on a mobile phone

Lyn is giving Ann instructions and warnings about finding her new house. Make the verbs in brackets into positive or negative imperatives.

ANN   Hi Lyn! I think I'm lost. I'm phoning you from St Mary's Church.

LYN   ....*Stay*........ ⁰ (stay) where you are. I'll come in the car. ....*Don't move*.... ⁰ (move).

ANN   ....¹ (wait) a moment! I'm enjoying the fresh air, and I'd like to walk. Just ....² (tell) me where to go.

LYN   OK, if you're sure. In a moment, you'll see a little bridge on your right, but ....³ (cross) it! It's very old and dangerous. After you've passed the bridge, ...⁴ (turn) left.

ANN   OK, I can see the bridge, and then a wood and a white house. Is that yours?

LYN   Yes. ....⁵ (go) into the wood, though. It's very dark. You'll get lost. Just ....⁶ (follow) the road up the hill.

ANN   OK, but Lyn, there's a big, black dog walking towards me. He looks angry.

LYN   Oh dear. That's Ben. He's not very friendly, so ....⁷ (touch) him. Just stand still and ....⁸ (enjoy) the fresh air. I'll come with a biscuit.

E   First day at university

Dr Sara Green is giving advice to new students. Add the following verbs to her advice. Use capital letters when you need to. There is one extra verb.

> lose   work   give   decide   go out   spend   ~~talk~~   be   have   stay

Welcome to the University of Yorkshire. Now, I'm sure you'll enjoy the next three years with us, but if you need help at any time, _talk_ ⁰ to someone at the Student Services office - don't just _____ ¹ at home in bed! And _____ ² careful with your money in the first few weeks. _____ ³ how much you can spend every week, and don't spend any more! Your studies, of course, will be the biggest part of your life. _____ ⁴ hard and you'll be OK. But don't _____ ⁵ all your time on your essays. Have a break when you feel tired - _____ ⁶ now and again and make friends. You'll meet students here from all over the world. And finally, please don't _____ ⁷ your university ID! You'll need it every day. Good luck, and _____ ⁸ a fantastic first year!

F   A barbecue

We use the imperative to ask people to do things; to make offers and suggestions; to finish conversations; to give instructions; to give warnings; and to give advice. Glenn and Nigel are having a barbecue. Add these phrases to their conversation:

If you don't know these words, look them up in your dictionary: *a barbecue, a fire, to burn oneself.*

WORD FOCUS

> Don't eat   Look at   Don't go   ~~Come into~~   But use   Put your   Have a

GLENN Hi Molly! _Come into_ ⁰ the garden. _____ ¹ coat on this chair. Have you met Nigel?

NIGEL Nice to meet you, Molly. _____ ² glass of water or some orange juice. The food will be ready later.

MOLLY Thanks. I'll have some juice, please. Wow! _____ ³ that barbecue! It's very big!

NIGEL Hey Tom! _____ ⁴ that meat. It isn't ready yet.

MOLLY Can I put a piece of bread on the fire? I want some toast.

NIGEL Well, all right. _____ ⁵ that big fork. _____ ⁶ too near the fire.

Now add these phrases:

> have some   help yourself   don't eat   don't burn
> but ask   be careful   put it   give Sally

GLENN Tom, _____ ⁷ to some more salad.

TOM Thanks. Have you seen Sally?

GLENN No, _____ ⁸ Julie. She lives with Sally. Or _____ ⁹ a ring. I'm sure she's going to come.

NIGEL Molly, _____ ¹⁰. That fire is really hot - _____ ¹¹ yourself!

MOLLY OK. My toast is ready. Oh! It's black.

TOM It looks horrible - _____ ¹² it, Molly. You'll be sick.

GLENN Tom's right - _____ ¹³ in the fire, and _____ ¹⁴ salad instead!

OVER TO YOU Now go to page 124.

1 Some examples of phrases with **have got** and **have**:
I've got a good friend in Australia. He's having a great time there.

2 Here are the positive and negative forms of **have got** and **have**:

POSITIVE
I/you/we/they **have got**/**'ve got** he/she/it **has got**
I/you/we/they **have** he/she/it **has**

NEGATIVE
I/you/we/they **have not**/**haven't got** he/she/it **has not**/**hasn't got**
I/you/we/they **do not have**/**don't have** he/she/it **does not have**/**doesn't have**

➔ For more information on questions with **have got** and **have**, see p. 46.
Note that the word **got** in **have got** never changes:
*I've **got**; you've **got**; he/she/it's **got** etc.*

3 We use **have got** for things we own/possess, for family and for illnesses:
*I've **got** a cold / headache / stomach ache etc.*
*We **haven't got** a garden.*

We can use **have** instead of **have got**, but **have got** is more common:
*I **have** a headache.*

4 We use **have** (NOT ~~have got~~) with these activities:

> have a bath/shower   have breakfast/lunch/dinner
> have a meal/a pizza/a sandwich/a cup of tea etc.
> have a holiday   have a good/great/bad etc. time
> have fun   have a walk/dance/swim/game

We can use the **present continuous** of **have** with these activities:
*Dave's **having** a bath. Can he phone you later?*
*They're **having** a game of tennis at the moment.*

> When you're saying goodbye to someone, say *'Have a good time/holiday/meal/game!'* or just *'Have fun!'* TIP

➔ For more information on **make**, **do** and **get**, see p. 72.

Grammar in action

1 We use **have got** to talk about our possessions, family and friends:
She's got two sisters and five cats.
John hasn't got blue eyes. He's got brown eyes!
Have you got any money with you?

2 We use **have got** to talk about illnesses:
He's got a cold.

3 We use **have** for things we do every day at home: (have a bath/shower, have breakfast etc., have a sandwich etc.):
We normally have tea at 4 o' clock.
Where's Sheila? Is she having a shower?

4 We use **have** for freetime activities (**have a holiday**, **have a good** etc., **time**, **have fun**, **have a walk**, etc.):
She has a dance every time she hears that song.
We're having a great time in Corfu. (on a postcard)

A   Possessions, family and friends

Sally is talking about her sister. Add these words to what she says:

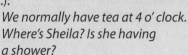

> she's   got   've got   's got   got   hasn't   I've   haven't

I haven't ____got____ ⁰ any brothers, but _____¹ got a sister called Kiki. She lives in Canada now; _____² got brown eyes and short black hair. She's pretty. She _____³ two big black dogs, but she _____⁴ got a husband or kids. I can't email her, because I _____⁵ got a computer, but I talk to her on the phone every day. We haven't _____⁶ much money, but we're both happy. We _____⁷ a good friend in Florida called Mabel, and we spend the summer there in her house.

B Possessions, family, friends and illnesses

Today is Kelly's first day at college in London. She's in the cafeteria. Add positive, negative or question forms of *have got* to the conversation. Use short forms, and capital letters where necessary.

KELLY Excuse me, but _have you got any aspirin?_ [0] (you/any aspirin?)

JULIE Sure. _____ [1] (you/a headache?)

KELLY Yes, it's very noisy here, isn't it? Is this your first day here?

JULIE Yes. My name's Julie. I don't know anyone. _____ [2]
(you/any friends at this college?)

KELLY I'm Kelly. No, I _____ [3] (I/not/any friends here),
but my brother lives in London, so I'm staying with him. It's good.
_____ [4] (He/lots of DVDs) and a big TV.
What about you? Where are you from?

JULIE East Anglia. _____ [5] (My parents/a farm there),
so London will be a big change for me.

KELLY Yes, I'm sure it will. _____ [6] (you/any brothers or sisters?)

JULIE Two sisters, but one is a baby! Shall we get another coffee before our first meeting?

C At home

It's Sunday morning. Jacob is at home with his parents and sisters. He's writing an email to his friend. Add a form of *have* (*having*, *have*, or *has*) eight times.

> having
> I'm / a sandwich, because I'm bored. Can I come over? Sunday morning is always the same in my house.
> Mum always a bath and Dad a walk. Sonia and Diana breakfast together. Then Dad comes home and a
> shower. Next, Mum and Dad a cup of tea together. Then Dad reads the papers. Then Mum, Dad, Sonia
> and me lunch together. Diana doesn't lunch with us because she goes to the gym. Anyway, what are you
> doing at the moment? Are you breakfast? Do you want to go for a swim or something?

D Freetime activities

Sara is phoning Maria, who is on holiday in Sweden with her friend Agneta, and Agneta's family. Add the correct form of *have* and complete the nouns in this conversation. Use capital letters where necessary.

SARA Hi, Maria. It's Sara here. _Are you having_ a good t_ime_ [0] (you) on holiday?

MARIA It's great, thanks. _____ f_____ [1] (you) at home?

SARA No, not really. _____ a bad t_____ [2] (my sister) at work at the
moment. She doesn't like her new boss.

MARIA Oh dear. Do you want me to speak to her?

SARA No, it's OK. _____ a w_____ [3] (she) in the park. I'll give her
your love. Anyway, how's Agneta?

MARIA She's fine. _____ a g_____ [4] (she) of tennis with her father at
the moment.

SARA And her brother?

MARIA Isak? He's fine too. _____ a s_____ [5] (he) in the lake. Well, I'd
better go. I'll speak to you later this week.

5 Some examples of **make, do** and **get**:
*I'm **making dinner** for some friends, and Tom is **doing**
the **washing**. We're both **getting tired**.*

6 **Make** sometimes means 'create':
*They **make** great **carpets** in Turkey.*
*Our company **made** a lot of **money** last year.*

We use **make** with food and drink, and with some
nouns (see 'Grammar in action' for a list):
*I'm going to **make a pizza** on Sunday night.*
*Can you **make** me **a cup of tea**, please?*
*She's **making a phone call** at the moment.*
*I think I've **made a mistake**.*

7 We use **do** for work in general, and for jobs at home:
*Can you be quiet, please? I'm **doing** some **work**.*
*We **did** three **exams** last month.*
*Who's going to **do the washing-up**?*

We also use **do** for 'personal' jobs:
*She's **doing her hair** right now.*
***Do your teeth** before you go to bed!*

And we use **do** with **something, nothing, anything**
and **everything** and with **well** and **badly**:
*I think she's **doing something** on the computer.*
*Kate **did** really **well** at college.*

8 **Get** can mean 'receive', 'obtain', 'catch' or 'buy':
*I **get** a hundred **emails** a day. (receive)*
*Shall I **get** you **a cup** from the kitchen? (obtain)*
*She **gets a taxi** to work sometimes. (catch)*
*James **got some flowers** for his mother. (buy)*

or 'become':
*Can we go home? I'm **getting tired**.*

Grammar in action

⑤ We can use **make** and **do** for activities in the house:

> make food   make a cake/a pizza/a cup of tea etc.
> make (some) breakfast/lunch/dinner
> make a phone call   make a noise   make a mess

> do the dishes/washing-up
> do the washing   do the cleaning
> do the ironing   do the cooking
> do (your) hair/teeth
> do something/nothing etc.

*The kids are doing the cooking, but
they're making a mess!*

⑥ We can use **make** and **do** at school and at work:

> make an effort   make progress   make a mistake
> make a decision   make a phone call
> make money   make a (new) product

> do some work   do a job
> do an exercise/test/exam
> do (your) homework
> do well/badly   do business

*I think I made some progress
yesterday.*

⑦ We use **get** for 'receive', 'obtain', 'catch' or 'buy', or for
'become' with these words:

> get tired   get angry   get bored
> get lost   get cold   get wet
> get better   get old   get washed
> get ready   get dressed
> get hungry   get married
> get divorced

We got lost four or five times!

E   Making dinner on Saturday night

**Paul, who shares a flat with Matt, Martin and Dave, gets a call from Milly. Circle the
correct verb forms.**

PAUL   Hi, Milly. I'm fine, thanks. I'm *making/doing*⁰ dinner, because it's Saturday. Here
at the flat, I *do/make*¹ the cooking at the weekend, and Matt *makes/does*² the
washing-up. Then Martin *makes/does*³ breakfast for us all on Sunday morning.

MILLY   And what does Dave do?

PAUL   Dave? I'm sorry, I can't hear you very well. Matt's *doing/making*⁴ a noise with his
        new CD player. Dave *makes/does*⁵ the washing - sometimes. Anyway, what are
        you and Jo doing?

MILLY   Jo says she's *done/made*⁶ a cake, but actually, she's *made/done*⁷ a mess in the
        kitchen. I'm *doing/making*⁸ nothing at the moment. Shall I come round?

F   Life in Kyoto

**Anne is learning Japanese in Kyoto. If the verbs are correct, put a tick (✓). If they're
wrong, cross them out and write the correct verb (*make*, *do* or *get*) in the correct form.**

Hi Joe,

I hope you're well. I'm making _____✓_____ ⁰ progress in Japanese, but it's not easy. I ~~do~~ _get_ ⁰ a bus
to class every morning, and I make _____ ¹ two or three exercises with my teacher, but I do _____ ²
mistakes all the time with the *kanji* (Japanese characters). I'm going to get _____ ³ a dictionary tomorrow,
so I can do _____ ⁴ some work at home. Kyoto is a really amazing place! There are so many temples.
Yesterday I made _____ ⁵ lost four times! Anyway, I got _____ ⁶ an email from Boris yesterday. He made
_____ ⁷ his final exams at Cambridge last week. He thinks he got _____ ⁸ well. I hope so, because he
made _____ ⁹ a really big effort! I must go now, Joe. I'm going to do _____ ¹⁰ ready for a meal at my
teacher's house. Write back soon!

Love, Anne

G   A business hotel in Karachi

**Alice and Tim are in a hotel in Karachi, waiting for their boss, Clara, and two
colleagues, Monty and Alan. Add the correct verb forms.**

ALICE   That was a really long day! Where's Monty?

TIM   He's _having_ ⁰ (making/doing/having) a shower. Monty _____ ¹ (gets/'s got/
        makes) a brother here in Karachi, you know. He's called Pandit.

ALICE   Really? Perhaps we'll meet Pandit this evening at dinner. I'm _____ ² (getting/
        doing/having) hungry. What about you?

TIM   Sure. Where's Clara?

ALICE   She's _____ ³ (making/doing/getting) her hair, I think. Clara says we're
        _____ ⁴ (doing/making/having) well in Karachi. It's a difficult market, but she
        says we're _____ ⁵ (doing/making/getting) progress.

TIM   Yes, I think so, too. We're meeting a lot of people, anyway. I _____ ⁶ (get/
        make/'ve got) ten business cards in my pocket.

ALICE   That's good. Look, there's Monty by the stairs. Is Alan coming with us this
        evening?

TIM   I'm not sure. He _____ ⁷ (gets/has/does) very tired when it's hot like this. He
        normally _____ ⁸ (makes/has/'s got) a swim at the end of the day, and then he
        _____ ⁹ (gets/has/makes) some phone calls to his children. He's _____ ¹⁰
        (getting/having/making) divorced, you know.

ALICE   Oh dear. That's very sad. I know his wife quite well.

OVER TO YOU **Now go to page 125.**

19 Verb + infinitive
Learn to cook; promise to write

1 Look at this example:

> **verb + infinitive**
>
> *I want to watch TV.*

2 We use an **infinitive** after these verbs:

> agree hope offer remember begin/start
> learn plan try decide manage
> promise want forget need refuse

> *I **need to speak** to the manager.*
> *Sara **is trying to learn** Chinese this year.*
> *They **refused to move** their car.*

Grammar in action

1 We use **decide**, **hope**, **need**, **plan** and **want** to talk about our hopes and plans. Here, we're talking about the New Year:

> *I've decided to get a new car.*
> *We're hoping to move to Spain in July.*

> *Sandra needs to learn Spanish for her job.*
> *Bill's planning to buy a flat.*
> *I want to have a really good holiday at Easter!*

2 We often use **begin/start**, **forget**, **learn**, **manage**, **remember**, and **try** to talk about the efforts we make. We might talk about a difficult week:

> *I've begun to paint the bedroom. It's hard work.*
> *Dan forgot to take his laptop to work.*
> *I'm learning to drive. I had my first lesson on Monday.*
> *We managed to get tickets for the concert.*
> *Did you remember to buy a new CD player?*
> *We tried to find a cheap restaurant, but couldn't!*

3 We use **agree**, **offer**, **promise**, and **refuse** to talk about the things we do (and don't do) for other people. Here are some flatmates talking:

> *Bill agreed to help me with my essay, and I offered to cook dinner for him.*
> *Do you promise to do some cleaning at the weekend?*
> *Tom has refused to wash up again. What shall we do?*

A Talking about our hopes and plans

Lucy and Adam are with their friends Ravi and Mina on New Year's Eve (31 December). Add the correct phrases to their conversation.

> planning to do   decided to change   ~~want to spend~~
> hoping to open   needs to write

MINA So, what are your plans for the New Year, Adam?

ADAM Well, we ..*want to spend*.. [0] a month in Spain in June. Lucy .... [1] her final essay for her university degree, and I'm .... [2] some fishing at sea! What about you two?

MINA Ravi has big plans. He's .... [3] his job.

RAVI That's right. I'm .... [4] a small bookshop.

LUCY That's fantastic. But will you make enough money?

> hoping to see   planning to create   wanted to look
> need to find   wants to open

RAVI I don't know! I'm .... [5] a website at the same time. It's possible that I'll sell more books on the internet than in the shop!

MINA He .... [6] the shop in March.

RAVI I .... [7] the right place, of course, but there's an empty shop on Queen Street.

LUCY Great, but what about you, Mina? You .... [8] for a new house.

MINA I know, but I've decided to wait. New houses are so expensive. Later in the year, though, I'm .... [9] my grandmother in Mumbai. That'll be exciting.

LUCY Good. Well, it's almost midnight. I hope it will be a great year for all of us!

B Talking about the efforts we make at home and at work

Mia's had a bad week. Look at her blog. Add the infinitives in brackets to each day of her week.

Monday	I forgot _to take_ / my purse to college, so didn't have any money all day. I managed _to borrow_ / £3 from Nick at lunchtime for a sandwich, but I was pretty hungry by the evening. (to borrow, to take)
Tuesday	I'm learning at the moment, and I went to my evening class. I tried my partner's hand, but we were dancing too fast and we both fell over! Maggie took a photo on her phone. (to hold, to dance)
Wednesday	I started some spaghetti at home for my sister, but then the phone rang and it was Claire from New York, and I forgot the spaghetti, and it burnt. Oh dear! I made a real mess. (to cook, to watch)
Thursday	I remembered Susie and Maisie in town for coffee, but I didn't know the name of the café, so I spent twenty minutes looking for them. I managed Maisie in the end, though. (to text, to meet)
Friday	I tried an important essay for college on Friday morning, but my neighbour, Ross, is learning the drums and it was impossible to work, so I took a photo of him instead, and then I went to the college library. (to finish, to play)

C Talking about the things we do for other people

To text means 'to send a written message on a mobile phone.' There is an example in exercise B.

Why did Sophie go to Paris? Read this conversation, and add the following infinitives:

to say   to drive   to meet   to help   to marry   to answer

CHARLOTTE	Sophie rang me on Thursday, and I agreed _to meet_ ⁰ her at Heathrow at 11.30.
OLIVIA	What did she say?
CHARLOTTE	Nothing. I offered _____ ¹ her all the way to her house in Cambridge, but she didn't tell me anything about her trip.
OLIVIA	Do you know where she went?
CHARLOTTE	No. She refused _____ ² my questions.
OLIVIA	So she agreed _____ ³ Bill in October, and then she went to Paris the same day, and now she's back in England. Charlotte, do you promise _____ ⁴ nothing to Sophie?
CHARLOTTE	OK, I promise.
OLIVIA	When Sophie was ill, I offered _____ ⁵ her at her house. When I was in the kitchen, the phone rang and a girl with a French accent said, 'Hello, this is Anne, Sophie's daughter.'
CHARLOTTE	Oh! She was probably in France to tell Anne about Bill then!

3 Look at this short dialogue:
It's nice to see you, Paolo. ~ Thanks. *I'm pleased to be* here again, Sue.

4 We use **it is / it's + adjective + infinitive** with these common adjectives:

> nice good interesting crazy silly
> wrong easy difficult/hard impossible

It's silly to spend all day in one museum.
It's impossible to find cheap clothes here.

We can also use **it was** or **it will / it'll**:
It was good to read your letter.
It'll be difficult to go home at the end of this holiday!

5 We use **I/you** etc.**+ be + adjective + infinitive** with these adjectives:

> glad happy pleased
> afraid sad surprised

I'm happy to meet you at the station.
She was surprised to see a dog in her garden.

Grammar in action

④ We use **it + adjective + infinitive** to give an opinion. We might be in town:
It's impolite to push in if people are waiting in a queue.
It's nice to go shopping with your friends, but it's easy to spend all your money!

⑤ We use **I/you** etc. **+ adjective + infinitive** to describe our feelings. We might be with our family:
We were sad to say goodbye.
Gran is afraid to go out at night.
I'm so glad to hear you like your present.

D Giving opinions about a new job

Brendan has just started a new job. Kevin, his manager, gives him all the pieces of advice below on his first day. Add *it's* and *to* to the phrases below, and then match your phrases with these endings:

> crazy/go to…   interesting/visit other…   hard/say that you've…
> wrong/send an email if…   easy/use the photocopier, and…
> impossible/finish…   good/talk to…

0 ...It's good to talk to... your colleagues - they often know more than you.
1 .... all your work before you go home.
2 .... it's easy to break it, too.
3 .... made a mistake, but you often do make mistakes!
4 .... offices and see how they do things there.
5 .... Tokyo for a meeting - have a video conference instead!
6 .... you can talk to a colleague instead.

E Describing our feelings when we see our friends

Oliver and Emma are meeting their South American friend Miranda at the airport. Complete the words in the spaces using *I/You* etc. *+ adjective + infinitive*. Use short forms where possible. Explanation 5 above will help you.

EMMA   Hi, Miranda. I 'm so g lad to see ⁰ you again! How was your flight?
MIRANDA Fine, thanks. I .... h .... b ....¹ in England again. How are you?

EMMA	I'm well, thanks. Let me introduce you to Oliver, my new husband.
OLIVER	Hello, Miranda. _____ very pl_____ m_____ [2] you. Emma has told me so much about you! Can I take your suitcase? It looks very heavy.
MIRANDA	Thanks, Oliver. Well, it's a beautiful day here in London, isn't it? Look at that blue sky! _____ su_____ s_____ [3] the sun in England in November.
OLIVER	It doesn't rain all the time here! Shall we all get a coffee?
EMMA	Yes. The café is this way. Miranda, w_____ w_____ sa_____ _____ h_____ [4] that Carlos is ill.
MIRANDA	Yes. It's not serious, and he really wanted to come, but h_____ w_____ a_____ [5] travel. It's not nice to be in a plane if you're ill.
EMMA	That's right. Anyway, we_____ g_____ wel_____ [6] you to London, and, in half an hour, to our house!

F Looking for a new job

We use a verb + infinitive to talk about our hopes and plans; the efforts we make; the things we do for other people; to give opinions; and to describe our feelings.

Look at these emails between Ella and her French friend, Vincent. First, add words or phrases to Ella's message.

> trying   want   decided   difficult to   forgot to
> offered to   promise to visit   pleased to hear

Hi Vincent
How's life? I ___forgot to___ [0] send you a Christmas card, so now I'm writing to you instead. I was _____ [1] in your last message that you've _____ [2] to finish your course at college. I'm glad. You need a degree if you _____ [3] to find a good job. I'm looking for a new job myself at the moment. I had an interview for a job on my local newspaper last week. I answered all the questions, and I _____ [4] start work immediately, but unfortunately, I didn't get the job. It's _____ [5] get a job on a newspaper, because a lot of young British people are _____ [6] to find work in the media these days. Anyway, I hope you're OK. I _____ [7] you later this year! What about Easter? Bye for now!
Ella

Now put these words in the right order, and add them to Vincent's reply:

> to/afraid/I'm/buy   get/was/It/nice/to   hear/to/hope/I
> give/My parents/to/have refused   I/hear/to/surprised/was

Hi Ella!
It was nice to get [0] your message this morning. I hope you're well. _____ [8] that you didn't get the newspaper job - you would be a very good journalist. Yes, life at college is very hard. Sometimes _____ [9] a new shirt or jumper, because I won't have enough money at the end of the month to pay for my flat. _____ [10] me any more money, so I'm doing some weekend work as a waiter. Anyway, I'm OK really, and it would be good to see you at Easter. _____ [11] from you again soon. Bye for now!
Vincent

OVER TO YOU Now go to page 125.

20 Articles and nouns
A, *an* or *the*

1 a or an

We use **a** before words that begin with a **consonant**
(b, c, d, f, g, etc.):

a fast car   *a meeting*   *a good friend*

and before **u**, when **u** sounds like 'you':

a university   (but *an uncle*)

and before **eu**:

a European city

We use **an** before words that begin with a **vowel**
(a, e, i, o, u):

an old house   *an ice cream*   *an apple*

and before words that begin with a silent **h**:

an hour   (but *a holiday*)

2 a/an or the

Look at this example:

*I've bought you **a** cake and **a** DVD. ~ Lovely!*
*Can you put **the** cake in **the** fridge, please?*

When we talk about something for the first time, we
often use **a/an** ('a cake'), but when we know which
one it is, we use **the** ('the cake'). We say **the fridge** in
this example, because we already know which one -
there's only one in the room!

If we say to someone 'I'm going to **the** supermarket',
we mean 'the supermarket that we both know – our
normal supermarket.' We also say '**the** Taj Mahal', '**the**
Thames', '**the** sun', etc. because we know which one
they are.

TIP

We use **the** when we talk about musical
instruments:

*Can you play **the piano** or **the guitar**?*

Grammar in action

1 We use **a/an** to describe people,
places and things. Here, we're talking
about a friend:

My friend George is a teacher.
He's got a black beard, and he
lives in a small flat with a roof
garden in Cambridge.

2 We use **a/an** to talk about numbers,
prices and how often something
happens. We might talk about a
beach barbecue on holiday:

There's a barbecue twice a week
here. Normally, there are a hundred
people, and you can buy beer or
lemonade for a pound a litre. It's great!

3 We use **the** to talk about things we know about
already, and **a/an** to talk about 'new' things. Here,
we're talking about our house:

Let's buy something for the house! The kitchen and
the bathroom are OK, but the living room is boring!
Shall we buy a painting or a new sofa?

A   Describing people, places and things

Laurent is writing about his home town, Saint-Paul-lès-Dax, in south-west France.
Write *a* or *an* in the gaps.

Saint-Paul-lès-Dax is ....*a*............ ⁰ nice, small French town. We don't have

...................¹ airport or ....² university, but we do have the normal

things like ....³ internet café and ....⁴ cinema and

...................⁵ hairdresser's. If you are visiting south-west France, and you want to

see a typical small town, come to Saint-Paul-lès-Dax for ....⁶ afternoon or

even ....⁷ hour! And if you want to know more about this part of France,

there's ....⁸ useful website, http://www.dax-tourisme.com. But remember

to bring ....⁹ umbrella - it rains a lot here!

B Talking about numbers, prices and how often things happen

Anne and Sue are on a camping holiday in Germany. After the example, add *a/an* fourteen more times.

UWE   Welcome to our campsite! For small tents like yours, it's only twelve euros ^{*a*}/ night.

ANNE   Great! It's big site, isn't it? How many people are there?

GREG   Well, there are hundred and eighty tents, so we have around six hundred people, I suppose. There's small supermarket, and someone comes once day to sell fresh fish.

SUE   That's nice. Can we wash our clothes here?

GREG   Sure. There's washing machine in every shower house. It costs euro hour to use.

ANNE   Is that farm next to the campsite?

GREG   That's right. You can buy apples there for two euros kilo. We've got little cinema as well. There's film three times week. Are you both students?

SUE   I'm student, but Anne is actor.

GREG   Really? Well, I'll show you where to put your tent. Come on!

C New things, and things we know about already

Rhys has arrived home from college. His flatmate, Lisa, is in the kitchen. If you think the underlined words are correct, put a tick. If you think they're wrong, cross them out and write the correct word.

WORD FOCUS

1 When you keep money at the bank, you have an *account* in your name.
2 A *competition* is a kind of game with prizes (a holiday or a car, for example) if you win.

LISA   Rhys! I didn't hear you at a ___the___ ⁰ door. How's it going? Do you want a ___✓___ ⁰ cup of tea?

RHYS   Yes, please. I've just been to the _____ ¹ bank, actually, for some advice on my account.

LISA   I hope things are OK. By the way, there's the _____ ² letter for you in the living room.

RHYS   Really? Thanks. What have you done today?

LISA   I went for the _____ ³ walk in the _____ ⁴ park. It's the first time I've been at lunch time. I met Joe.

RHYS   Joe? The guy who plays a _____ ⁵ piano so well?

LISA   That's right. We had the _____ ⁶ interesting conversation about music.

RHYS   That's nice. (*Rhys goes to the living room.*) Where's a _____ ⁷ letter? I can't find it.

LISA   On a _____ ⁸ television.

RHYS   (*A moment later*) I don't believe it! I think I've won a _____ ⁹ prize!

LISA   (*Entering the living room*) How? Did you enter a competition?

RHYS   Yes, and I've won a _____ ¹⁰ tour of China!

LISA   Fantastic! When does a _____ ¹¹ tour start?

RHYS   In two months. The letter says I'll see a _____ ¹² Great Wall of China on my second day and then the Forbidden City in Beijing!

3 Look at the **plural nouns** in this dialogue:
*What's on your shopping list? ~ A few **things** for my dinner party tomorrow: some **flowers**, four wine **glasses**, two new **knives**, some fish and some **tomatoes**.*

4 We usually make **plural nouns** by adding -s:

> one ball → two ball**s**
> one metre → three metre**s**
> a car → some car**s**
> a question → any question**s**?

5 With nouns that end in -s, -ss, -sh, -ch, and -x, we add -es:

> bus → bus**es**   glass → glass**es**   dish → dish**es**
> beach → beach**es**   box → box**es**

6 With nouns that end in a **consonant** (**b, c, d, f** etc.) + -**y**, we change the -**y** to -**ies**:

> baby → bab**ies**   family → famil**ies**
> city → cit**ies**   country → countr**ies**
> story → stor**ies**

but we **don't** change the **y** after a vowel (**a, e, i, o, u**):
days, **journeys**, etc.

> The plural form of **penny** is **pennies**, but we normally use **pence** or **p**:
> > *That's ten pence, please.   Can you lend me 50p?*
>
> Or, if we're talking about pounds and pence, nothing:
> > *That's six pounds seventy.*

7 With nouns that end in -f or -fe, we change the -f/-fe to -ves:

> leaf → lea**ves**   loaf → loa**ves**   life → li**ves**
> wife → wi**ves**   knife → kni**ves**

8 Most nouns that end in -o have -s: **kilos**, **photos**, **radios**, etc. But three common nouns have -**es**:

> potato → potato**es**   tomato → tomato**es**
> hero → hero**es**

9 Some nouns have irregular plural forms:

> man → men   woman → women
> child → children   person → people
> foot → feet   tooth → teeth   fish → fish
> sheep → sheep   mouse → mice

10 Some nouns only have plural forms:

> clothes   trousers   jeans
> pyjamas   glasses   scissors

> **Team** and **family** can be singular or plural:
> > *My team is/are winning.*
> > *My family come/comes from Scotland.*

Grammar in action

4 We can use **plural nouns** when we tell someone about the actions we have completed. This might be at work:
Have you had a busy morning? ~ Yes - four visitors, two meetings, fifteen emails and six phone calls!

5 We can use **plural nouns** when we talk about the things that we want to buy, or that we own. We might talk about a shopping trip:
I need some new clothes. ~ What do you need? ~ Trousers for work, a pair of jeans and some new pyjamas. ~ I'll come with you. I need to get three loaves of bread from the baker's and some tomatoes.

6 We can use **plural nouns** to describe the number of people or things we can see. This example is a radio ad:
There are about five thousand people here. Men, women and children are enjoying the sunshine and the music. Come to the Hyde Park Festival!

D A short advertisement

Cross out the noun plurals that are wrong in this radio advertisement for a large store, and rewrite them.

0 ....*men*....   2 ....   4 ....   6 ....
1 ....   3 ....   5 ....

Come to 'Lacey's'! We've got clothes for ~~mans~~ and ~~womans~~. We've got toys for children. We've got sofas for families! ~~Persons~~ come from all the ~~citys~~ in UK to 'Lacey's'. Are your ~~foots~~ uncomfortable? Have a look at our shoes. Are you always late for work? Have a look at our ~~watchs~~. At 'Lacey's' we make people's ~~lifes~~ better!

E Shopping

Josie and Juan are at Borough Market in London. Add plural forms of these words to their conversation:

| sandwich | potato | pound | piece | tomato | penny | fish | loaf | person |

JUAN Is this the market, then? There are so many ....*people*........ 0 here!

JOSIE It's very popular. Shall we get some bread first? Excuse me, could we have two small brown ....¹, please?

MAN Certainly, Madam. That's three ....², sixty, please. (*Josie gives him four pounds.*) Thank you, and here's forty ....³ change for you. Don't spend it all today!

JUAN I'm really hungry, Josie. Is that woman selling ....⁴?

JOSIE Yes. I'm hungry too. Can you get me a chicken sandwich? (*Josie goes to the fishmonger's.*) I'll buy some ....⁵ for tonight.

WOMAN Morning, love. I've got some nice haddock today.

JOSIE All right. Could I have two small ....⁶ of haddock, please?

JUAN Here's your sandwich, Josie. Shall I get some ....⁷ - we could have chips with the fish tonight.

JOSIE Good idea. There's a greengrocer's over there. Could you get some ....⁸ at the same time? We could have a tomato salad.

WOMAN That's three pounds for the fish please, darling.

JOSIE Here you are. Thanks very much.

OVER TO YOU Now go to page 125.

1 Look at these examples:
> **There's** a cash machine at the supermarket.
> **There aren't** many people here.
> **Are there** any Brazilian students in your class?

2 **There is/are**: if the **noun** after **there** is **singular** or **uncountable**, we use the **singular form** of **be**:
> **There's a** good **film** at the cinema.
> **There isn't** any **sugar** left, I'm afraid.

If the **noun** is **plural**, we usually use the **plural form** of **be**:
> There **are two pizzas** in the fridge.
> There **aren't** any **shops** open now.

3 To make questions, we put **be** before **there**:
> **Is there** a supermarket near here?

and we use **was/were** after **there** to talk about **the past**:
> **There weren't** any tickets left.

4 We often use these words after **there + be**:

> a/an   any   some   much/many/a lot of/lots of
> two/three/hundreds etc.

> **There's a** cat under the car.
> There wasn't **any** science homework last week.
> There were **three hundred** people at their wedding.

> We sometimes use **there + be** with **a problem**:
> **There's a problem** at work. I may be late
> home.

Grammar in action

1 We use **there + be** to talk about where things or people are. We might talk about our town:
> There are a lot of police in the town centre today.
> There's a new cinema outside town.
> Is there a car park near the High Street?

2 We use **there + be** to talk about when things happen. Here, we're making plans:
> There's a good play at the theatre next week. Or there are one or two new films at the cinema. ~ OK. And is there a market on Sunday?

3 We use **there + be** to talk about numbers. We might talk about parties:
> There were a lot of guests at the party, but there weren't any famous people.
> There are two parties tonight. Which one shall we go to?

4 We often use **there + be** to talk about which items we have at home. Here, we're talking about food and drink:
> Is there any butter left?
> There are some biscuits in the cupboard.

And we use **there + be** to talk about the types of food that are in a meal:
> Don't worry. There isn't any meat in the pasta.
> Is there any sugar in the coffee?

A   Where things are and when things happen

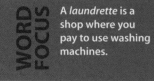

Fabio is talking to Fukiko in the kitchen of his university hall of residence. Put the words in brackets in the correct order, and add them to the conversation.

FABIO   How long have you been here?

FUKIKO All summer.

FABIO   Great, can I ask you some questions? For example, *are there any buses* ⁰ (buses/any/there/are) that go into town?

FUKIKO Yes, ...¹ (bus stop/a/there's) outside the hall. The journey into the town centre only takes ten minutes. And if you want to go to a concert or something in Bristol, ...² (bus/another/there's) from the centre, or you can take a train.

FABIO   That's fine, but ....³ (a/there/is/supermarket) on campus?

FUKIKO No, ...⁴ (a/was/shop/there) here in the summer but it's closed now. But ....⁵ (good supermarkets/there/four or five/are) in town.

FABIO   OK, my last question – ....⁶ (a/there/laundrette/is)?

HOLLY   Well, there's a room with washing machines, but you don't pay - you just take some washing powder with you. So, are you ready for your first classes?

FABIO   I think so – .... ⁷ (is/anything/there) tomorrow?

HOLLY   Another question! Well, ... ⁸ (isn't/there/anything) in the morning, but .... ⁹ (two/are/lectures/there) in the afternoon.

B Talking about numbers

It's nearly Christmas. Holly is sending an email to her friend Glenn. Put '/' in the four places where the word *there* is missing.

Hi Glenn,

How are you? Are you looking forward to Christmas? I know that / are lots of things to do, but it's fun, isn't it? We had our Christmas lunch at work today, and were thirty-five of us in a very small Italian restaurant! Then I went shopping, but I didn't buy many presents, because were thousands of people on Oxford Street. Anyway, are only six days left until Christmas now. The kids will be excited this weekend. Perhaps I'll take them to the cinema - are one or two new Christmas films at the moment. Do you want to bring your two boys if we go to something? Let me know. Bye for now!

C Talking about food and drink

Sam and Tom return to Tom's flat after an evening football match. Add the following phrases to their conversation. You will need to use two phrases more than once. Use capital letters where necessary.

WORD FOCUS

First match these words with the correct pictures of food:

omelette ....
chillies ....
garlic ....
herbs ....
sauce ....

there isn't	there aren't	there are	is there	are there	there were	there's

SAM   ...Is there... ⁰ anything to eat?

TOM   No, ... ¹ nothing, I'm afraid.

SAM   Are you sure? .... ² always something!

TOM   .... ³ two pizzas in the freezer, but I ate them at the weekend.

SAM   (*Looking in the fridge*) Well, ... ⁴ any eggs, so we can't make an omelette.

TOM   Wait a moment! .... ⁵ some tomatoes in the fridge and there's one onion in the cupboard.

SAM   OK. .... ⁶ any pasta?

TOM   Yes, ... ⁷ a lot of pasta, actually.

SAM   Well, that's fine. .... ⁸ any chillies or garlic or anything like that?

TOM   .... ⁹ two green chillies at the bottom of the cupboard, and we've got some herbs, but .... ¹⁰ any garlic, I'm afraid.

SAM   Don't worry. I think we've got enough.

TOM   OK, but what are you cooking?

SAM   It's an Italian sauce called 'arrabiata'. It's delicious.

5

This is my father and that's my grandmother.

6 Here are forms of **this, that, these, those**:

SINGULAR	PLURAL
this chair	**these** chairs
that chair	**those** chairs

7 We use **this, that, these, those** with nouns:
> *This shop is nice, but these jeans are expensive!*

We also use them without nouns, when the meaning is clear, and with **one/ones**:
> *Those are my books.* (**Those** = the books)
> *Look at these watches. That one at the back is cheap.*
> (**That one** = that watch)

Grammar in action

5 We use **this/these** (sometimes with **here**) for things that are near to us, and **that/those** (sometimes with **there**) for things that are not so near. To say where things are in a shop, we can say:
> *These blue flowers here smell quite nice, but those pink flowers in the window look fantastic!*

6 We use **this** and **these** to talk about our present and future activities. We might talk about our plans:
> *What are we going to do this evening? ~ Can we stay in? I'm enjoying this film.*

And we use **that** and **those** to talk about the past. Here, we're talking about a class that's just finished:
> *That was a really difficult class! Did you understand anything? Those written exercises were horrible!*

7 We use **this** and **that** when we speak on the phone:
> *Hello, this is Dave here. ~ Dave, is that your mum on the phone? Can I speak to her later?*

And we use **this** and **that** to talk about friends and family when we meet people:
> *Steve, this is my husband, Mike. That's our daughter, Sally, over there.*

> **TIP**
> We use **that's right** to say that a piece of information is correct:
> *You work at the university, don't you? ~ Yes, that's right.*

D   A food shop

Marcus is buying some food on his way home. Complete what he says using *this, that, those* or *these*.

'Hello. Can I have ___that___ ⁰ tin of biscuits, please? Oh, and could I have some of ___these___ ⁰ eggs, too? And perhaps I could have some of _____ ¹ French cheese? I'd also like two of _____ ² packets of your coffee, and _____ ³ small jar of strawberry jam. Oh and two of _____ ⁴ chicken legs, and how much is _____ ⁵ wonderful chocolate cake over there?'

E A holiday apartment in Italy

Sam, who works for Sun Holidays, is showing the Robertson family (Lucy, David and their children Lily and Jack) their holiday apartment in Italy. Add *this*, *that*, *those* or *these* to their conversation.

SAM   So, ___this___ ⁰ is your apartment. It's nice, isn't it? ___That___ ⁰ 's the swimming pool over there.

LILY   Why are _____¹ children in our pool, then?

SAM   Well, you share the pool with _____² apartment behind _____³ trees, Lily. Now, _____⁴ is your front door. _____⁵ are the keys, Mrs Robertson. But don't worry if you lose them. Just come and see me at the office.

DAVID   Is _____⁶ the town over there, Sam?

SAM   Yes. Can you see _____⁷ shops? There's a good supermarket there, and a baker's.

JACK   Look, Lily! _____⁸ 's the sea over there. Can you see _____⁹ boats?

SAM   OK. I think that's everything. Have a great holiday!

(Later, inside the apartment)

LUCY   _____¹⁰ is a nice apartment, isn't it, kids? What are we going to do _____¹¹ afternoon?

LILY   I want to go to the beach!

LUCY   OK, Lucy. But put some of this sun cream on your face and arms, first. Do you remember _____¹² time when you got burnt in Spain?

DAVID   After the beach, we could have a meal in one of _____¹³ restaurants that we saw _____¹⁴ morning.

JACK   I want some fish and chips!

LUCY   You can have fish and chips _____¹⁵ evening, but you have to try some local Italian food _____¹⁶ week too, Jack!

F A phone call from school

Martin is meeting his wife Sophie at work. Add *there*, *this* or *that* to their conversation.

WORD FOCUS

1 Look up *stomach ache* before you begin if you don't know it.

2 A *nurse* is a person who helps you if you're ill, usually in a hospital.

SOPHIE   Hi, Martin. I'm almost ready. ___This___ ⁰ is my colleague, Brian. Brian, _____¹ is my husband, Martin.

BRIAN   Pleased to meet you, Martin. _____² 's some coffee in the machine.

MARTIN   Thanks. (*Martin's mobile phone rings.*) Excuse me. Hello, _____³ is Martin here. Yes, _____⁴ 's right. I'm Ella's dad. Is _____⁵ a problem at school?

SOPHIE   Is _____⁶ Ella's school on the phone, Martin?

MARTIN   Yes. Ella went to the painting club, but she's not feeling very well. But don't worry. _____⁷ 's a nurse at the school. Do you want to speak to Ella? (*Martin gives the phone to Sophie.*)

SOPHIE   Ella? _____⁸ is Mummy. Are you OK, darling?

BRIAN   It's natural to worry when the school rings, but normally it's nothing.

MARTIN   _____⁹ 's right. Ella's got a stomach ache, that's all. _____¹⁰ was a birthday party at school, and Ella ate too much ice cream.

SOPHIE   Well, it's not serious, but we'd better go, Martin.

OVER TO YOU Now go to page 125.

22 Countable and uncountable nouns
Countable and uncountable; *a, some, any, no*

1 Nouns with plural forms are **countable nouns** - because we can count them:

a/one car   two cars   three cars

We can use **a/an**, **some** and **the** with countable nouns

	SINGULAR	PLURAL
a:	**a** cat	–
some:	–	**some** cats
the:	**the** cat	**the** cats

2 Some nouns - **uncountable nouns** - normally have no plural forms:

moneys   homeworks   furnitures

Other common uncountable nouns are:

> information news advice
> travel petrol traffic
> food bread rice pasta milk cheese cake meat
> weather snow rain ice thunder lightning

We do not use **a**, or **one**, **two**, **three** before uncountable nouns:

We need to buy ~~a~~ bread.
*Would you like **some** toast?*
*Look at **the** rain! We're going to get wet!*

3 With some **uncountable nouns**, we can use **a piece of** or other words in front of them:

> a piece of + information, luggage, news, advice,
>   homework, furniture, chicken, cheese, toast
> a slice of + bread, beef, pork, lamb
> a glass/bottle of + water, milk
> a spoonful of + coffee, sugar   a cup of + coffee, tea
> a packet of + tea, coffee, rice, pasta, sugar

4 We normally use **some** before **uncountable nouns** and **plural countable nouns** (e.g. **books**, **bikes**, **cities**) in **positive sentences**:

*I've got **some** exciting **news**!*
*I got **some books** from the library yesterday.*

5 We can also use **some** in **questions**, when we're making offers and requests:

*Would you like **some tea**?*

6 We normally use **any** before **uncountable** and **plural countable nouns** in **negative sentences** and questions:

*There aren't **any yoghurts** in the fridge.*
*Did your dad give you **any advice**?*

> We sometimes use **no** instead of **not any**:
>   *There are no hotels in this part of town.*
>   *We have no fish left, I'm afraid.*

Grammar in action

1 We use **a**, **some** and **any** with nouns to talk or ask about the amount of something. We might talk about food:

*Have you got **any** tomatoes or meat? I could make a pasta dish. ~ Good idea, I've got an onion and some cheese we could use too*

2 We use **a/an** and **some** with nouns when we make requests. We might be in a restaurant:

*We'd like **some** water, please, and some bread. I'd also like a glass of cola, please. ~ Of course, and I'll bring **some** menus for you.*

3 We use **some** with nouns when we offer something in particular. Here, we're talking to some guests at home:

*Would you like **some** sandwiches or some cake? ~ No, thanks, we're not hungry.*

A   A corner shop

David works in his family's corner shop. Here are some of the things people ask for during the day. Choose the right words.

0 Can I have a ___bottle___ (slice/bottle/packet) of milk, please?

1 Have you got a small _____ (spoonful/glass/piece) of chicken, please?

2 Could I have a _____ (packet/piece/bottle) of brown rice?

3 I'd like a _____ (piece/cup/packet) of white coffee with two _____ (slices/spoonfuls/bottles) of sugar, please.

4 Can I have four _____ (slices/glasses/packets) of beef?

B Will's Weather and Travel Website

It's 8 a.m. Look at Will's Weather and Travel Website. There's one wrong plural form in each part of the country. Cross out the wrong forms and write the correct words at the end.

Will's Weather and Travel

| TODAY | TOMORROW | THE WEEKEND | CONTACT US | ● HOME

NORTH OF SCOTLAND: I haven't got much ~~informations~~ for travellers in this part of Britain. It's going to be windy, if you're on the top of a mountain, but for most people it's a nice but cool day. *information* 0

SOUTH OF SCOTLAND: There will be some very heavy rain here today. There isn't much traffics right now between Glasgow and Edinburgh, but there are two football matches tonight in Glasgow. 1

NORTH OF ENGLAND: Take your umbrellas if you're going out today in Manchester, Liverpool and Preston. There aren't many clouds in the sky at the moment, but it there will be rains later today. 2

WALES: Three cars have crashed outside Cardiff. The Police haven't given us much advices, but it's a good idea to listen to Radio Cardiff this morning, if you're driving in south Wales. 3

NORTHERN IRELAND: There will be some ices on the road in the early morning in Northern Ireland, but there will be blue skies for most of the day. Drive to work carefully! 4

EAST ANGLIA: Some petrol stations will be closed today in East Anglia, so if you didn't buy petrols yesterday, don't drive too far! 5

SOUTH OF ENGLAND: There are problems on the underground in London. If you're travelling to Heathrow with a lot of luggages, remember that you can check in your suitcases at Paddington station. 6

C In a café in the park

Marsha is ordering food for David and their kids, Zoe and baby Ryan. Circle the correct options to complete the conversation.

MARSHA This is a nice café for *a/-* 0 families, David. I'll order *a/some* 0 food. You can sit down with the kids.

DAVID Let's find *a/some* 1 table, kids. Can you see *some/any* 2 other men here? I think I'm the only one!

WOMAN Hi! Can I help you?

MARSHA Sure. You can look after *a/the* 3 children for the next ten years if you like! I'll ask my husband. David! What would you like? *Some/A* 4 sandwich?

DAVID No, I've had too much *breads/bread* 5 this week. Have they got *any/a* 6 rice?

ZOE I'd like some *toasts/toast* 7, Daddy! I don't want *a/-* 8 rice!

DAVID How many *pieces/piece* 9 of toast would you like, Zoe?

MARSHA Two *coffee/coffees* 10 please, some fried rice and *a/some* 11 toast, please.

ZOE I've got *one/some* 12 *homeworks/homework* 13 to do, Daddy. Can you help me? First, where do *a/-* 14 tomatoes come from? And second, is it cold in Canada?

DAVID Yes, it is. There's a lot of *snow/snows* 15 there in winter, Zoe.

MARSHA Here's the food! David, *a/the* 16 bread looks lovely. Do you want to try my sandwich?

7 Look at these examples:

*We don't have **much** pasta left.*
*There aren't **many** students in class today.*
*I've got **a lot of** problems at the moment.*

8 **Much**, **many** and **a lot of** mean **a large quantity of**. If you say *She's got **a lot of** money*, you mean 'she's rich.'

9 We use **many** with **plural countable nouns** and **much** with **uncountable nouns**:

*I haven't seen **many tourists** in London this year.*
*How **much information** do you need?*

→ For more information on **countable/uncountable nouns**, see p. 86.

10 We can use **a lot of** with **plural countable nouns** and **uncountable nouns**:

*He's taking **a lot of exams** at the moment.*
*I listen to **a lot of music** at the weekend.*
*Toby doesn't play **a lot of golf** these days.*

Exams are countable; **music** and **golf** are uncountable.

Grammar in action

④ We can use **a lot of** in positive sentences, negative sentences and questions. Here we're talking about a day out in London:

London has a lot of museums.
We didn't spend a lot of money at Harrod's because it was so busy.
Did you buy a lot of gifts?

⑤ We normally only use **many** or **much + a noun** in negative sentences and questions. (In positive sentences, we prefer to use **a lot of**: *I've got ~~much~~ a lot of work to do.*) Here, we're talking about food and free time activities:

How many onions and how much bread have you got?
Are there many golf courses in that part of Spain? ~ Yes, but I was busy, so I didn't play much golf in the end.

⑥ But we sometimes use **many** in positive sentences when we write. We might write about the UK:

The UK has many small fishing ports.

And we can also use **much** and **many** in positive sentences after **so** and **too**. Here, we're talking about school:

Our teacher was great. He gave us so much advice.
I can't come tonight. I've got too much homework to do.

D   Talking about school days

Read this article about a small school in Scotland. Add *much* or *many* to the spaces. A 'pupil' is a child at school.

When I was a child there were ......*many*...... [0] small schools in villages in Scotland. There were only fifteen pupils in my school, for example, and .... [1] children lived nine or ten miles miles from our village. Our teacher didn't give us .... [2] homework in the summer, because we had to work on our parents' farms. And sometimes in the winter there was too .... [3] snow, and we couldn't come to school. My teacher was called Mrs McCraig. She read so .... [4] books and newspapers, and she gave us so .... [5] information about America and China and Africa! I met her .... [6] years after school, and she still remembered me.

E Talking about food and free time activities

Mike and his neighbour Debbie are in Mike's garden. They're going to have a dinner party. Add the correct words or phrases.

MIKE Here's your orange juice. It's not very cold. There wasn't .... much .... ⁰ (much/many) ice, I'm afraid.

DEBBIE It's lovely here. Shall we eat outside when our guests come? I could bring some garden chairs.

MIKE It's a nice idea, but how .... ¹ (much/many) garden chairs have you got, Debbie?

DEBBIE I'll have a look in my shed. I bought .... ² (a lot of/much of) them last summer for a wedding. What about a barbecue?

MIKE But we're going to have a Spanish omelette! You can't cook an omelette on a barbecue.

DEBBIE I've got .... ³ (much/a lot of) fish, and it's ready to eat. We can have fish instead, with some salad.

MIKE I haven't got .... ⁴ (much/many) salad.

DEBBIE I'm sure we'll be OK. How .... ⁵ (many/much) lettuce have you got, and how .... ⁶ (many/much) tomatoes?

MIKE I'll have a look, but I think it's going to rain. There are .... ⁷ (much/a lot of) clouds in the sky.

WORD FOCUS
1 A *shed* is a small wooden building in the garden.
2 Look up the word *lettuce* if you need to.

F Buying food in a delicatessen

Megan is in a delicatessen (a shop where you can buy good quality cheese, bread, meat, etc.) Add the correct words from the brackets.

MEGAN Hello! I'd like to buy ...... some ...... ⁰ (some/any) of the cold beef, please. It looks nice. How much is it?

MAN It's £4.50 for .... ¹ (some/a) kilo. The cooked prawns are good, too. I don't normally have .... ² (a lot of/much) prawns, but they're cheap at the moment.

MEGAN I'll have .... ³ (some/any) beef, please. Six slices will be fine. Have you got .... ⁴ (any/many) fresh pasta today?

MAN Oh dear. We haven't got .... ⁵ (no/much) pasta today, I'm afraid. I've got .... ⁶ (some/any) delicious cheese from Wales, though, and .... ⁷ (some/a) brown bread from a local farm.

MEGAN The bread looks nice, too. I'd like to buy .... ⁸ (any/some). Can I have .... ⁹ (a/some) loaf, please? And can I try .... ¹⁰ (much/some) cheese?

MAN Of course you can. Is there anything else? I haven't got .... ¹¹ (many/much) eggs today, I'm afraid - there are only two left.

MEGAN Don't worry. The cheese is fantastic. I'm sure you sell .... ¹² (a lot of/any) of it. Could you give me half a kilo, please?

MAN Certainly. I'll give you .... ¹³ (a/any) bag to carry everything. Can I give you .... ¹⁴ (an/some) advice too? Make sure the cheese is warm when you eat it. It tastes much better!

WORD FOCUS
Prawns are a type of seafood.

OVER TO YOU Now go to page 125.

1 Look at this:

subject	+	verb	+	object	
Did	Sam	phone	Anne?		
No,	**he**	met	**her**	in town.	

The second time we talk about Sam, we use **he**; the second time we talk about Anne, we use **her**.

2 Here are the **subject and object pronouns**:

SINGULAR		PLURAL	
Subject	**Object**	**Subject**	**Object**
I	me	we	us
you	you	you	you
he	him	–	–
she	her	they	them
it	it	–	–

> **TIP**
>
> Usually, it's wrong to leave out these pronouns:
>
> *No, I don't like it.*   (NOT *No, I don't like.*)
> *We are leaving today.*   (NOT *Are leaving today.*)

3 We can use **object pronouns** after these **verbs + prepositions**:

> agree with   belong to   laugh at   listen to
> look at   play with   reply to   smile at   stay with
> speak to   talk to   wait for   write to

*That bike belongs to **me**.*
*I smiled at **them**, but they didn't speak to **me**.*
*My grandmother stays with **us** every summer.*

Grammar in action

1 We use **subject and object pronouns** in daily conversation when it is clear which person or thing we are talking about. We might talk about our family:
> *I saw Mark yesterday. I drove him home after work. We talked about Mum. He agrees with me. We need to visit her more often.*

2 We use **it** to talk about things and animals. Here, we're talking about a visit to the zoo:
> *I went to London Zoo yesterday. It's in Regent's Park. I saw a baby elephant. It was so sweet.*

3 We use **it** to talk about the weather, time, days, dates, and distances. Here, it's breakfast time:
> *Good morning! It's Monday, and it's the sixth of March. You're listening to Radio Bristol.*
> *It's nine o' clock. Get up! It's a lovely day.*
> *How far is it to your new college? ~ Don't worry. It's only a couple of miles. I'll go by bike after breakfast.*

4 We use **you** when we talk to groups of people in lectures and presentations, and at weddings or birthday parties:
> *Can you hear me at the back?*
> *You're all welcome to visit me in my new house!*

5 We use **you** to talk generally about people. Here, we're talking about food and drink:
> *You need a teapot for a good cup of tea!*
> *On a cold day, you need a good, hot breakfast!*

A   Daily conversation

Marco is staying with the Petts family (Geoff, Linda and their children, Lewis and Kylie) in Warwick. It's Saturday morning. Cross out the underlined words and put a single subject or object pronoun in their place.

LINDA   Hi Marco. Geoff didn't bring me a cup of tea this morning. Have you seen ~~Geoff~~ ....*him*.....⁰ or Kylie?

MARCO   Yes, ~~Geoff~~ ....¹'s playing with ~~Kylie~~ ....² in the garden.

LINDA   Thanks. I'll call ~~Geoff and Kylie~~ ....³ for breakfast. It's a lovely day. Have you got any plans?

MARCO   Yes. I'm playing football in the park with Lewis. I'm waiting for ~~Lewis~~ ....⁴ at the moment.

LINDA   Good luck! Lewis likes his bed. (*Marco goes upstairs, and then Geoff brings Kylie into the kitchen.*) Hi Geoff! How's Kylie today?

GEOFF   <u>Kylie</u> .... ⁵ 's fine, Linda. <u>Kylie and I</u> .... ⁶ played on the lawn, and <u>Kylie</u>
          .... ⁷ wanted to have a look in the shed. Then I put <u>Kylie</u> .... ⁸ in the
          wheelbarrow. Where are the boys?
LINDA   Upstairs. <u>Lewis and Marco</u> .... ⁹ are going to play football in the park.
GEOFF   Well, it's a nice day. Perhaps we should take Kylie, and we can all watch the game.

B   Talking about things, animals, the weather, times, days, dates and distances

Carrie and Jude are listening to the radio in their car. They're driving to a wedding. Add the correct words from the brackets to their conversation.

A *reward* is money or something nice that you get because you've done something good.

WORD FOCUS

RADIO   Good morning. ....*You're*........ ⁰ (It's/You're/They're) listening to BBC Radio
          Yorkshire. .... ¹ (He's/We're/It's) Saturday the tenth of March, and
          .... ² (it's/it/he's) going to be a sunny day…
CARRIE   Good. Mark and Steff will be happy. How far is .... ³ (it's/it/he) to
          the church now?
JUDE   About ten miles, I think. Have you got a present? What did .... ⁴
          (it/you/us) buy?
CARRIE   .... ⁵ (It's/She's/He's) a silver teapot. I bought .... ⁶
          (her/it/him) in Selfridge's. Do you remember what they bought
          .... ⁷ (it/we/us) for our wedding?
JUDE   They gave .... ⁸ (me/I/it) a tie, and they gave you a dress.
CARRIE   Look, Jude! Slow down! What's that on the road? Is .... ⁹ (he/she/
          it) a dog?
JUDE   I think so. It's OK. .... ¹⁰ (It/It's/You) just crossing the road. We'll
          wait.
CARRIE   OK, but what time is .... ¹¹ (he/it/it's)? Are we going to be late?
JUDE   No, don't worry. .... ¹² (It's/It/He's) only ten past eleven. We've got
          plenty of time. Relax.
RADIO   …so if you see Benjamin, Lord Stafford's favourite dog, phone us, and you'll get a
          £1,000 reward…

C   Talking to groups of people, and talking generally about people

It's the end of a Saturday course at an art gallery in Edinburgh. The teacher is talking to the class. Put '/' in the ten places where the word *you* is missing.

Ladies and gentlemen, can I ask / to sit down for a moment, please? I'd like to talk to for a minute before you go. Thank you. I hope that will agree with me that we've had an interesting day. When look at paintings carefully, you understand more about the people around you, don't you? And as you relax at home tomorrow, perhaps will think again about some of the beautiful paintings you've studied today. After all, paintings tell you stories about yourselves, your friends and your families. I want to ask you, before go, to look at one final painting, one of my favourites. What do think about when see it? Look at this successful man. Look at the flowers. What do see? I won't give you the answers. I don't have the answers, anyway. But isn't it true that when you get older, understand that some things are important, and some things aren't important? Thank for coming.

4 Look at this:

*That's **my** phone. ~ No, it's **mine**. **Yours** is blue.*

5 Here are the possessive adjectives and pronouns:

OBJECT PRONOUN	POSSESSIVE ADJECTIVE	POSSESSIVE PRONOUN
me	my	mine
you	your	yours
him	his	his
her	her	hers
it	its	its
us	our	ours
you	your	yours
them	their	theirs

6 We use **my**, **your**, etc. (possessive adjectives) with nouns:

my cat   **your** bag

They do not change with singular or plural nouns:

their books (NOT ~~theirs~~ books)

and we use **mine**, **your**, etc. (possessive pronouns) instead of **my cat**, **her bag**, etc.:

*I've got my coat. Is this **yours**? (**yours** = your coat)*
*I can't believe this house is finally **ours**!*

TIPS

1 Don't use **a/an** or **the** with **my**, **mine** etc.
This is ~~the~~ your desk - ~~the~~ mine is over there.

2 Say *Tom and **his** girlfriend/**his** wife/**his** daughter*, not ~~her girlfriend~~ etc.

3 **Its** is different from **it's** (= **it is**): *It's half past seven. Have you given the dog **its** dinner?*

Grammar in action

6 We use **my**, **your**, etc. to talk about about family members, friends, flatmates, and work colleagues:

My parents are coming to London tomorrow.
David is his boss, not his friend.

7 We use **my**, **your**, etc. for parts of the body:

Have you brushed your hair?
He's closed his eyes, but he's not asleep.

8 We use **my**, **your**, etc. and **mine**, **yours**, etc. to talk about things that belong to us. Tom is talking about the room that he shares with his brother:

My brother Mike is at work at the moment, but this room is ours. All those CDs in the corner are mine, but the suits in the wardrobe are his. ~ Is that your CD player? It's nice. ~ No, it belongs to my parents, actually. The TV is theirs too!

9 We use **my**, **your**, etc. and **mine**, **yours**, etc. to talk about personal facts and information. We might be at work:

This is his office. Shall we knock?
Here's my email address. Can I have yours?
This is Sue's desk, and this is mine.

D Talking about family members, friends etc., and parts of the body

Michiko, Pilar, Yuanjian and Guus are sharing a flat in Sydney. Add *my, your* etc. to their conversation.

MICHIKO .... *My* .... [0] mother is arriving this afternoon, Guus, and my room is in a mess. Where's Pilar? Perhaps she can help me.

GUUS She's brushing .... [1] teeth. .... [2] boss has asked her to work today. What time does .... [3] mother arrive?

MICHIKO 2 p.m. Guus, can you help me? I'll help you when .... [4] parents come next time.

GUUS I'm sorry, I can't help you. I'm washing .... [5] hair this morning.

MICHIKO What? Men don't wash .... [6] hair! I mean, they do, but it only takes five minutes.

GUUS I'm sorry, but Yuanjian and I are meeting .... [7] new girlfriends today. We have to look good.

MICHIKO Yuanjian's got a new girlfriend? What about .... [8] girlfriend in Beijing? Where is he?

GUUS   He's cooking some eggs and chips for me.

MICHIKO   The most important thing in your life is .... [9] stomach, Guus.
I hope .... [10] new girlfriend knows this.

E Talking about things that belong to us, and about personal facts

Dieter has arrived at Heathrow airport. A customs officer asks him to open his suitcase. Add the words to the conversation. You will need to use some words more than once.

| my | mine | ~~your~~ | yours | his | hers |

OFFICER What's ..*your*.. [0] name, sir?

DIETER   Dieter Mann. Here's .... [1] passport.

OFFICER Is this suitcase .... [2]?

DIETER   Yes, it's .... [3]. It's just a small case for .... [4] holiday. I'm staying in London for a week.

OFFICER OK. Open .... [5] suitcase please. (*Dieter opens it.*)

DIETER   Here you are. These are .... [6] clothes, and these are some books.

OFFICER Is everything .... [7]?

DIETER   Well, all the clothes are .... [8], but I borrowed one or two things from my brother. This dictionary is .... [9], for example. Oh, and I borrowed something from my sister, too. This computer game is .... [10]. Is it important?

OFFICER No, that's fine. OK, you can close .... [11] case. Have a good holiday.

F Do the cups belong to us or them?

Emily and Tom are leaving Nora and Brian's flat after five years. Brian is emailing Nora, who is on a business trip to India. After the example, there are five mistakes in the first message, and five in the second. Cross out the wrong words and rewrite them.

Hi Nora,

Tom left this morning but her / [*his*] books are still here! I'll text him tomorrow. I asked Emily for hers key to the flat. But I'm not sure if the blue cups in the kitchen are ours cups or theirs - you forget these things when he live with people for a long time, don't you? By the way, your mum rang this morning. She's going to visit we at the weekend. Is it sunny in Mumbai? I don't know what time he is in India, but I'm going to bed here! Bye!

Hi Brian,

Thanks for your message. Its Monday morning in Mumbai. I've just washed the hair, and I'm looking out of the window. There's a small bird in the hotel garden, and it's singing an Indian song! Anyway, I'm travelling to Delhi later today. It's about two hours by plane. The name of mine hotel in Delhi is 'The Metropolitan'. I hope things are OK now at the flat. Did you text Tom? I think some of those books are my, actually. And the blue cups are our! Your sister gave them to us. And is my mother arriving on Friday or Saturday? Bye for now!

OVER TO YOU Now go to page 125.

24 Possessives (2)
's and s' possessive

1 Look at these examples:
> This is Lucy, **Isobel's** daughter.
> Excuse me, but where are the **men's** clothes?
> This is a photo of my **grandparents'** house.

2 Here are the rules for using the **apostrophe** ('):

- We use **'s** with **names** and **singular nouns**:
> Have you seen **Ben's** passport anywhere?
> My **boss's** office is over there.

- We use **'s** with **irregular plural nouns** such as *women, men, children* and *people*:
> The **women's** toilets are next to the door.

- We use **s'** with **regular plural nouns**:
> The **footballers'** coach is coming!

Grammar in action

1 We normally use the **apostrophe** with people, to say that something belongs to someone:
> Those are Phil's CDs. (his CDs)

We use it to talk about other people's things, and their friends and family:
> Lily's dress is wonderful, isn't it?
> Is that your sister's new boyfriend?

We can also use it with animals:
> My dogs' names are Victor and Hugo. (their names)

2 We usually use **of** (not an apostrophe) with things:
> What's the name of the road? (NOT ~~the road's name~~)

particularly after words like **beginning, end, back, front, top, bottom.**

We might talk about a visit to the cinema:
> Did you have a good time? ~ Not really. We arrived late, we sat at the back of the cinema, and we didn't see the beginning of the film. (NOT ~~the cinema's back~~ or ~~the film's beginning~~)

3 But we sometimes use the **apostrophe** with places and companies in the news, or in business:
> Madrid's new Museum of Modern Art will open in February.
> Betty Santo is Coca Cola's new boss in Europe.

4 We can use the apostrophe without a noun, if the meaning is clear:
> This is my camera, but where is Jack's?

We do this when we talk about visiting some shops, our dentist and our doctor:

> I'm going to the dentist's tomorrow.
> Did you get some chicken from the butcher's? ~ Yes, but I forgot to get any tomatoes at the greengrocer's.

When we say **the chemist's** etc., we mean 'the chemist's shop'.

5 We use the **apostrophe** to talk about time. Here, a businesswoman is talking to her colleague:
> Next month's trip to New York will be interesting.
> Did you enjoy yesterday's lunch?

A **Talking about other people's things, and their friends and family**

Matt, Lucy and their children Thomas and Daisy are having a picnic with their Brazilian friends, Julieta and Rafi, and their boys, Lucas and Sabino. Add two-word phrases with 's or s'.

LUCY Daisy, have you got _Daddy's camera_⁰ (camera/Daddy) in your bag? We could take a nice picture.

RAFI Can you pass me ....¹ (shoes/Sabino), Julieta? We'll go for a little walk in a minute.

JULIETA I can't reach them, Rafi, but I think they're under ....² (coat/Lucas).

LUCY OK, smile everyone! Thomas, don't eat ....³ (sandwich/ your sister). It's been on the ground.

MATT What a lovely day for a picnic! Where's the ....⁴ (football/boys), Rafi? We could have a game.

RAFI   Good idea, but Sabino needs the toilet first. Are there any .... ⁵ (toilets/men) in the park, Matt?

MATT   Yes, they're in the café. See you in a minute!

DAISY   Daddy, I've lost my cup. Can I have a drink from .... ⁶ (cup/Thomas), please?

MATT   Of course you can. Lucy, can we use the .... ⁷ (coats/children) as goal posts in the football game?

LUCY   Yes, OK. But don't play too close to the food, darling.

B   Visiting shops

Henry is leaving a phone message. Add the correct shop names. You don't need to use one of them.

Write the shop names in exercise B in the correct spaces in the picture. WORD FOCUS

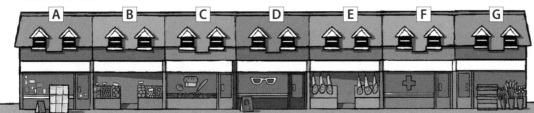

baker's   butcher's   greengrocer's   florist's   newsagent's   chemist's   optician's

'Rosie? I've lost my shopping list, but I think I've got everything. I got some oranges and some onions at the _greengrocer's_ ⁰. I got a loaf of brown bread at the .... ¹. I couldn't get your magazine at the .... ², because they didn't have any left. Then I went to the .... ³ and bought some more aspirin. Then I picked up your new glasses at the .... ⁴. Then I remembered the steaks, and I went back to the .... ⁵. Anyway, I'll be in town for the next twenty minutes. Give me a ring if you get this message. Bye!'

C   Talking about news, politics, business and time

This is the homepage of a news website, showing the main 'stories' of the day. Add 's five more times after the example.

Articles, nouns, pronouns, and determiners | 95

3 Look at this:

> *What are you doing this weekend? ~ Well, **some friends of mine** are going camping and they've invited me.*

Some friends of mine means 'some of my friends'.

4 We form these phrases like this:

a/some etc.	+ noun	+ of	+ mine, yours, etc.
some	friends	of	mine
a	neighbour	of	ours
a	classmate	of	yours

A neighbour of ours means 'one of our neigbours'.
A classmate of yours means 'one of your classmates':

> *Hi David. **A classmate of yours** phoned an hour ago.*

5 Instead of **mine, yours**, etc., we can say **my brother's** or **Sara's** etc.:

> *It was a good idea of **Sean's** to go to Paris.*
> *An old friend of **my mother's** phoned last night.*

An old friend of my mother's means 'one of my mother's old friends'.

Grammar in action

6 We use phrases like **some friends of mine** to talk about our friends and family, and the things they're doing:

> *Hello Nick. This is Fran. She's a flatmate of ours.*
> *A friend of Sally's has started to work in my office.*

D   Talking about the things our friends and family are doing

Izzy is writing an email to her friend Rebecca. Use the words in brackets to help you to make phrases with *mine, yours, my Dad's*, etc.

Hi Rebecca,

I hope you're enjoying your new job. I think it was <u>a good idea of yours</u> [0] (your idea was good) to go to America. I'm sure it's really interesting there. Things are OK here. Some .... [1] (some of my friends) are going skiing next month, and I'm planning to go with them. Then, in the summer, a .... [2] (one of my dad's friends) has invited all the family to his new house in France. I think it will be fun. By the way, do you remember a .... [3] (one of our schoolfriends), Katie Gray? Well, a .... [4] (one of her flatmates) is a singer, and he's just made a CD! It's actually in the shops now. Can you believe it? Anyway, there's one more piece of news. A .... [5] (one of Paul's colleagues) has asked me to a party on Saturday night. I don't really know him, so I hope it was a .... [6] (my idea was good) to say 'yes'! I'll tell you about it in my next message. Bye for now!

Izzy

E   Amy's party

We use the apostrophe to talk about other people's things, family and friends; to talk about shops; to talk about news, business, politics and time; and to talk about the things our friends and family are doing. Amy is having a twenty-first birthday party. If the underlined phrases are wrong, rewrite them. If they're right, put a tick (✓).

DAVE   Did you go to <u>the jeweller's today</u> ....✓........... [0]? I hope you didn't spend too much! We aren't rich, you know.

MAISIE   Yes. Don't worry. I've got <u>Amy bracelet</u> *Amy's bracelet* [0] in my pocket. Who's that tall man in the corner?

DAVE   I don't know. I suppose he's a <u>friend of Amy's</u> .... [1]. Why?

MAISIE   I'm sure he was on <u>yesterdays' TV news</u> .... [2]. Anyway, here comes the birthday girl.

AMY   How nice to see you both! I'm putting <u>guest's coats</u> .... [3] in the bedroom. Can I take yours?

MAISIE   Dave will take them. Your necklace is beautiful, Amy. Is it a present?

AMY   It is, actually. <u>Marcus's brother</u> .... [4] gave it to me. Have you met him? Daniel! (*The tall man comes over.*) Daniel, this is Maisie, a good <u>friend of my</u> .... [5]. Maisie, this is Daniel.

MAISIE   Pleased to meet you, but I'm sure I saw you yesterday on TV.

DANIEL   Hi, Maisie. You probably saw the opening of my <u>company's new shop</u> .... [6] on Oxford Street. It's the biggest <u>jeweller's in</u> .... [7] central London now. So, if you ever want some new earrings, or your boyfriend wants to buy you a diamond ring, come and see us! In fact, you must come to <u>next's month big sale</u> .... [8]. We'll have some very special prices.

MAISIE   I'll introduce you to my husband in a moment, Daniel, but he isn't <u>Londons' number one</u> .... [9] shopper!

F   A conversation with a friend in the street

Mandy and her son Freddie meet Toby in the street. Cross out any words that need an apostrophe, and rewrite them above. Look up the word 'lottery' before you do this exercise, if you don't know it.

MANDY   Hi, Toby! How are you? How are things going?

TOBY   Well, Mandy. There's not much happening really. My ~~brother~~ / *brother's* wife, Shelly, is going to have her fifth baby in June. The other four are girls, so she's hoping for a boy. Then, my best friend son has decided to go and live in India. He wants to make carpets, I think. And then, do you remember my sisters? Kate and Mirabelle? They have a florist in Birmingham. Well, Kate boss won two million pounds in last week lottery, and she gave Kate a hundred thousand pounds, and now Kate and Mirabelle are going to travel around the world, and my dad is going to buy my sister shop. What about you? Any news?

MANDY   No, my life is really boring at the moment. I've just spent half an hour at the dentist. That's not very interesting, is it? And I've just been to the shoe shop as well and changed a pair of Freddie shoes, because they were too small. And then Carly, a friend of mine, is going to Spain on holiday next week. I think that's all. No, wait a moment. Do you remember my parent house in Cornwall?

TOBY   Yes?

MANDY   Well, I've got a photo of it. Would you like to see it?

OVER TO YOU   **Now go to page 125.**

25 Adjectives
Red; small; square

1 Here are some common adjectives:

> nice   black   new   little

We use these words to describe people and things:
> It's a **nice** day, isn't it?
> She's got a **little black** dog.
> Your car looks **new**. Have you just bought it?

2 The form of adjectives never changes:
> a **good** book   two **good** books
> (NOT ~~two goods books~~)

and when you use an adjective with a noun, the adjective normally comes first:
> We had a **wonderful** holiday.
> (NOT ~~a holiday wonderful~~.)

3 We don't normally use **and** when we put two adjectives before a noun:
> a **friendly old** man (NOT ~~a friendly and old man~~)

except for colours:
> a **black and white** cat

4 In writing, you can decide to separate adjectives with **commas** (,):
> It's a **beautiful, sad** song.

but it's not necessary:
> It's just a **cheap old** coat.

5 We use adjectives to describe colour, size, shape, our opinions, what something is made of and nationality.

→ For more information on the order of adjectives and adjectives after a noun or a verb, see p. 100.

Grammar in action

1 We use **adjectives** to describe colour. We can tell our friends about something new that we've bought or have received:
> What does Steve want for his birthday? ~ A very expensive red and white bike, I'm afraid.

2 We use **adjectives** to describe size. Here, we're talking about a person's appearance:
> Which one is Keira? ~ She's the tall woman in the corner with short blonde hair.

3 We use **adjectives** to describe shape. This might be when we buy something for our home:
> We're looking for a dining room table. ~ Round or square, Madam?

A   Colour, size and shape

(i) Underline all colour, size and shape adjectives in this email.

Hi Milly,
I can come round to your house in the evening, but I'm shopping during the day. I'm looking for a <u>white</u> jacket to wear with my blue and green dress at Julie's wedding. I also want two square Japanese plates, some red roses, a small, round lamp, and a short yellow skirt for my holiday. It's a long list, isn't it? I'd better go!
See you later, Kate.

(ii) Now write the adjectives in the correct spaces below.

1 Colour adjectives: _white_ ....

2 Size adjectives: ....

3 Shape adjectives: ....

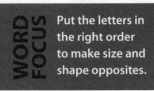

WORD FOCUS Put the letters in the right order to make size and shape opposites.

SIZE   ~~igb~~   _big_ 0   little

SIZE   gihh   ....¹   low

SHAPE	edwi	.... [2]		narrow	
SIZE	gheu	.... [3]		tiny	
SHAPE	aft	.... [4]		nith	.... [5]
SIZE	lalt	.... [6]		rhtos	.... [7]

B Colour and size

Jamie and Marie have been invited to a summer party with their new neighbours. Add these words to their conversation:

> tiny black and   blue and red   high   ~~short man~~   tall
> green table   yellow dress   long blonde   huge house

MARIE It's a nice party, but we don't really know anyone, do we? For example, who is that _short man_ [0] by the window?

JAMIE Oh, that's Phil. He's got a .... [1] Ferrari. But what about the .... [2] woman with .... [3] hair? Do you recognize her?

MARIE I think so. She lives in the .... [4] at the end of the road, with a .... [5] wall.

JAMIE Of course! And she's got a .... [6] white dog, hasn't she?

MARIE That's right. Anyway, I'm hungry. Is there anything to eat?

JAMIE I think so. That girl in the .... [7] has got a sandwich.

MARIE Look! There's a large .... [8] in the garden with lots of food and drink. Let's go and eat!

C Size and shape

Look at the picture on the right, and then put the phrases below in the correct order to finish the advertisement for a new town called Springville.

> tall, and the streets are   parks and a huge round
> ~~Wouldn't you like to live in a nice town~~   welcome when you arrive.
> lake? In our new town the trees are   wide. Make a short
> with two beautiful small   journey to Springville. We'll give you a big

Wouldn't you like to live in a nice town… ....

....

....

....

....

6 When we use more than one adjective before a noun, there is normally a correct order. For example:

a new French restaurant
(NOT ~~a French new restaurant~~)

7 Adjectives that give our **opinion**, like **nice**, normally come before other adjectives that describe **facts**, like **hot**, so we say:

*a **nice hot** bath* (NOT ~~a hot nice bath~~)

More examples of words to give our opinion:

> good   nice   important   special   wonderful
> great   fantastic   beautiful   funny
> (un)friendly   bad   horrible   awful

8 When you have more than one fact adjective, we normally put them in this order before the noun:

SIZE	AGE	SHAPE	COLOUR	NATIONALITY	MATERIAL
an	old		blue		jumper
a	small		German		town
a	round		glass		table

Here are some common **nationality adjectives**:

> American   Australian   Chinese   Dutch
> English   French   German   Greek   Indian
> Irish   Italian   Japanese   Portuguese   Russian
> Scottish   Spanish   Turkish   Welsh

and some **adjectives to describe materials** (what something is made of):

> cotton   silk   gold   silver   metal
> plastic   leather   wooden

9 We can use an adjective on its own after **be** and also after:

> look   seem   feel   taste   smell   sound

For example:
*This cake **is delicious**!*
*Some languages **seem difficult**.*
*Your exam **sounds horrible**!*

Grammar in action

4 We use **adjectives** to describe our opinions, what we see, hear, taste and smell, or how we feel:
You smell fantastic! ~ I know. I bought a wonderful new perfume today.
I feel awful today. ~ Go home and have a good rest.

5 We use **adjectives** to describe nationality. Here we're telling someone about our family history:
My mother is Canadian and my father's Italian. ~ Really? My grandparents were both Russian.

D   Did you have a good summer?

If the opinion and fact adjectives are in the correct order, put a tick (✓). If they're wrong, cross them out and re-write them.

BELLA   Hi Craig! Did you have a good summer?

CRAIG   Not bad, thanks. We had a ~~new special~~ _special new_ ⁰ project at work, but I still had time for a *fantastic short* _____✓_____ ⁰ holiday in Greece. The weather was beautiful. What about you?

BELLA   Well, we stayed in a *Scottish wonderful* _____¹ castle for a week in August, and then we visited my brother in his *old horrible* _____² flat in Edinburgh! But it was nice to see him.

CRAIG   Really? I know a *fantastic little* _____³ hotel in Edinburgh. It's a friendly city, isn't it?

BELLA   Sure, but busy in the summer. Anyway, we found a *Portuguese great* _____⁴ restaurant near the Royal Mile, so we were quite happy!

E For sale ads

Sometimes people advertise things they want to sell in local shops. Look at these 'ads' (advertisements) and put the adjectives in the correct order.

(leather/green) _Green leather_ [0] handbag (Harrods's) £10;

ring Stephanie
on 07700900173

(Welsh/tall) .... [1]
wardrobe, good condition,
only £30!
Email: joe45@yeah.co.uk

(old/beautiful/silk) Three
.... [2] blouses
(two cream, one white) £12 each;
phone Mo on 0207 9460650

(narrow/wooden)
.... [3] table:
£20 - great for barbecues!
Email: lola@lolaprice.com

(Turkish/red and green/fantastic)
.... [4] carpet.
Talk to Kev
on 07700900214

(silver/wide) .... [5]
belt, £5 - excellent condition.
Ring Fay
on 07700900761

F A meal in an international restaurant

Carol and Mark are looking for a place to eat. Choose the correct verb, and add an *s* if you need to.

CAROL This restaurant ...._looks_........ [0] (smell/look) friendly, and the menu
.... [1] (seem/taste) interesting. Shall we go in?

MARK Sure. After you. (*They enter.*) Is it Spanish or African or what?

CAROL I don't know. The music .... [2] (sound/look) South American, actually.

MARK But the food .... [3] (taste/smell) Indian! Shall we sit down?

WAITER Welcome! You both .... [4] (feel/look) hungry. You've come to the right place. Table for two here by the window?

CAROL Thanks, but it .... [5] (feel/sound) a little cold here. Can we sit over there?

WAITER Of course. Here's something to eat. I'll get you the menus and some water.

CAROL This dish .... [6] (taste/look) a bit funny. You can try it first, if you like!

MARK OK. (*He eats some.*) It .... [7] (taste/sound) quite nice - Mexican, perhaps?

OVER TO YOU Now go to page 125.

1 Look at this conversation:
> *Where do you want to eat tonight? At the hotel or in town? ~ It'll be* **cheaper** *and* **more interesting** *in town. Have you been to Paulo's? ~ No. Is it good? ~ Well, it's* **noisier** *than the hotel, but it's* **better** *fun.*

2 The words **cheaper**, **more interesting**, **noisier** and **better** are **comparative adjectives**. To form them:

- For short adjectives (one syllable), add **-er**:

small → smaller	short → shorter
tall → tall**er**	old → old**er**
new → new**er**	slow → slower

  or, if the adjective ends in **-e**, add **-r**:

nice → nice**r**	wide → wide**r**	late → late**r**

- For short adjectives, ending in one vowel and one consonant, we double the consonant before adding **-er**:

big → bi**gg**er	sad → sa**dd**er
hot → ho**tt**er	fat → fa**tt**er
thin → thi**nn**er	wet → we**tt**er

- These short adjectives are irregular:

good → **better**	bad → **worse**	far → **farther**

- For most long adjectives (two syllables or more), we put **more** first:

important → **more** important
expensive → **more** expensive

- For long adjectives ending in **-y**, we use **-ier**:

happy → happ**ier**	early → earl**ier**

3 We often use **than** with comparative adjectives:
> *Scotland is wetter* **than** *England.*

but it's not necessary:
> *It's colder today, isn't it?* (= it's colder than yesterday)

4 We use comparatives to compare two things:
> *England is bigger than Scotland.*

> **TIP**
> We sometimes use **a lot/much** or **a bit/a little**:
> *You can lift it. You're* **a lot** *stronger than me!*
> *The exam today was* **a bit** *easier, wasn't it?*

Grammar in action

1 We use **comparative adjectives** to compare things that we buy, and services that we use:
> *I like this jumper better, but it's more expensive.*
> *Don't drive. It's faster by train.*

2 We use **comparative adjectives** to compare places:
> *Her new flat is nicer than her old one. It's much bigger.*
> *Spain will be sunnier than France at Easter.*

3 We use **comparative adjectives** to compare people. We might talk about how a friend has changed:
> *Tom is much friendlier than he was when we were at school. He looks different too: he's taller than me now, his hair is longer and he seems happier.*

A Comparing things we buy and services we use

Fareed is buying a new laptop. Change the underlined words into comparative adjectives.

WOMAN These two, the Helix 400 and the VKC 28, are very popular at the moment, sir. The VKC 28 is a little <u>new</u> _newer_ [0], but the Helix is <u>cheap</u> .... [1].

FAREED Can I touch them? Which one is <u>heavy</u> .... [2]?

WOMAN The VKC is <u>light</u> .... [3] than the Helix, but it's also <u>wide</u> .... [4].

FAREED Yes, you're right. The VKC is <u>big</u> .... [5], but much <u>thin</u> .... [6]. And I suppose it's <u>powerful</u> .... [7] too, if it's newer.

WOMAN   It's <u>fast</u> .... [8], yes. But the Helix is still a good computer. We sell hundreds every week.

FAREED You said the VKC was <u>expensive</u> .... [9]. What's the difference in price?

WOMAN   The Helix is £400 and the VKC is £600.

FAREED Thanks. I think the VKC is a little <u>good</u> .... [10], but I'll take the Helix!

B   Comparing places

'Visit England' is a magazine in English for Polish students. In this article, the writer is comparing study holidays in Liverpool, a big city in Lancashire, and in Beverley, a small town in Yorkshire. Circle the correct comparative adjectives.

Of course, Liverpool is much *bigger*/*biger* [0] than Beverley. It's also *famouser*/*more famous* [1], much *noisier*/*noisyer* [2], and, when I was there, *weter*/*wetter* [3]! (It rained every day!) I spent two weeks in the Lancashire city last March, and I loved it. I stayed in the more *old*/*older* [4], *busier*/*busyer* [5] part of the city, near the river Mersey. I went on the Beatles tour, and I watched Liverpool FC play against Newcastle. (Newcastle won.) It was a good game, but football matches in England are much more expensive *than*/*as* [6] in Poland – I had to pay £45 for a ticket. Then I spent a week in Beverley at a *smaller*/*more small* [7] language school. Beverley is *beautifuller*/*more beautiful* [8] than Liverpool, and the people were *more friendlier*/*friendlier* [9] to me. It's a *richer*/*more rich* [10] and *cleaner*/*cleanner* [11] place too, – but perhaps Liverpool is *more interesting*/*interestinger* [12] in the end.

C   Comparing people

Dan is having breakfast with his 10 year-old daughter Amy and his 4 year-old son, Josh. Use the words in brackets to make phrases with comparative adjectives. Use short forms of the verb *be*.

DAN   ....*You're earlier for breakfast*....... [0] (You/be/early/for breakfast) today, Amy. Is it a normal day for you?

AMY   No. Mr Brown is teaching us today and tomorrow. .... [1] (He/be/bad/than) Mr Samson. .... [2] (He/be/fat), too.

DAN   I'm sure Mr Brown isn't fat, Amy.

AMY   .... [3] (Mr Samson/be/nice and funny), and .... [4] (he/be/intelligent).

DAN   All your teachers are intelligent, Amy. I'm sure it's a very difficult job for Mr Brown, with a class of 10 year-old kids.

JOSH   .... [5] (Be/it/difficult/than) your job, Daddy?

DAN   I don't know. .... [6] (I think/I/be/lucky), because I can work at home.

AMY   Daddy, ... [7] (be/I/pretty/than) the girl on 'Top TV'?

JOSH   .... [8] (You/be/silly/than) her!

DAN   You're both pretty, Amy. Are you ready for school?

JOSH   Yes, but I want some more toast, please.

DAN   .... [9] (You/be/hungry/than) usual this morning, Amy.

AMY   Because .... [10] (it/be/cold) today. Daddy, do you think Mr Brown eats a lot because he's cold?

5 Look at this example:

'Paulo's' is **the best** restaurant in town. Their pizzas are **the biggest** and **the most delicious**!

6 **The best**, **the biggest** and **the most delicious** are superlative forms. To make **superlative adjectives**:

- For short adjectives and long adjectives ending in **-y**, take away the final **r** of the comparative form, and add **-st**:

  small → smaller → the small**est**
  nice → nicer → the nic**est**
  big → bigger → the bigg**est**
  happy → happier → the happi**est**

- For long adjectives, change **more** to **most**:

  important → more important
  → the **most** important

- Irregular forms:

  good → better → the **best**
  bad → worse → the **worst**
  far → farther → the **farthest**

7 **Before superlative adjectives**, we usually use **the**:

Picasso is **the most famous** Spanish painter.

After superlative adjectives, we sometimes use **of**:

Sunday is the best day **of** the week!
It's the smallest **of** the three hotels.

but we use **in** for places and groups of people:

She's the richest woman **in** Britain. (NOT ~~of Britain~~)
Dave is the funniest student **in** the class.

8 We use **superlatives** when we're comparing more than two things:

There are four countries in the UK. England is the biggest.

> We sometimes use the present perfect with **ever** after the superlative form:
> What is **the worst** meal **you've ever eaten**?
> This is **the most beautiful** park **I've ever seen**!
>
> TIP

Grammar in action

4 We use **superlative adjectives** to talk about the best, worst or most interesting places, people and things:

Heathrow is the busiest airport in Europe.
This is the most comfortable room in the house.
It's the fastest family car in the UK.
It's the saddest film we've ever seen.

D **Talking about the best things about the Seychelles**

Look at the home page of the website for 'Seychelles Holidays'. Change the underlined words into superlative adjectives.

Seychelles Facts (and Opinions!):

- The Republic of Seychelles is the <u>small</u> *smallest* [0] African country, and it's the <u>good</u> .... [1] place in the world for your holiday!

- The <u>big</u> .... [2] of the hundred and fifty five islands is Mahé, with an international airport.

- The Seychelles Islands have the <u>beautiful</u> .... [3] beaches you've ever seen, and the <u>warm</u> .... [4] seas.

- The <u>sunny</u> .... [5] times of year are December and January (but they're also the <u>expensive</u> .... [6] times to visit).

- The <u>peaceful</u> .... [7] island is La Digue - it's like a journey into the past!

- The <u>nice</u> .... [8] restaurant in the Seychelles is 'André's' in Anse Lazio. (Another free meal, please, André!)

- The best Creole music is by the <u>famous</u> .... [9] Seychelles musician, the wonderful Jean-Marc Volcy!

E Choosing a flat in London

We use comparatives to compare things we buy; services we use; places; and people. We use superlatives to talk about the best, worst or most interesting places, people and things. Sean and Thierry want to share a flat in London. They've looked at three flats, and now they're in a café. Add these words to the conversation:

If you rent a flat, your *landlord* or *landlady* is the person you pay every month.

WORD FOCUS

ever	in	most	of	the	than	dirtier	expensive	friendlier	nearer

SEAN   What did you think about the two flats in Camden?

THIERRY   The first one was bigger, but it was ___dirtier___ [0] too.

SEAN   You can clean a flat though, can't you?

THIERRY   Sure, but the second one was nicer, and the landlord was _____ [1].

SEAN   Perhaps, but it was also noisier _____ [2] the first one, because it was _____ [3] to the road.

SEAN   They weren't the best flats we've _____ [4] seen, were they? What about the one in Crouch End?

THIERRY   It was the _____ [5] comfortable _____ [6] the three flats.

SEAN   I agree. But it was also the most _____ [7]. We haven't got enough money, have we?

THIERRY   Shall we have another coffee? They make _____ [8] best cappuccino _____ [9] north London here. We can look at some more flats this afternoon.

F Choosing a singer for a musical

Desmond and Jilly are trying to find a singer for a new musical. They saw three singers this morning. Change the underlined adjectives into comparatives or superlatives.

Hi Desmond,

What did you think about the guys this morning? Charlie was the <u>loud</u> ___loudest___ [0] singer I've ever heard! My ears are still hurting. He's probably got the <u>strong</u> _____ [1] voice in London. I liked him, but Luke was a <u>good</u> _____ [2] dancer than him, and his voice was good too. But Luke hasn't sung in a big show before. Matt, the <u>tall</u> _____ [3] guy today, looked great, but his voice was <u>weak</u> _____ [4] than Charlie's. We've got to decide soon, but we could see them again tomorrow. What do you think?

Jilly

Hi Jilly,

It was <u>difficult</u> _____ [5] today with the guys than yesterday with the girls. Luke is the <u>young</u> _____ [6], isn't he? He was also the <u>good</u> _____ [7] dancer this morning, but I don't think he's ready. It's hard to sing every night for six weeks, isn't it? Matt is <u>old</u> _____ [8] than Luke, and he's got the right face, but he's also got the <u>bad</u> _____ [9] voice of the three, I'm afraid. In my view, Charlie is the <u>good</u> _____ [10] of the guys. We can teach him to dance later!

Desmond

OVER TO YOU Now go to page 125.

1 Look at this conversation:
*Are you driving to the match? ~ Yes. I don't think we'll win today, because we're playing so **badly** at the moment. ~ Well, drive **carefully**. The roads will be busy.*

2 **Badly** and **carefully** are **adverbs of manner**. We form them from adjectives:

For most adverbs, add **-ly** to the adjective:

clear → clear**ly**		correct → correct**ly**	
loud → loud**ly**		perfect → perfect**ly**	
polite → polite**ly**		proper → proper**ly**	
quick → quick**ly**		quiet → quiet**ly**	
secret → secret**ly**		serious → serious**ly**	
silent → silent**ly**		slow → slow**ly**	

For adjectives ending in consonant (**b**, **c**, **d**, etc.) + **-y**, change **-y** to **-ily**:

angry → angr**ily**	easy → eas**ily**
heavy → heav**ily**	noisy → nois**ily**

For adjectives ending in **-ful**, double the **l** before adding **-y**:

beautiful → beautifu**lly**	careful → carefu**lly**
successful → successfu**lly**	

For adjectives ending in **-le**, take away **-e**, and add **-y**:

simple → simp**ly**	terrible → terrib**ly**

3 **Adverbs of manner** tell us **how** things happen. They normally go **after the verb**:
*It **rained heavily** all morning.*
*You need to **walk carefully** in the snow.*

or **after the verb + direct object**:
*He **sang the song beautifully** at the concert.*
(The word 'song' is a direct object.)

Grammar in action

1 We use **adverbs of manner** to describe how things happen. Here, a boss is talking about her employee:
She does her job perfectly. She speaks clearly and she works quickly. She sells our products successfully.

2 We use **adverbs of manner** to tell people how to do things, such as instructions for cooking:
Add the eggs and flour carefully, then stir the mixture slowly.

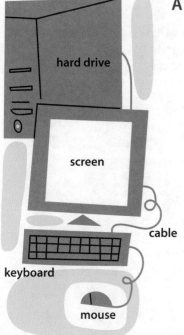

hard drive

screen

cable

keyboard

mouse

A Describing how things happen (1)

Karen is at home with her flatmates, when her phone rings. Cross out the adjectives and add their adverb forms to the conversation.

KAREN Hello? Shula? I'm sorry, I can't hear you. My friends are talking so ....*loudly*........ ⁰ (~~loud~~). Just a moment. Mike, Joss! Shut up! That's better. They're talking ....¹ (quiet) now. Yes, I'm OK, but I've got a problem. I bought a new computer yesterday. I think I've fixed it ....² (correct), but it doesn't work very well. What? You'll come round? That's very kind, but you know it's raining ....³ (heavy)? OK. Thanks. See you later.

KAREN *(Ten minutes later)* Thanks for coming, Shula. I fixed the computer and the printer ....⁴ (careful), but something is wrong. Do you think there's a problem with the hard drive?

SHULA I'll have a look.

KAREN I'm sure I did it ....⁵ (proper).

SHULA Everything looks OK. I'm going to try to print something.

KAREN It's printing very ....⁶ (noisy), isn't it?

SHULA   Yes, but it's only because the cable is in the wrong place. Don't worry. Can you lift
        the keyboard .... [7] (slow), please? I'll hold the mouse.

KAREN   The noise has stopped. How did you do it so .... [8] (easy)?

SHULA   Because I'm fantastic! Can you make me a cup of tea now, please?

B Telling people how to do things

Sarah is going to work as a tour guide for tourists visiting her home town, Gloucester. Debbie, her boss, is giving her some advice. Use the first two letters of the adverbs in brackets to add the full words to the conversation. All of the adverbs are in the lists on page 106, but try to do this exercise without looking back.

DEBBIE You have to speak (cl) _clearly_ [0], of course, so everyone understands you,
        and you should also speak (co) .... [1]. People will tell you if you make
        grammatical mistakes!

SARAH   I'll remember that. When we're in the town centre, can we go into the market?

DEBBIE Yes, that's a good idea, but there's a lot of noise in there, so you have to talk
        (lo) .... [2]. And after the market, you can go towards the cathedral, but walk
        (sl) .... [3] - there's a lot to see on the way.

SARAH   OK. I can show them some of the old shops. By the way, I think people have to
        pay something when they enter the cathedral, don't they? What should I do?

DEBBIE Don't worry. Just ask the group (po) .... [4] to put some money in the
        glass box. It won't be a problem. And remember to talk (qu) .... [5] in the
        cathedral! They don't like noisy groups.

SARAH   Do you think the group will know it's my first time as a guide?

DEBBIE Don't worry. You'll be great. I'm sure you'll do it (be) .... [6].

C Describing how things happen (2)

Now Sarah is emailing Debbie to tell her about her first tour. First make these adjectives into adverbs:

proper ......_properly_......   quick ....   slow ....
loud   ....   angry ....   heavy ....

Then add them in order into the underlined parts of the text.

>   _properly_
> The tour went well, I think. <u>I hope I did it</u> /. [0] I met the group at the bus station at nine thirty. <u>We walked into the town centre,</u>[1] and I took them to the market. We had a really good time there. <u>Then we walked to the cathedral.</u>[2] But there was one problem in the cathedral. <u>One of the tourists asked a question,</u>[3] and <u>a tall woman said something.</u>[4] But it was OK in the end. We had a good visit. <u>Unfortunately, it rained on the way back to the bus station,</u>[5] but most of the group had umbrellas!
>
> Best wishes,
>
> Sarah

4 Well

The **adverb of manner** from the adjective **good** is **well**:
*She plays most sports **well**.*
*I slept **well** last night.*

We often use **very** and **quite** with **well**:
*Fran speaks Chinese **very well**.*
*I **don't** remember films **very well**.*
*Tom and I both swim **quite well**.*

➔ For more information on **very/quite + adverb**, see Unit 28 on p. 110.)

To do well means 'to be successful':
*He's **doing well** at university.*
*The company isn't **doing** very **well** this year.*

But remember that **well** can also be an adjective:
*How are you? ~ **I'm** very **well**, thanks.*

and a word we use when we start to speak:
*What are you doing this evening? ~ **Well**, I think we'll just watch TV.*

> Look at the way we use the expression **well done**:
> *I passed the exam. ~ Well done!*
>
> **TIP**

5 These adverbs of manner have the same form as their adjectives:

early	late	fast	hard

*The bus is **late** again. (late = adjective)*
*We mustn't arrive **late**! (late = adverb)*

Here are some more examples of these adverbs:
*Do you get up **early**?*
*He drives very **fast**. It's dangerous.*
*We're all working **hard** for the exams.*

Grammar in action

3 We use **well** to talk about our ability to do things. Here, a teacher is talking about a student's progress at school:
He can't dance well, I'm afraid, but he speaks French well and is doing well in chemistry.

4 We use **early** and **late** to talk about when things happen, and **fast** and **hard** to talk and ask about how we do things, such as on a journey:
That's our bus! It's arrived early!
How fast can you run? We don't want to miss it!

D   Talking about our ability to do things

Molly is sending an email to Dave on Saturday morning. After the example, add *well* five more times.

Hi Dave

I went to Marie's concert yesterday evening. She sang 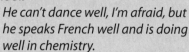 /. She plays the piano very, too. I'm not very good

at music, as you know, but I can cook quite, and I can paint, so I'm lucky, aren't I? Anyway, do you want to

meet later today? I don't really want to go to Sammy's party this evening. I didn't sleep very last night, so

I feel tired today. We could go to that new Japanese restaurant on Dean Street. Greg says that it's doing.

Hope to hear from you later.

E   When things happen and how things happen

Dave is replying to Molly's email. Add the correct adverbs to their conversation.

Hi Molly,

I had a terrible day yesterday. First, I got up very ___late___ **0** (hard/late) so I had to eat my breakfast
_____ **1** (fast/early). Then I cycled to work, but it was raining _____ **2** (hard/fast), so I got
very wet. Anyway, I worked really _____ **3** (hard/early) all morning, and I ate lunch _____ **4**
(hard/early), at about twelve o'clock. After lunch, the sun was shining, so I went for a walk, and I forgot about my meeting
with my boss at twelve thirty! I ran _____ **5** (fast/early) back to the office, but I arrived fifteen minutes
_____ **6** (late/early). He wasn't happy. The rest of the day was OK. I just cycled home, ate my dinner and
went to bed _____ **7** (early/hard)! Shall I meet you at the restaurant at one o'clock? I won't be late!

F   A skiing holiday

We use adverbs of manner to talk about the way things happen; to tell people how to do things; and to talk about our ability to do things. Ben is at an internet café with his friend Candy on Friday evening. If there is an adjective in brackets at the beginning of a line, add its adverb form in the correct place.

BEN   (good) Can you ski /ᵂᵉˡˡ, Candy?

CANDY   Yes, I'm pretty good. Why are you asking?

BEN   (early) There's a skiing holiday here for two in
          Switzerland for £50, if we leave in the morning.

CANDY   Really? Why is it so cheap? Is there any snow there at
          the moment?

BEN   (hard) Yes, it snowed last week in Austria and
          Switzerland.

CANDY   (quick) Can we pack enough? It's nine o'clock already.

BEN   (bad) I think so. But there is one problem. I ski very,
          I'm afraid.

CANDY   (fast) Oh. Well, there will be a ski school. I'm sure
          you'll learn.

BEN   Give me some advice.

CANDY   (correct) You have to move. That's the important thing.

BEN   (slow) And you have to turn, don't you?

CANDY   And you have to fall in the snow ten times an hour!
          Come on, let's go home and pack.

OVER TO YOU   Now go to page 126.

1 Look at these examples:

*She speaks **very quietly**. I can't understand her. I'm **quite hungry**. Shall we stop for a sandwich?*

2 **Very** and **quite** are **adverbs of degree**. We can use these adverbs before adjectives:

*I loved the film. It's **very funny**.*

or before other adverbs:

*He spoke **quite angrily** to us.*

3 We use **very** to make the adjective stronger. We can also use **really**:

*It was **very kind** of you to help me.*
*I'm **really tired**. I could sleep for hours!*

4 **Quite** is not as strong as **very**. We use it to make the adjective weaker. We can also use **fairly** or, in informal English, **pretty**:

*Harry is **quite good** at tennis.* (= He's good at tennis, but not wonderful.)
*The exam today was **fairly easy**.* (= It was OK, but not simple.)
*You don't need a coat. It's **pretty warm** outside.* (= The weather is warm, but it isn't hot.)

5 We can also use **really** and **quite** with these verbs:

> really + enjoy, like, love, want, need, hope, hate
> quite + enjoy, like

Here are some examples:

*My mum **really loves** the Beatles.*
*He **really hates** fish.*
*We **quite enjoy** musicals.*
*I **quite like** Shakespeare, but I prefer modern writers.*

We can't use **very** in this way:
~~I very enjoy football.~~

Grammar in action

1 We use **very**, and **really** to say things strongly, when we want to give extra emphasis to what we say. We can do this when we tell a friend about a particularly good or bad experience we've had:

The roads were really busy and we arrived very late at the church. I felt really terrible. But the bride was really beautiful and we were very pleased to be at the wedding.

2 We can use **quite**, **fairly** and **pretty** to say things less strongly. Here we are telling a friend about a book:

This book isn't fantastic but I quite like the story. It's fairly long and quite complicated, and the characters are pretty boring.

A Saying things about our lives more strongly

Naomi, Etsuko and Henry are meeting in a café after work. Put the words in brackets in the correct order and add them to the conversation. Use capital letters where necessary.

ETSUKO I'm really tired **0** (tired/I'm/really). How was your day, Henry?

HENRY OK thanks, Etsuko. .... **1** (very/is/my new colleague Simon/friendly). What about you, Naomi?

NAOMI Terrible! .... **2** (important/meeting/really/for a/I was late) in the morning, and then I had a headache all afternoon.

ETSUKO That's too bad. .... **3** (need/I/another coffee/really). I'll get three more.

HENRY What did your boss say, Naomi, when you were late?

NAOMI .... **4** (very/she/angry/was), because we had visitors from France, and they arrived an hour early!

HENRY Oh dear. Anyway, it's Friday tomorrow. .... **5** (I/weekends/love/really)!

NAOMI Me, too. I want to find a new sofa, but .... **6** (cheap/to be/very/it's got). I don't have much money left after my holiday.

HENRY Well, ... **7** (you find one/hope that/really/I).

B Saying things less strongly

Paul is a British student studying for a semester in Toronto. Look at his blog. Rewrite the underlined parts of the text, adding the adverbs in brackets.

I've just finished my first month in Toronto. <u>It's been hard</u>. (quite) <u>It's been quite hard</u> [0]. It's a new country for me, after all. <u>I was lucky.</u> (fairly) .... [1]. I arrived late, but <u>I got a flat quickly.</u> (quite) .... [2]. My new flatmate is called Billy. <u>He's funny,</u> (pretty) .... [3], so we laugh a lot. It's good. And <u>I like the food here</u> (quite) .... [4] – you get a great burger in the college café, for example. Billy has a car, so he gives me a lift to college sometimes, and <u>the bus service is good</u> (quite) .... [5] – but it takes about an hour. <u>Our teachers are young,</u> (fairly) .... [6], but there are about a hundred students in my class, so you can't really ask questions. Oh, <u>and it's cold here!</u> (pretty) .... [7]! I bought some warm clothes, <u>but they were expensive.</u> (quite) .... [8]. Anyway, I've got to go now. Billy wants me to watch an American football game with him. Bye for now!

C Giving extra emphasis or saying things less strongly

Liz's company is going to sell a new type of car, called the 'Sunflower'. Liz is talking to Charlie and George. Say things more strongly (M) or less strongly (L) by crossing out the wrong adverb.

LIZ (M)[0] When do you think we should launch the Sunflower? It's ~~quite~~/really important to find the right time of year.

CHARLIE (L)[1] Sure. August would be quite/very good, I think.

GEORGE (L)[2] No, that's late, Charlie. It's a summer car, I know, but consumers buy cars fairly/really early.

LIZ OK, we could launch the car in May, then.

CHARLIE (M)[3] All right, but that's pretty/very soon. We need to finish the TV ad.

GEORGE (L)[4] I saw the idea for the advert yesterday, Charlie. It's quite/very serious, isn't it?

CHARLIE Yes, but I think people will remember it.

LIZ (M)[5] Sure, they'll remember it, Charlie. It's fairly/very beautiful.

GEORGE (L)[6] But it's also really/pretty sad. My question is: do we want a sad ad?

LIZ George may be right. It is a summer car after all, Charlie. Summer normally means holidays. It's a happy time.

CHARLIE (M)[7] But we've got Sam Taylor in the ad. He's really/quite famous!

GEORGE He's a wonderful actor, Charlie, but he's a wonderful actor in some very sad films.

LIZ (M)[8] George is right. Charlie, I'd like you and George to work together on this. Is that OK? I think you could be fairly/very special together. What do you think?

CHARLIE I'm sure it will be fine, thanks, Liz.

6 When we use **quite** with an adjective and noun, we normally put **quite** before **a/an**:

	quite	+ a/an	+ adjective	+ noun
It's	quite	a	long	journey.

But we put **very**, **really**, **fairly** and **pretty** after **a/an**:

	a/an	+ very, really, etc.	+ adjective	+ noun
It's	a	really	good	film.

We can also use **quite** with **a lot of**:
> I've bought *quite a lot of vegetables*.

(We can't use **very**, **really**, **fairly** and **pretty** in this way.)

> With some adjectives, like **right** and **true**, **quite** means 'completely':
> *That's quite true.* (= That's completely true.)
>
> TIP

Grammar in action

D We normally use **quite** before **a/an** + **adjective** + **noun**, and we also use **quite** with **a lot of** to add more detail when we describe something. Here, we are describing a trip to the cinema:
> *It was quite a good film. We ate quite a lot of popcorn.*

D Quite a hard life

Read the beginning of this magazine article. Then add the correct adverbs from the brackets.

My husband and I have a hotel in France. It's _____ *quite* [0] (fairly/quite) a hard life. We get up early because there are _____ [1] (quite/pretty) a lot of things to do every day. After breakfast, I go to the local market. All my friends go to the market, and I _____ [2] (very/really) enjoy it. There's a good butcher's there, and a _____ [3] (fairly/quite) cheap greengrocer's. Back at the hotel there are _____ [4] (fairly/quite) a lot of sheets, pillowcases, towels and basins to clean! It's a _____ [5] (pretty/quite) difficult job, because we don't have a washing machine at the

moment! We have _____ [6] (quite/pretty) a small restaurant at the hotel, but it gets busy at lunchtime. My husband cooks in the kitchen, and I make sure that everything is OK in the restaurant. _____ [7] (Fairly/Quite) a lot of local people come for their lunch, and we _____ [8] (fairly/really) like to give them a good, hot meal at a _____ [9] (pretty/quite) low price. After lunch, I usually sleep for half an hour, and then the afternoon begins! It's always a _____ [10] (quite/really) long day, but we love it here!

E   A gallery opening

Ben, Angie and Derek are at a 'gallery opening' (the first night of an art show) in Glasgow. Decide if the adverbs of degree have been used correctly. If they have, put a tick (✓). If not, write the correct word(s).

If you wear a *wig*, you don't have your own hair.

WORD FOCUS

BEN   The colours in her paintings are quite ....._✓_....⁰ good, you know.

ANGIE   Oh yes. I ~~fairly~~ _really_⁰ love her paintings!

DEREK   I don't agree. Look at this painting, 'The Evening Sea', for example. The sky is quite ....¹ nice, I suppose, but the sea is pretty ....² horrible.

ANGIE   You may not like it, but someone will pay pretty ....³ a lot of money for it!

BEN   Sssh! She's here tonight, you know.

DEREK   I very ....⁴ hope she is! I can give her my opinion.

ANGIE   She comes to all her first nights, but she wears a very ....⁵ long wig!

DEREK   I don't believe you!

ANGIE   Look! I'm fairly ....⁶ sure that's her in the corner.

DEREK   Really? She's fairly ....⁷ a young woman, then.

BEN   Do you very ....⁸ want to speak to her, Derek?

DEREK   Well, I can tell her that the sky in her painting is pretty nice ....⁹, can't I?

F   An interview in central London

A journalist is interviewing people who work in central London. Add the adverbs in brackets in the order in which you see them.

WOMAN   You work in a travel agent's at Oxford Circus. What's it like?

MAN   (pretty, really) Well, it's _pretty_ / busy, of course, but I _really_ / like this part of London.

WOMAN   Why is that?

MAN   (quite, quite, very) First of all, it's a friendly place, in fact. For example, there are a lot of cafés where people go with colleagues for coffee, lunch, etc. That's nice.

WOMAN   (quite, fairly) And I suppose you see a lot of famous people. The headquarters building of the BBC is close to Oxford Circus.

MAN   (quite) Yes, but I'm more interested in the shops. They're expensive, but you can get any new CD or DVD immediately!

WOMAN   So are there any problems here?

MAN   (really, pretty, very) Yes. The underground is busy in the morning, but if you drive to work, it's hard to find a parking space! Sometimes I arrive early at work, but it's still fairly busy.

WOMAN   Well, thanks very much for your time.

OVER TO YOU   Now go to page 126.

29 Prepositions
Prepositions of place (*at, in, on, above, behind, under*)

1 Look at this conversation:
*Darling, where are you? ~ I'm **at** Heathrow. Why? ~*
*You've left your passport **in** the living room. ~ Oh no.*
*~ I'm afraid so. It's **on** the table.*

2 Place

We use **at**, **in** and **on** to say where people/things are.

We use **at** to talk about a point where something happens.

We use **in** with enclosed spaces and countries.

We use **on** with surfaces, or with lines like a river or road.

3 Here are some more examples of **at**, **in** and **on**:

at the bus stop	at the train station	at the office
at the doctor's	at the supermarket	at a party
at Sue's (house)	at the door	at the front/back

in the library	in the park	in London	in Spain
in the pool	in the photo	in a book	in the car

on the chair	on the shelf	on the train
on the road	on the beach	on the first floor
on the left/right	on page seven	on the menu
on the internet		

4 Sometimes we don't use **the**:

at home	at school	at college	at work
in bed	in town	in hospital	

5 We also use **above**, **behind** and **under** to say where things are:

Hi Dave,
*I'm very comfortable in my new room. I've put a nice painting **above** the desk. Fifi, my cat, is sleeping **under** the bed and all*
*my empty suitcases are **behind***
the sofa!
Love, Debbie

Grammar in action

1 We often use **at**, **in** and **on** to talk about travel:
I'm on the train. Can you meet me at the station?
How long are you going to stay in Australia?
Shall we get off the train at Cardiff?

2 We normally use **at** to talk about where people are:
I'm at the office, Hugh. I'll be home about seven.
Sara's at the dentist's, but she'll be back later.
Is there someone at the door?

3 We often use **at**, **in**, **on**, **above**, **behind** and **under** to describe where we have put things at home:
My bag's at home! I think I've left it under the bed. Or it might be on the desk, or behind the piano, or in my wardrobe!

A   Talking about travel

Luke, Angie and Dave are on holiday in Goa. Luke and Angie are taking a local bus. Add the correct prepositions to their conversation.

ANGIE   It's a lovely day, isn't it?

LUKE   Of course. You're ___*in*___⁰ (at/in) India now, not England.

ANGIE   That's true. Are we going to get off the bus _____¹ (at/in) Sammi's café?

LUKE   OK. We could ring Dave, and have a picnic _____² (on/in) the beach this afternoon.

ANGIE   Good idea. (*She takes out her mobile phone.*) Dave? Hi! Luke and I are _____³ (at/on) the bus. Shall we meet later for a beach picnic? Excellent! I'll give you a ring.

LUKE A picnic in November! This is different life .... ⁴ (at/in) Glasgow, isn't it?

ANGIE Luke? Why is the bus stopping here?

LUKE Because there's a monkey .... ⁵ (at/on) the road. Have you got your camera?

ANGIE No. I left it .... ⁶ (in/on) the car, I'm afraid. I'll get it later.

LUKE Don't worry. We'll see more monkeys while we're here.

B Talking about where people are

Joe gets home and asks Mandy where their flatmates are. Use *at* and the pictures to complete the conversation.

JOE It's very quiet, Mandy. Where is everybody?

MANDY Well, Ethan's ~~at the greengrocer's~~ ⁰. He's getting some tomatoes, I think. Millie's .... ¹. She's working late this week. Dylan's father is arriving from America, so he's .... ². And Megan is having a problem with one of her teeth, so she's .... ³. Now Jake is .... ⁴, because he wants get the sports results, and Jasmine is .... ⁵. Does that answer your question?

C Talking about where things are

Phil is staying in Diana's house. Read her letter to him, and use the picture of her kitchen to add the correct prepositions.

| at | in | on | above | behind | under |

Dear Phil,

I hope you enjoy your week in Norfolk. Please use the food ....in.... ⁰ my kitchen. There's a bag of potatoes .... ¹ the table. They're from my garden. There's a loaf of brown bread .... ² a small cupboard .... ³ the fridge. I made it myself two days ago. I hope you like it. There's also a tin of biscuits .... ⁴ the table, and some fruit .... ⁵ the biscuits. Help yourself! And you'll find some vegetables under the window .... ⁶ the back of the kitchen. They're not from my garden. They're from a local farm. Finally, if you look through the window, you'll see some apple trees .... ⁷ the garden. The apples are delicious!

Best wishes,

Diana

Prepositions
Prepositions of time (*at*, *in*, *on*, *from*, *to*, *until*)

6 Time

We use **at**, **in**, **on**, **from** and **to/until** to talk about time.

7 We use **at** for 'clock' times and meals:
*The film starts **at** eight thirty.*
*Sleep well. I'll see you **at** breakfast.*

8 We also use **at** in these expressions:

> at night   at the weekend   at the moment
> at Christmas   at Easter

*I always lock the door **at night**.*

9 We use **in** for parts of the day, months, seasons and years:

> in the afternoon   in June
> in the summer   in 2001

*Have you ever been to Boston **in** the autumn.*

10 And we use **on** for days and dates:

> on Wednesday   on the thirteenth of August

*Shall we go shopping **on** Saturday afternoon?*

11 When we use **this**, **next**, and **every**, we don't use **at**, **in**, or **on**:
I wake up two or three times ~~at~~ every night.
We'll go to the match ~~on~~ next Saturday.

12 We use **from** or **from…to/until** to talk about periods of time:
*Call me later, Sam. I'll be at home **from** six.*
(= from six and for the rest of the evening.)

*The museum is open **from** 9 a.m. **to** 6 p.m.*
*I waited for you **from** 4 p.m. **until** 5 p.m!*

> **TIP**
> In spoken and informal English, we often use **till** or **'til** instead of **until**:
> *She played that CD from midday **till** midnight!*

Grammar in action

4 We can use **at**, **in** and **on** to talk about time. Here, we are making a plan to meet a friend:
I'll see you at the weekend. Shall we meet in the afternoon on Saturday? ~ I can be in town at 2 p.m. See you then!

5 We can use **from** and **to/until** to talk about a period of time, such as the opening times of a shop:
The library is closed from 1 p.m. until 2 p.m.
The supermarket is open from 10 a.m. till 4 p.m. on a Sunday.

6 We can use **from** and **to/until** to tell someone how long we do an activity for. We might talk about our daily routine, or our holiday plans:
I work from 9 to 5, but I'm always out at lunch from 12.30 to 1.00.

D   Arranging to meet at lunchtime

Carol wants to meet a business colleague for lunch. Cross out eight wrong words after the example in her message.

Hi Alex,
Can we meet today? I'm flying to Mumbai on Friday, and I'd like to talk to you about the trip. Who did you meet when you went there ~~on~~ in May last year? My trip to Mumbai is quite short. I'll be back on Thursday in next week. I'm trying to fix some meetings at in the moment, but I need your help! Anyway, I'm in a meeting on this morning until from ten till eleven, but we could meet on at lunch, if you like. I'm going to visit our Bristol office in this afternoon, so could we have an early lunch at in twelve o'clock perhaps? If that's not possible, maybe we could meet on in the evening? I hope to hear from you soon.
Best,

Caroline

E We use prepositions to talk about where people and things are; and to talk about travel, time, dates, and days. Leo is writing to his sister from a campsite in Italy. First, look at this picture of the campsite and the photo. Then add the correct prepositions.

Hi Sara!

We're looking forward to seeing you next Sunday ...._at_.... [0] (under/at/above) the campsite. We're having a good time. Sam and I run .... [1] (until/at/in) the mornings. Anna swims .... [2] (in/on/under) the pool, and Eve gets croissants for our breakfast .... [3] (on/at/to) a baker's in town. Then from about ten o' clock .... [4] (from/till/at) lunch, we do what we want. There's a wood .... [5] (above/from/behind) the campsite, so sometimes I go for a walk. We normally have lunch .... [6] (at/to/on) one o' clock, and then we go .... [7] (in/at/on) the car to the seaside. Sometimes we have a picnic .... [8] (above/on/in) the beach, or we drive to one of the towns or cities nearby. .... [9] (At/On/From) the moment, I'm emailing you from an internet café .... [10] (under/on/in) Perpignan. .... [11] (On/In/At) night, we cook a meal. I've attached a photo of our kitchen! .... [12] (On/In/At) the photo you can see there's a small fridge .... [13] (under/behind/above) the table, and there are lots of pots and pans .... [14] (under/on/above) the cooker! The weather is beautiful now, but the campsite manager says there was snow a month ago .... [15] (in/on/at) Easter!

See you soon,   Leo

F   A family meal

Peggy and her husband Bill are having dinner with their children and their guest from Colombia, Santiago. Choose the correct words from the brackets.

BILL   We're ...._in_.... [0] (in/on/at/above) the dining room, everyone! Dinner is
            .... [1] (in/on/at/above) the table! Where are the twins?

PEGGY   Tom's .... [2] (behind/at/in/on) town, Bill, and Katie's working .... [3] (above/until/at/on) eight every day this week to make some extra money.

SANTIAGO   Mia's .... [4] (at/in/behind/on) home, but I think she's .... [5] (on/in/at/above) her bedroom.

AMY   Where's my knife, Mummy?

PEGGY   It's on the floor .... [6] (above/in/to/under) your chair, darling. Give it to me. I'll wash it for you.

BILL   Did you get your ticket .... [7] (on/under/at/to) the travel agent's today?

SANTIAGO   No, Bill. I got there at a quarter to six, and it was closed. It's open .... [8] (to/at/in/from) nine thirty to five thirty. I'll go again tomorrow, or I'll buy it .... [9] (under/in/on/at) the internet. I hope to fly home .... [10] (in/on/till/at) the twentieth of June.

PEGGY   But you'll come back again .... [11] (on/at/this/until) September, won't you, Santiago?

SANTIAGO   That's right. I'm going to study economics .... [12] (on/at/in/to) university.

OVER TO YOU Now go to page 126.

1 Sentences in English always need a **subject** and a **verb**, but they can be quite short:

> **Tom is** reading.   **I love** chips!
> **She's** at work.   **I'm** tired.
> **You look** sad.   **He hasn't arrived**.

We make sentences longer with the conjunctions **and**, **but** and **or**:

> *I love chips, **but** I don't like fish.*

2 And

We use **and** to connect ideas and things:

> *I bought some trousers, a jumper **and** a shirt.*
> *I'm cold **and** hungry.*
> *Fran works in a bank, **and** Don teaches French.*
> *I did some homework, **and** then I went to bed.*

> We sometimes use **go and... + verb**:
> > *Shall we **go and get** a DVD?*
> > *I must **go and do** some work now.*
>
> TIP

3 But

We use **but** to connect two different ideas:

> *I worked really hard, **but** I didn't pass the exam.*
> *It's a nice shop, **but** why is it so expensive?*

4 Or

We use **or** to connect two possibilities:

> *Would you like a biscuit **or** a piece of cake?*
> *Shall we have a meal **or** see a play?*

We sometimes use **or** in negative sentences:

> *We haven't got any fruit **or** cheese, I'm afraid.*

5 Comma (,)

In lists with **and**, we use **commas** like this:

> *You'll need paper, a pen, your book **and** a dictionary.*

And we often use a **comma (,)** before **and** and **but** in longer sentences (sentences with a verb in each part, for example):

> *He finished his meal, **and** then he went out.*
> *I bought a new CD player, **but** it didn't work.*

6 We don't need to repeat unnecessary words:

> *Greg is watching TV, **and** ~~Greg is~~ eating a pizza.*
> *This coffee is hot **but** ~~it is~~ very weak.*
> *We could drive **or** ~~we could~~ take the bus.*

Grammar in action

① We use **but** to talk about contrasts (things that are different from each other). This might be when we're disappointed about a result:
> *We played quite well, but we lost six-one.*
> *I trained for six weeks, but I still finished last.*

② We often use **or** when we make offers and suggestions:
> *Would you like tea or coffee?*
> *Shall we have a pizza or a curry or something?*

③ We use a comma with **and** to connect ideas together in a list. This might be a shopping list:
> *I've bought balloons, paper cups and plates.*
> *We need sugar, bread and coffee.*

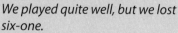

A   Talking about contrasts

Maggie is emailing her friend Linda. Put '/' in the four places where the word *but* is missing.

> Hi Linda,
>
> I've just got back from Scotland. It was fun, / it was also very tiring! It rained every day, of course, the mountains were beautiful. We camped in the Highlands near Inverness. The kids loved the campsite, it was pretty cold at night! We bought most of our food at the campsite shop. It took a long time to get our meals ready in the evening, they tasted delicious. After dinner the kids played games, and I read my book. I'm sure we'll return to the campsite one day, next time we'll go in August, not April!   Best wishes, Maggie

B Making offers and suggestions

Dave and Sheila are at home on Friday night, talking about the weekend. Add these phrases to their conversation:

| or a TV | or a cup | or read a | or any sugar | or a quiz | ~~or we could~~ |

DAVE   What shall we do tomorrow? We could go for a walk *or we could* ⁰ see a film.

SHEILA I don't know, Dave. I'm tired. Do you want a cup of tea .... ¹ of coffee or something?

DAVE   We haven't got any milk .... ² left.

SHEILA Perhaps we should go shopping tomorrow.

DAVE   OK. Have we got a newspaper .... ³ guide? I'll see what's on the telly.

SHEILA I've looked already. Apart from the soap operas, there's a war film, a nature programme .... ⁴ show.

DAVE   Is that all? I think I'll have a bath .... ⁵ book or something.

> **WORD FOCUS**
> 1 *Soap operas* are short TV programmes (shown two or three times a week) about the lives of a group of people.
> 2 *The telly* is the TV.

C Connecting ideas and talking about contrasts (1)

Read this short article from a magazine, and add the words in brackets, in order, in the correct place in the lines.

(but, and)	Our kids need to eat healthy food, *but* / we know they often prefer burgers, pizzas *and* / chips. Experts say that
(and, or)	we should all - kids adults - eat five portions of fruit vegetables every day, if we can. This may be a
(but)	good idea, what do we do when our kids say 'no'? That's the question. You can give your kid a piece of
(or, but)	fruit - a banana or an apple a pear - to take to school, you won't be there at lunchtime! Last week I
(and, but)	put an apple in my son's lunch box every day, he took it to school, then he brought it home again,
(and, or)	said, 'I wasn't hungry, Mum.' If you've got any good ideas, write to me email me!

D Connecting ideas and talking about contrasts (2)

Mike has invited his boss, Paul, to dinner. Add *and*, *but*, or *or* to the conversation.

MIKE   Paul, this is my wife Daniela, *and* ⁰ these are my sons, Reece .... ¹ Oliver.

PAUL   Pleased to meet you, Daniela. We've spoken on the phone, ... ² we've never actually met, have we?

DANIELA   No, that's right. Would you like another coffee, ... ³ a glass of cola?

PAUL   I'll just take some water, please.

MIKE   Reece is a dentist, Paul, ... ⁴ Oliver is a teacher.

OLIVER   Yes, normally I teach Spanish, ... ⁵ at the moment I'm also teaching maths, because the maths teacher is ill!

MIKE   Oliver went to Madrid, ... ⁶ stayed with Daniela's brother for six months when he was twelve. It was a great experience for you, wasn't it, Oliver?

OLIVER   Fantastic! I learnt Spanish, ... ⁷ I learnt how to cook paella!

MIKE   Well, I'll go .... ⁸ look at the food. I hope you're ready for Oliver's paella!

7 Because

We use the conjunction **because** to give the **reason** for something:

*We didn't walk very far **because**...*

REASON ➜ *...it was raining.*

*I went to bed **because** I was feeling ill.*

We sometimes put **because** at the beginning of a sentence:

***Because** the shops were really busy, we didn't stay long in town.*

8 So

We use the conjunction **so** to talk about the **result** of something:

I've got exams next week, …

RESULT ➜ *…so I don't have much free time.*

*I don't have any money, **so** I can't go on holiday.*

9 We use a comma when we put **because** at the beginning of a sentence:

***Because** we left late, we missed the last train.*

And we often use a comma before **so**:

*I've got to get up early tomorrow, **so** I think I'll go home now.*

Grammar in action

4 We use the conjunctions **because** and **so** to say why we do things:

I gave her some flowers because she helped me at work.

The programme wasn't very interesting, so I didn't watch the end.

E Saying why we do things

Max is telling his friends about his strange night. Add *because* or *so* to the sentences. (In one sentence, you will need to use a capital letter.)

I went downstairs ___because___ [0] I heard a noise in the kitchen at about 3 a.m. There was nothing in the kitchen, ___ [1] I went back to bed. An hour later, I heard a second noise, ___ [2] I went downstairs again. This time I put all the lights on ___ [3] I was sure there was something in the house. But for the second time, I couldn't see anything, ___ [4] I went back upstairs again. ___ [5] I was afraid after the two noises, I didn't switch the lights off. When I got back to my bedroom, I looked at my clock. It was half past four, ___ [6] I tried to go to sleep again. Suddenly, something jumped onto my bed - it was my neighbour's big, black cat!

F Working in a clothes shop

Mickey works in a clothes shop and studies at college in the evenings. He's talking to his boss, Sara. Add the following sentence endings to their conversation:

I'm sure we'll sell lots of them.   her mother is ill.   we'll close the shop for tonight.
~~I hope you can work both days, Mickey.~~   I need to work in the library on Thursday.
I could work on Sunday afternoon.   you could leave early then.   I'm going to a wedding.

SARA   I think we're going to be busy this weekend, so
___I hope you can work both days, Mickey.___ [0]

MICKEY Oh dear. I can't work on Saturday, I'm afraid, because
___ [1]

SARA   Well, what about Sunday?

MICKEY The wedding is in Wales, and I'm coming back on Sunday morning, so
___ [2]

SARA   All right. You know that Millie is away next week, don't you? She's going to Cornwall because .... 3 Can you work every day?

MICKEY I'm not sure. I've got an exam at college on Friday evening, so 4

SARA   Well, my son Phil is going to work in the shop on Thursday afternoon, so 5

MICKEY OK, that's fine. By the way, the new shirts for men arrived this morning, and I put them in the window because 6

SARA   Good idea. Anyway, our last customer has just left, so .... 7 I'll see you on Sunday. Take it easy at the wedding. I need you here next week!

The word *challenge* is used in exercise G. It means 'a new or difficult thing'.

WORD FOCUS

G   A job interview

We use *and*, *but*, *or*, *because* and *so* to connect ideas together. Janice Copland wants to leave her uncle's business in Bristol, and find a new job. This is her first interview - with Sally Prescott and Joseph Mifsud's company. Add the correct conjunctions.

SALLY   Are you ready, Miss Copland? Good. Now, why have you applied for this job?

JANICE Well, I wrote to you ....because.... 0 (because/but/so) your company is the most successful in the south west of England at the moment.

JOSEPH We're doing quite well, Miss Copland, but now we want to go .... 1 (and/because/or) find new challenges!

SALLY   Joseph's right. We want new business, ... 2 (because/or/so) we need new staff.

JOSEPH We know you like the company, Miss Copland, ... 3 (because/but/so) why did you apply for this particular job?

JANICE I've come here today .... 4 (because/or/so) I believe that I have the experience that you're looking for.

SALLY   I'm sure you've got the experience, Miss Copland, ... 5 (and/but/so) you haven't got any qualifications in business management, have you?

JANICE That's correct. I left school at eighteen .... 6 (and/because/or) joined my uncle's company. He offered me a fantastic job, ... 7 (but/or/so) I said 'yes'.

JOSEPH Well, we both agree that you've done very well in the family business. Why do you want to leave? We can't offer you more money, you know.

JANICE I'm not looking for more money .... 8 (because/or/so) a bigger car. I applied for this job .... 9 (because/or/so) I need a new challenge.

SALLY   All right, Miss Copland. In the next part of the interview, we're going to ask you to look at a problem we've got, ... 10 (and/because/or) then give us some of your ideas. Is that OK?

OVER TO YOU Now go to page 126.

Over to you

01 *Be*: Present simple

You are going to stay with a family in England; write an email to introduce yourself. See how much you can say about each member of your family or about your friends.

- Talk about yourself and your family, jobs and where you're from.

- Ask questions about the family you're going to stay with.

02 Present simple

Look at these notes:

> **FACTS:**
> 1. Bath/south England   2. English & French
>
> **REGULAR ACTIVITIES:**
> 1. Football/at the weekend
> 2. Cinema/on Mondays   3. Chinese food/often
>
> **LIKES/DISLIKES:**
> 1. ✓ French films   2. ✓ Holidays/hot countries
> 3. ✗ Politics

Now complete this short profile by adding these verbs: *eat, play, don't like, ~~come~~, love, speak, go*.

I ....*come*........ [0] from Bath in the south of England. I .... [1] English and one or two words of French. I .... [2] football at the weekend with my friends, and I normally .... [3] to the cinema on Mondays. I often .... [4] Chinese food at our local Chinese restaurant. I .... [5] French films and holidays in hot countries, but I .... [6] politics!

Check your answers, and then write notes and a short profile of yourself (*I come from…* etc.) AND one other person you know well (*My friend Carlos comes from…*)

03 Present continuous

We use the **present continuous** on the phone to say what we're doing, and what our friends family are doing, now and around now.

Try writing the beginning of a phone conversation between two friends. Try to use at least four examples of the **present continuous**. Before you start, look at the conversations in unit 3 (exercises A, E, and G), and, with a highlight pen or a pencil, mark examples of language that may be useful to you (e.g. beginnings *'Sally? It's Mandy here'* and questions *'What about you?'*, *'Is Clare in?'* etc.)

04 Present simple and present continuous

Write an introductory email to a new penfriend in England.

- Tell him/her some facts about yourself (*I come from Madrid* etc.)

- Tell him/her about some of your regular activities (*I go to the gym on Fridays* etc.)

- Tell him/her about some of the things in your life that are temporary/different from normal (*I'm learning Japanese at the moment*; *I'm studying for an exam this month* etc.)

- Tell him/her about some of the things you like and don't like (*I love shopping* etc.)

05 Present simple and present continuous questions

Imagine you're spending two weeks in London. On your first day, you go to a central London tourist office. Write down six questions you would like to ask. (e.g. *When does Buckingham Palace open in the morning?*)

Go to www.visitlondon.com for some ideas, and look at Exercise B for some useful question forms.

06 Past simple

1 Describe what you did (and didn't do) last weekend, e.g. *I got up early on Saturday morning, but I didn't do very much. In the afternoon, I…* or describe a holiday or trip, e.g. *In 2005, I visited my brother in America. First, I flew to Seattle. Then my brother and I travelled together to California…*

2 Write some questions for an interview with a writer about his/her early life e.g. *Where were you born? Did you write stories at school?*

07 Past continuous

Choose a day from the last two weeks. Describe what you did, using the **past continuous** form at least three times. Look at the examples in exercise F.

08 Present perfect

Use the present perfect to write down:

- three things that you have done today
- three things you've never done in your life
- three things that have happened this week in your country
- three questions to ask your favourite actor about things they have done in their life.

09 Past simple and present perfect

Imagine you are studying English in London. 'Coffee Time', your local coffee shop, is looking for a Saturday assistant to make coffee, to wash up and to clean tables.

Write a short letter saying why you would be a good person for the job. Use the **past simple** and the **present perfect** to talk about yourself and the past e.g. *'I've studied English for six years…I've never worked in a coffee shop, but I was a waiter in a restaurant in Italy last summer…'*

Begin your letter *'I'm interested in becoming a Saturday assistant at 'Coffee Time."* You may find it helpful to look at the letter Keiko wrote in exercise B on page 35.

10 The future with *going to*

In an email, tell one of your friends what you and your family are going to do this weekend. As well as *I'm going to*, try to use one or two of the other forms: *She's going to, my brother's going to, we're going to, Peter isn't going to, they aren't going to* etc. At the end of the email, use **going to** to ask your friend one or two questions about his/her plans.

11 The future with *will* and *shall*

Imagine that two friends are on the phone. They want to go out this evening. Write out their conversation as a dialogue.

- Use **shall we/I** to make suggestions (e.g. **Shall we go to the cinema?**)
- Use **will** for offers (e.g. *When does the film start? ~ I'll phone the cinema.*) and for saying what we think about the future (e.g. *I think the new film with Kiefer Sutherland will be good.*)
- Look through the exercises in unit 11, and use some of the language!

12 Questions

A questionnaire is a list of questions we ask people to find out about their lives, work, study, free time, routines etc. Make a list of questions that you could ask people in your town or city centre, using **What**, **Where**, **How**, and **When**. Here are some examples:

What: *What sort of books do you like?*

How: *How often do you play sports?*

Where: *Where are you going this morning?*

When: *When do you normally get up?*

13 *Can*

> ## CAMP CANADA
>
> **25 July - 31 August**
>
> Can you swim? Can you play sports? Can you sing and dance? Can you help young people to learn new skills in the countryside? If the answer is 'yes', we can offer you a job. We can't pay you very much, but we can give you a very interesting time this summer.
>
> *CAMP CANADA* organises an international camp for teenagers at Lake Superior every summer. We're looking for Student Assistants.
>
> Write to Dave Spurling at PO Box 56, Toronto, Canada, and tell us what you can do.

Write a short letter of application, starting with the sentence, *'I would like to apply for the post of Student Assistant.'* Answer the questions in the advertisement. If you can't do something, say so; for example: *'I can't dance, but I can play the guitar.'* Talk about other useful skills that you have, for example: *'I can also drive.'*

Use **can/can't** to say in the letter that you are not free to work in July, *'because I need to finish a university project.'* Ask if you can start on 1 August, and offer to work an extra week at the end of the camp *'if you need me.'*

14 *Could, was able to, managed to*

1   You're going to spend five days in a business hotel in London. Write a list of at least five polite requests you could make on the phone from your room, or in different parts of the hotel. Think about:
    using 'room service' (e.g. ordering a meal in your room, or getting an alarm call); using one of the restaurants or the gym/swimming pool; using the business centre; getting a taxi etc.

2   It's Thursday evening. Write an email to a friend. Make some suggestions about things you could do together at the weekend. Look at Exercise B for an example.

15 *Should*

An English friend, Holly, is going to spend two weeks in your country. It's her first visit. She wants to see as much as possible.

Write an email to Holly, using **should** to give her some advice on what to do. The second email in Exercise E may help you.

16 *Must* and *have to*

1   Write three sentences starting **'You must…'** to describe some of the things a tourist must do, when visiting your country (e.g. *'You must spend a few days in Scotland, because it's a beautiful country.'*)

2   Write three or four sentences about the things you **have to** and **don't have to** do every week at home or at work (e.g. *'I have to cook dinner on Friday evenings, but I don't have to wash up…'*)

17 The imperative

Look at this information for students visiting London:

> ☞ Visit the big museums - they're normally free.
>
> ☞ Take a boat trip on the Thames. You'll get some great views of London!
>
> ☞ Don't take taxis everywhere, because they're expensive.

Now write a list of at least six **imperative** points to help students from England visiting the capital city of your country.

18 *Have got* and *have*; *make*, *do*, and *get*

1 Use **have got** to write six sentences: two sentences about the things you possess (e.g. *I've got a new computer*); two sentences about your family (e.g. *I've got two brothers.*); and two sentences about what you or your family members look like (e.g. *I've got black hair.*)

2 Use **make**, **do**, **have** and **get** to write three sentences about the things you, your family and friends do regularly (e.g. *My brother sometimes does the washing-up*); and three sentences about the things they're doing at the moment (e.g. *My dad is making dinner.*)

19 Verb + infinitive

Imagine you're writing a blog on a Saturday morning. You can write about

- your efforts last week (e.g. *'I tried to go to the gym on Monday, but I got up too late.'*)

- your hopes and plans (e.g. *'I'm planning to visit Brazil in the summer.'*)

- the things people do for us (e.g. *'Sara offered to buy me dinner.'*)

- your opinions (e.g. *'it's difficult to learn a new language in the evening'*)

- your feelings (e.g. *'On Friday, I was surprised to get an email from my American friend, Stu.'*)

20 Articles and nouns

1 Write a very short story (true or untrue). Exercise B may help you.

2 Look at Exercise F. Imagine you are Juan and describe your visit to Borough Market. Start your description with the sentence, *'We went to Borough Market yesterday.'*

21 *There is*, *there are*; *this*, *that*, *these*, and *those*

It's Friday evening. Write a short email to a friend, making plans for the weekend. Use **there + be** (e.g. *'There's a good film at the cinema…'*) and **this/that** (e.g. *'I liked that restaurant on George Street. Shall we go there again?'*)

22 Countable and uncountable nouns

Write out a phone message that you might leave with your husband/wife/friend, saying what you need from the supermarket. Use the phrases: *'We need some/a/an/a lot of/two etc.…'*; and *'We haven't got much/many/any…'* with **countable** and **uncountable** food and drink words.

23 Pronouns and possessives

Write an email to a new English friend. Talk about

- the weather where you are.

- yourself, your friends and/or your family

- something that belongs to you or someone else

Try to use at least two object pronouns (**me**, **you**, **him** etc.), two possessive determiners (**my**, **your**, **his** etc.), and one possessive pronoun (**mine**, **yours**, **his** etc.)

24 Possessives (2)

Write an email to an English-speaking friend, telling him/her what you, your friends and/or family members are doing at the moment. You may find the language in exercises D and F useful.

Try to use *'s* two times, a phrase like **a friend of mine** once, and **s'** once (if you can.)

25 Adjectives

Imagine you're on holiday. Write a postcard to an English friend, describing your hotel and the town where you're staying. Try using different types of adjectives. Make sure you put two **adjectives** before a noun at least twice in your postcard!

26 Comparative and superlative adjectives

1 Write a very short text (two or three sentences), comparing two towns/cities in your country. Use three or four **comparative adjectives**. Exercise B may be helpful.

2 Write a second very short text about a great holiday place in your country. Use two or three **superlative adjectives**. Exercise D may be helpful.

27 Adverbs of manner

1 Write a short list of the things you do/can do **well**, the things you do/can do **quite well**, and the things you don't do/can't do **very well** (e.g. sports, hobbies, cooking, languages).

2 Use **adverbs** to write about four people that you know (e.g. *My friend Steve plays music very loudly*).

28 Adverbs of degree

Use adverbs of degree (including **quite** before **a/an** + **adjective** + **noun**, and with **a lot of**; and **really** and **quite** with verbs) to write about your job, or your life at school, or college/university (e.g. *I'm working very hard at the moment, because we have exams next month. My teachers give me quite a lot of homework…*)

It may be useful to look at Exercise E.

29 Prepositions

Imagine you're working in an office in London. Write a short email to a colleague. Explain that you want to see him/her, but you can't meet today, because you are the only person in your office. Say where your colleagues are, e.g. *Julie is in Spain at our Madrid office.* Then try to fix a meeting for tomorrow, e.g. *I'm in a meeting from nine to eleven, but could we meet at 11.30?* You may find exercises A and E useful.

30 Conjunctions

First, look at this job ad on the internet:

'The Shakespeare Academy is a language school in Stratford-upon-Avon. We're looking for an assistant for our multi-national Summer School. The successful person will organise weekend trips to different parts of the UK, and help our students with their problems. If you are interested, email us. Tell us why you are applying for this job. Describe your education and skills. Tell us about any other jobs you've had. If we like your message, we'll ask you to come for an interview in April. Email Karen Brown at info@ shakespeareacademy.com'

Now write the email, using the conjunctions **and**, **but**, **or**, **because** and **so**.

Form tables

A   Plural nouns

	SINGULAR	PLURAL
+ -s		
With most nouns, we add **-s** to make them plural:	car	cars
	mistake	mistakes
	photo	photo**s**
+ -es		
With nouns that end with **-s, -ss, -sh, -ch** and **-x**, we add **-es**:	bus	bus**es**
	glass	glass**es**
	wish	wish**es**
	beach	beach**es**
	box	box**es**
-f/-fe → -ves		
We change **-f/-fe** to **-ves** in the plural:	life	li**ves**
	knife	kni**ves**
	but roof	roof**s**
-y → -ies		
With nouns that end with a consonant* + **-y**, we change the **-y** to **-ies**:	story	stor**ies**
	city	cit**ies**
	family	famil**ies**
Irregular nouns		
	man	men
	person	people
	child	children

B   Present simple

	I/YOU/WE/THEY	HE/SHE/IT
+ -s		
After **he/she/it**, we add **-s** to most present simple verbs:	work	work**s**
	write	write**s**
	say	say**s**
+ -es		
We add **-es** to verbs that end with **-ss, -sh, -ch, -o** or **-x**:	pass	pass**es**
	finish	finish**es**
	teach	teach**es**
	do	do**es**
	mix	mix**es**
-y → -ies		
We change **-y** to **-ies** with verbs that end with a consonant* + **-y**:	try	tr**ies**
	marry	marr**ies**
	fly	fl**ies**

* Consonants
b c d f g h j k
l m n p q r s t
v w x y z

Vowels
a e i o u

Syllables
|*hit*| = 1 syllable
|*vi*|*sit*| = 2 syllables
|*re*|*mem*|*ber* = 3 syllables

C *-ing* forms

	INFINITIVE	*-ING* FORM
+ -ing		
With most verbs, we add **-ing**:	walk	walk**ing**
	eat	eat**ing**
-e + -ing		
With verbs that end with a consonant* + **-e**, we delete the **-e** and add **-ing**:	make	mak**ing**
	come	com**ing**
	write	writ**ing**
-ie ⟶ -ying		
With verbs that end with **-ie**, we change **-ie** to **-ying**:	lie	**ly**ing
	die	**dy**ing
	tie	**ty**ing
-t ⟶ -tting		
With verbs that end with one vowel* + one consonant (e.g. *get, hit, stop*), we double the consonant:	sit	si**tting**
	run	ru**nning**
	swim	swi**mming**
+ -ing		
But note that we do not double the consonant, 1) when it is **y** or **w** (e.g. *play*) 2) when the last syllable* is not stressed (e.g. *reMEMber, VISit*):	play	play**ing**
	happen	happen**ing**
	listen	listen**ing**
	remember	remember**ing**

D Regular verbs: Past simple and past participle

	INFINITIVE	PAST SIMPLE	PAST PARTICIPLE
+ -ed			
With most verbs we add **-ed**:	cook	cook**ed**	cook**ed**
	finish	finish**ed**	finish**ed**
+ -d			
With verbs ending with **-e**, we add **-d**:	live	live**d**	live**d**
	close	close**d**	close**d**
-y ⟶ -ied			
With verbs that end with one consonant* + **-y**, we change the **y** to **-ied**:	study	stud**ied**	stud**ied**
	carry	carr**ied**	carr**ied**
	try	tr**ied**	tr**ied**
-p ⟶ -pped			
With verbs that end with one vowel* + one consonant (e.g. *stop*), we double the consonant:	stop	sto**pped**	sto**pped**
	plan	pla**nned**	pla**nned**
+ -ed			
But note that we do not double the consonant, 1) when it is **y** or **w** (e.g. *play*) 2) when the last syllable* is not stressed (e.g. *LISten, HAppen, Open*): Note that in British English **l** is usually doubled, even if the syllable in unstressed (e.g. *travel*)	stay	stay**ed**	stay**ed**
	happen	happen**ed**	happen**ed**
	open	open**ed**	open**ed**
	visit	visit**ed**	visit**ed**
	cancel	cance**lled**	cance**lled**
	travel	trave**lled**	trave**lled**

E Irregular verbs: Past simple and past participle

INFINITIVE	PAST SIMPLE	PAST PARTICIPLE
be	was / were	been
become	became	become
begin	began	begun
break	broke	broken
bring	brought	brought
build	built	built
buy	bought	bought
catch	caught	caught
choose	chose	chosen
come	came	come
cost	cost	cost
cut	cut	cut
do	did	done
drink	drank	drunk
drive	drove	driven
eat	ate	eaten
fall	fell	fallen
feel	felt	felt
find	found	found
fly	flew	flown
forget	forgot	forgotten
get	got	got
give	gave	given
go	went	gone
grow	grew	grown
have	had	had
hear	heard	heard
hide	hid	hidden
hit	hit	hit
hold	held	held
hurt	hurt	hurt
keep	kept	kept
know	knew	known
learn	learnt/learned	learnt/learned
leave	left	left

INFINITIVE	PAST SIMPLE	PAST PARTICIPLE
lend	lent	lent
let	let	let
lose	lost	lost
make	made	made
meet	met	met
pay	paid	paid
put	put	put
read	read	read
ring	rang	rung
run	ran	run
say	said	said
see	saw	seen
sell	sold	sold
send	sent	sent
show	showed	shown / showed
shut	shut	shut
sing	sang	sung
sit	sat	sat
sleep	slept	slept
speak	spoke	spoken
spell	spelt / spelled	spelt / spelled
spend	spent	spent
stand	stood	stood
steal	stole	stolen
swim	swam	swum
take	took	taken
teach	taught	taught
tell	told	told
think	thought	thought
throw	threw	thrown
understand	understood	understood
wake	woke	woken
wear	wore	worn
win	won	won
write	wrote	written

F Comparative and superlative adjectives

	ADJECTIVE	COMPARATIVE	SUPERLATIVE
+ -er/-est			
We add **-er/-est** to short adjectives (one-syllable* adjectives):	warm	warm**er**	the warm**est**
	tall	tall**er**	the tall**est**
	young	young**er**	the young**est**
+ -r/-st			
We add **-r/-st** to adjectives that end with **-e**:	late	late**r**	the late**st**
+ -g → -gger			
With short adjectives that end with one vowel* and one consonant* (e.g. *big*), we double the consonant:	big	bi**gger**	the bi**ggest**
	hot	ho**tter**	the ho**ttest**
	wet	we**tter**	the we**ttest**
-w + -er/-est			
We don't double **w**:	low	low**er**	the low**est**
more/most			
We use **more / the most** before adjectives of two or more syllables*:	expensive	**more** expensive	the **most** expensive
	famous	**more** famous	the **most** famous
	beautiful	**more** beautiful	the **most** beautiful
-y → -ier/-iest			
But note that with adjectives ending with **-y** (e.g. *happy*), we change **-y** to **-ier/-iest**:	happy	happ**ier**	the happ**iest**
	lucky	luck**ier**	the luck**iest**
	easy	eas**ier**	the eas**iest**
Irregular adjectives			
	good	**better**	**the best**
	bad	**worse**	**the worst**
	far	**farther**	**the farthest**

G Adverbs

	ADJECTIVE	ADVERB
+ -ly		
With most adverbs, we add **-ly** to the adjective:	quick	quick**ly**
	correct	correct**ly**
	slow	slow**ly**
Exceptions		
Adjectives that end with **-y** (y → **-ily**):	happy	happ**ily**
	lucky	luck**ily**
Adjectives that end with **-ble** (**e + y**):	remarkable	remarka**bly**
Irregular adverbs		
	good	**well**
	fast	**fast**
	hard	**hard**
	late	**late**

***Consonants**
b c d f g h j k
l m n p q r s t
v w x y z

Vowels
a e i o u

Syllables
|*hit*| = 1 syllable
|*vi*|*sit*| = 2 syllables
|*re*|*mem*|*ber*| = 3 syllables

Verb tenses

infinitive: **to start**

	POSITIVE *full forms (short forms)*	NEGATIVE *full forms (short forms)*	QUESTIONS
Present simple			
I/you/we/they	start	**do not** start (I **don't** start)	**Do** I start?
he/she/it	start**s**	**does not** start (it **doesn't** start)	**Does** he start?
Present continuous			
I	**am** start**ing** (I**'m** starting)	**am not** starting (I**'m not** starting)	**Am** I starting?
you/we/they	**are** start**ing** (we**'re** starting)	**are not** starting (**'re** not/**aren't** starting)	**Are** you starting?
he/she/it	**is** start**ing** (it**'s** starting)	**is not** starting (**'s** not/**isn't** starting)	**Is** she starting?
Past simple			
I/you/he/she/it/we/they	start**ed**	**did not** start (**didn't** start)	**Did** you start?
Present perfect			
I/you/we/they	**have** start**ed** (I**'ve** started)	**have not** started (**haven't** started)	**Have** they started?
he/she/it	**has** start**ed** (he**'s** started)	**has not** started (**hasn't** started)	**Has** she started?

Answer key

01 Be: Present simple

A(i)
1	'm	5	are	9	's
2	's	6	are	10	'm not
3	's not / isn't	7	're		
4	's	8	's		

(ii)
1 I'm a student. / They're both teachers.
2 My father's from Brazil. / She's Irish.
3 Paul and Simon are my brothers.

B
1	is	4	're	7	'm
2	's	5	're	8	're
3	's	6	're		

C
1	's	7	's	13	sea
2	is	8	's not / isn't	14	're not / aren't
3	near	9	's	15	is
4	's	10	sunny		
5	's not / isn't	11	south		
6	cold	12	're		

D
1 Are you a student here?
  Yes, I am.
2 What's your name?
  It's Ming Yifeng.
3 How old are you?
  I'm twenty two.
4 Are you from Hong Kong?
  No, I'm from Shanghai.
5 Where is your ID card, please?
  Here it is.
6 What's your address in the UK?
  It's The Hyde Park Hotel, Queensway, London W2 3BJ.
7 Is this your first day here, too?
8 are you from?
9 Am I in the correct classroom?
10 Is this the bus to Queensway?
11 is the Hyde Park Hotel, please?
12 is breakfast tomorrow morning?

E
1	Are you	5	It's	9	You're
2	It's	6	it isn't	10	I'm not
3	I'm	7	this is	11	I'm
4	are you	8	we're	12	it's

F

ASIF Look at the time. It's two in the morning. Where *are* we?

KATIE On Burley Street, I think. *Are* you hungry, Asif?

ASIF No, I'm *not* hungry, but I'm tired. Where's the bus stop?

KATIE Look, it's there! Come on!

ASIF Excuse me. *Is* this the bus stop for Rayne's Park?

DIETER Yes, I hope so. It's a cold night.

KATIE Hi. I'm Katie and this *is* my friend Asif.

DIETER Pleased to meet you. I'm Dieter. *Are* you students?

KATIE No, we're *not* students. We're doctors. And you?

DIETER I'm a waiter at the Hamburger restaurant on Park Street.

ASIF Where *are* you from? *Are* you German?

DIETER No, I'm Austrian, but I'm in Leicester for six months. It's an interesting city.

KATIE Look, the bus *is* here! I hope it's warm inside. After you, Dieter. Come on, Asif. Let's go home.

02 Present simple

A
1	drive	4	lives	7	make
2	has	5	come	8	sleeps
3	fixes	6	speaks	9	teaches

B(i)
1	go	4	arrives	7	gives
2	have	5	finishes	8	do
3	start	6	fly	9	try

(ii)
1	goes	3	starts	5	does
2	has	4	flies	6	tries

C
1	work works	4	plays play	7	spends
2	spends spend	5	work	8	play
3	speaks speak	6	speak		

D
1	hate	6	know
2	don't think	7	love
3	doesn't like	8	don't like
4	doesn't understand	9	want
5	don't know		

E (i)
1	don't doesn't	5	✓
2	✓	6	meets meet
3	have has	7	✓
4	go goes	8	✓

(ii)
1	don't eat	5	understand
2	love	6	don't speak
3	think (or undertstand)	7	don't meet
4	studies	8	takes

03 Present continuous

A
1. 'm sitting
2. 's/is shining
3. 're enjoying
4. 'm thinking
5. 're having
6. 's/is swimming
7. splashing
8. 's/is running
9. 's playing

B
1. 're walking
2. 's/is sinking
3. 's splashing
4. 's/is shouting
5. 're standing

C
1. 's/is arriving
2. 's/is stopping
3. 's/is getting out
4. 's wearing
5. 's/is giving
6. 's smiling
7. 's talking
8. is coming

D
1. Dave, I think the owner is looking at you.
2. Yes. She's walking towards us now
3. Hello. My husband and I are having a cup of coffee on the deck.
4. it's getting late.

E
1. She isn't/'s not staying
2. her sister's/is moving
3. Galina's/is helping
4. I'm not working
5. I'm learning
6. You're learning
7. I'm writing
8. We aren't/'re not living
9. they aren't/'re not playing
10. Alexander's/is studying
11. Fedor's/is teaching

F
1. enjoying
2. getting
3. staying
4. buying
5. eating
6. living
7. having

G
1. 'm watching
2. are spending
3. 'm looking
4. 's/is eating
5. 's/is playing
6. 's visiting
7. 're eating
8. isn't/'s not spending
9. 's meeting
10. 's playing
11. 're driving
12. 're working
13. 'm thinking
14. 're looking

04 Present simple and present continuous

A
1. I normally work
2. I'm visiting
3. I live
4. I'm staying
5. I usually drive
6. I'm walking
7. my English is improving

B(i)
1. I speak
2. I'm studying
3. I'm doing
4. My dad works
5. I'm studying
6. I play
7. It rains
8. We have
9. I'm learning
10. My mum teaches
11. that man is shouting

(ii)
1. The sun's/is shining
2. I go to
3. I do
4. Khan comes
5. he's studying
6. He's spending
7. He's doing
8. He's painting
9. He speaks
10. my Spanish is getting

C
1. 's walking
2. 's wearing
3. 's singing
4. 's falling
5. comes
6. has
7. watches
8. goes
9. isn't/'s not eating
10. 's dancing

WORD FOCUS 1 violin 2 piano 3 trumpet

D

DIANA (the = 0) Hello, my name's Diana. I'm studying here at 0 moment.

JULIE (every = 1) Hi! I'm Julie. I come to these concerts 1 week. What instrument do you play?

DIANA (this = 2) Well, I normally play the violin, but I'm learning to play the trumpet 2 year, too.

JULIE I love violin music. But the trumpet is a difficult instrument, isn't it?

DIANA (on = 3) Yes! I have a class 3 Tuesdays. It isn't easy. What about you? Do you play anything?

JULIE (is = 4) Not really. My husband 4 teaching me the piano at the moment. He plays every day.

DIANA It's not easy to find the time, is it?

JULIE (these = 5) We're all working very 5 hard days. Too hard. But these concerts after work are great.

DIANA (have = 6) Good. We sometimes 6 concerts at lunchtime, too.

JULIE Lunchtime! What's that?

DIANA (at = 7) Oh dear! You're working much too hard 7 the moment!

E

1 ✓
2 ~~are liking~~ like
3 ✓
4 ~~build~~ are / 're building
5 ~~are thinking~~ think
6 ✓
7 ~~are wanting~~ want
8 ~~work~~ are / 're working
9 ✓
10 ~~make~~ are / 're making

F

1 you like
2 I don't know
3 I love
4 you're studying
5 I'm learning
6 The waiter's / is coming
7 Michiko doesn't like
8 We're looking
9 Chris and I teach
10 I don't understand
11 I get up
12 I go
13 I play
14 The waiter's / is bringing

05 Present simple and present continuous questions

A

1 Do you like the local shops?
2 Do you play sports in Madrid?
3 Do you have a map of Madrid?
4 Do metro tickets cost a lot of money?
5 When does college start?
6 Do you cook Spanish food?
7 Does the college library open at the weekend?
8 Does the local bank change money?
9 Do the local restaurants cook traditional food?
10 How much does the cinema cost?

B

1 How do we find Dublin Castle?
2 Does / Is it open on Sundays?
3 when does / is the National Gallery open?
4 Does the train go to Dublin Bay?
5 How much does the train cost?

WORD FOCUS 1 chocolate fudge cake 2 banana split 3 apple pie 4 lemon cheesecake

C

1 Do you want some more water?
2 Do you want some cheesecake?
3 Does he want a banana split?
4 Do we want coffee afterwards?
5 Do you want some more orange juice?

D

1 What is she doing?
2 Is he cooking in the kitchen?
3 What are you listening to?
4 Are we leaving now, Joe?
5 Is Cova resting upstairs?
6 Are you coming downstairs?

E(i)

1 staying
2 come
3 work
4 job
5 studying
6 do
7 like

(ii)

1 What sort of things do you do in your free time?
2 What sort of job do you do?
3 What sort of food do you like?
4 Where do you come from?
5 Do you live near here?
6 Do you work near here?
7 Are you studying anything?

F

1 Do you want a ticket?
2 Does the bus leave soon?
3 When does it go?
4 Are you waiting for the bus to Mumbai?
5 Are you staying in New Delhi at the moment?
6 What sort of work do you do there?
7 Are you travelling around India?
8 Do you want a cold drink?
9 Where are you going?

06 Past simple

A

1 they stayed
2 We talked
3 we saw
4 we ate
5 it was
6 I went
7 I met
8 we did
9 we watched
10 They lost
11 I took

B

1 was
2 found
3 went
4 bought
5 cooked
6 read
7 played
8 enjoyed
9 took
10 left

C

1 wore
2 drank
3 caught
4 told
5 spent
6 sold
7 woke
8 became
9 lost
10 married
11 stayed
12 came

D

1 I didn't do anything
2 Did you see Jenny
3 she wasn't at home
4 Was she OK
5 she didn't talk very much
6 Did you invite her to our party
7 What did you do all afternoon,
8 Did you make a wonderful dinner
9 When did they leave
10 I didn't get any milk this morning,

WORD FOCUS A lock B feed C check

E
1 Did you forget
2 I didn't have time
3 Was your passport under the bed
4 Did you email Sally
5 Did you give her a key
6 I didn't check the windows upstairs
7 Were they open
8 No, I didn't pack my laptop

F
1	arrived	5	stayed	9	put
2	didn't	6	was	10	broke
3	what	7	walk	11	carried
4	were	8	made	12	fixed

07 Past continuous

A
1	were dancing	4	was working
2	was eating	5	was sleeping
3	wasn't / was not playing		

B
1 Where were you going?
2 We were meeting an old friend.
3 Lorna was sleeping.
4 But she wasn't / was not ringing from Moscow.
5 What was Svetlana doing in London?
6 No, she wasn't / was not working.
7 I think she was joking.

C
1 Were you walking home?
2 I wasn't going home.
3 What was he doing?
4 Was he jogging?
5 he wasn't running.
6 was he walking?
7 he wasn't walking.
8 Was he sleeping?
9 He wasn't sleeping.
10 What was he wearing?

D
I hope you've had a better day than me! It *0*
raining hard when I got up, so I didn't go jogging. Then, *1* I
was having breakfast, my boss phoned. … I was writing the
first sentence when Mike *2* on my door, and said he was
feeling really ill. So I *3* downstairs again and phoned for the
doctor, and while we were *4* for her, Mum arrived and said,
'If you're not doing anything this weekend, perhaps you'd
like to help me. I'm painting the kitchen.'
Thanks for your message. … I *5* buying a new CD in town *6*
I saw a really good TV for £150, so I bought it for the flat. …
While I *7* waiting in the queue for my cappuccino, I *8* Julie
and she invited me to her party tonight! … He *9* looking for
a flat, when his brother got a job in America. …

E
1	wasn't / was not enjoying	4	were looking for
2	was travelling	5	was doing
3	were getting off	6	was helping

F
1	I ate / was eating	4	sat was sitting
2	ran was running	5	drove was driving
3	walked was walking	6	rained was raining

08 Present perfect

A
1	's sent	4	's travelled	7	's been
2	've lived	5	have met	8	's made
3	's spent	6	's done		

WORD FOCUS 1 crocodile 2 monkey 3 elephant
4 giraffe

B
1 The kids have seen
2 She's taken
3 she's lost
4 He's just been
5 I've done
6 I've written
7 I've spoken
8 Vincent's just paid
9 Josie and Stella have run

C
1	's broken	4	's travelled	7	've written
2	's left	5	's won		
3	's gone	6	've started		

D
1 Steve hasn't emailed his new photos
2 I haven't done my homework.
3 Have you eaten?
4 Have you talked to Luke?
5 He hasn't finished work.
6 Have you ever seen it?
7 Has Steve spoken to you about a holiday in Greece?
8 I've never been to Greece.
9 Have you seen any photos of the house?
10 Steve hasn't been there.

E
1	d	3	a	5	c
2	f	4	b		

F(i)
1	never	3	made	5	ever
2	been	4	returned	6	have

(ii) (3) … to your message. Diana isn't at home because she's
been to London. Mum is ill, I'm afraid. We tried to phone
you lots of times. Has you lost your mobile again? Ring me
back.
(4) Good afternoon, Mr Daw. This is Brian Hart from the
Country Kitchen. We haven't make a mistake, I'm afraid.
Someone used your card and your name on 17 December. I
am just spoken to our manager, Greg Turner…

1	gone	3	made
2	Have	4	have / 've

09 Past simple and present perfect

A
1 I phoned Clare
2 She's lost
3 Her husband gave
4 what did you do
5 I met
6 I went
7 I've just asked
8 Have you spoken
9 I saw
10 He's bought

B
1 've worked
2 spent
3 was
4 sold
5 've lived
6 've started
7 passed
8 've used

C
1 Have you spent
2 I lived
3 My parents returned
4 I haven't worked
5 Have you visited
6 I've been
7 I went
8 I travelled
9 Did you go
10 we stayed
11 have you talked

D
1 ~~has sold~~ sold
2 ~~bought~~ has bought
3 ~~has visited~~ visited
4 ~~returned~~ has returned
5 ~~has gone~~ went
6 ~~has bought~~ bought

E
1 ever
2 just
3 never
4 in
5 ago
6 in
7 last

F
1 've had
2 Did you have
3 wasn't
4 showed
5 drove
6 've never seen
7 worked
8 haven't seen
9 's just bought
10 Have you ever been
11 went
12 haven't been

10 The future with *going to*

A
1 I'm going to have a swim
2 I'm going to get
3 You aren't going to buy an English paper
4 Jamie and I are going to spend the morning
5 Lily and I are going to do some shoppping
6 I'm going to go cycling
7 What are you going to do
8 I'm not going to go cycling

B
1 I'm going to put some old suitcases
2 I'm going to tidy my clothes
3 I'm going to wash the bath
4 I'm going to clean the windows
5 I'm going to vacuum the carpet
6 I'm going to cut the grass

C
1 I'm not going to work
2 I'm going to go
3 I'm going to spend
4 Are you going to have
5 Abigail and I are going to find
6 what are you going to do
7 Abigail is going to stay
8 I'm not going to look
9 We're going to teach

D
1 Careful! The traffic lights are going to change.
2 The old man is going to win again.
3 It's going to be a hot afternoon.
4 Are you going to have an icecream?
5 She's going to break her leg!

E
1 I'm going to work
2 I'm going to meet
3 I'm not going to do
4 I'm going to get up
5 Are you going to go
6 We're going to cook
7 Lucy is going to spend
8 he's going to say

F
My brother Luke and I have got plans, of course, for the New Year. First, we're both *going* to learn Chinese, because China is now the most important country in the world. In fact, I'm going to fly to Beijing , if I can find the money. Luke is going *to* visit Mr Xu at our local Chinese restaurant, Hot Wok, to get some information about China etc. Next, we're going to paint our bedroom. The walls *are* going to be green and red, and the ceiling is going to *be* dark blue with stars, like the sky at night. Luke *is* going to talk to Dad about this. Finally, I'm going to *do* better at school. I'm *not* going to work harder, because I work hard enough already - I'm going to use a new system, called the 'System of Seven': I'm going to learn seven new things every day, and write them down in a special book. Are *you* going to do anything interesting this year? Send me an email.

11 The future with *will* and *shall*

A
1 I think it'll last about an hour.
2 You'll finish at twelve.
3 It won't be busy at that time, Lauren.
4 Do you think they'll ask me about my year in Africa?
5 I'm sure you'll do well.
6 When will you get the result?
7 They'll tell me at the end of the interview.

B
1 I'll open
2 we'll drive
3 I'll have a glass
4 we'll have a bottle
5 I'll bring
6 Adam will fix it
7 I'll order

C
I'm so sorry to hear about the flood in Gloucester, and to see the photo of your house. They say the weather / get better on Thursday and Friday. I hope so, but life / be difficult for you in the next few days. I saw the Prime Minister on TV in Gloucester yesterday, but / you get any help from the government? They need to spend more money. I'm sure we / see more floods in the UK in the future. Anyway, I listened to the news this morning. The roads near you / be OK at the weekend, so Tom and I / come over on Saturday morning. We / help you to clean your floors, and Tom / buy us all some fish and chips on Saturday night!

D
1 Shall we have
2 Shall I drive
3 Shall we park
4 Shall we get
5 Shall I take
6 Shall I make

E
1 'll / will
2 will
3 Shall
4 Will
5 'll / will
6 Shall
7 'll / will
8 Will
9 'll / will
10 Shall
11 'll / will
12 Shall

F
1 shall we do
2 I'll / will be
3 Will you see
4 Shall I ask
5 I'll / will see
6 Shall we see
7 'CIA Blues' will be
8 Santiago won't be
9 I'll / will call
10 he'll / will stay
11 Shall I bring

12 Questions

A
1 Why are
2 How are
3 How do
4 How did
5 Why are
6 How do
7 Why do

B
1 When do the classes begin in the morning?
2 When did you get up this morning?
3 Where am I going to sleep?
4 Have you slept in a tepee before?
5 where is the bathroom?
6 Did you bring a towel with you?
7 When will I meet the other students?
8 Where did you leave your bag?
9 Shall I go to my tepee now?

C
1 Are
2 many
3 did
4 far
5 going
6 old
7 much

D
1 Yes, it was.
2 Yes, I am.
3 No, he doesn't.
4 No, we haven't.
5 Yes, we are.
6 Yes, he has.
7 No, we won't.
8 Yes, I do.
9 No, we don't.

E
1 What is he going to buy?
2 What do you normally buy at this market?
3 Shall I get two small loaves?
4 Which loaves do you want?
5 Have you seen Isabelle, Pierre?
6 What did she say?
7 Whose phone is this?
8 Who are you looking for?

F
1 How
2 Who
3 Where
4 Which
5 When
6 Why
7 Whose
8 What

13 *Can*

WORD FOCUS 1 basketball 2 baseball
3 ice skating 4 snooker

A
1 I can make
2 I can't do
3 Can you play
4 I can't play
5 I can skate
6 Can you play
7 she can play
8 she can speak

B
1 Can you hear the sea
2 Can you see a kettle
3 I can see a lot of old newspapers
4 I can't see any cups
5 I can hear a noise
6 I can't hear anything
7 can you smell fish
8 can you see anything

C(i) …We could have something to eat. I / can't see you at the weekend, because I'm going to visit my dad in Wales. He's ninety now. He *can* get to the shops every day, so he always has enough to eat, but he *can't* do all the jobs around the house. Anyway, email or ring me!

(ii) Thanks for your message. I *can't* see you on Monday evening, because I'm flying to Sweden on business on Monday morning, but thanks for asking me. I *can* do something with you next weekend, though. Do you want to see a film or go for a walk? I know I'm working too hard at the moment, but I *can't* stop because this is my first big project, and my boss is watching me! I hope …

D
1 I can take you
2 I can make some food
3 Can I do anything
4 Can you take some books
5 Can I give them
6 Can I help
7 can you bring

E

TRANG Good evening, sir. Can I ~~can~~ help you?

JAMES Yes, I hope so. Can ~~you~~ I have a single room for two nights, please?

TRANG Of course, sir. I can ~~have~~ give you a room on the top floor, if you like. You'll have a great view!

JAMES That's fine, thanks.

TRANG Can you fill in this form, please?

JAMES Sure. Can I ~~buy~~ pay by credit card?

TRANG Of course, sir. No problem. Can ~~you~~ I see your card now, please?

JAMES Here it is. By the way, is it possible to use the internet here?

TRANG Certainly, sir. It's on the seventeenth floor. You can check your email there at any time, but you ~~can~~ can't send faxes after 10 p.m. Now, can I ~~show~~ see your passport, please?

F
1 Can I
2 I can
3 Can you
4 can you
5 You can't
6 I can't
7 Can you

14 *Could, was able to, managed to*

A
1 Could you tell us the way to the bus station, please?
2 Could we have some information about the trip to Ayers Rock, please?
3 Could you give us a timetable, please?
4 Could we have two return tickets for tomorrow, please?

B
Thanks very much for your message. I'm glad you're free at the weekend. We / drive to Newquay around ten in the morning. It takes about four hours from my house. I / bring some sandwiches. We'll be hungry before we arrive. In the afternoon we / cycle along Watergate Bay, perhaps. It's beautiful there. You / take some fantastic photos with your new camera! Then, in the evening, we / eat at 'Mickey's', if you like, the small fish restaurant in Newquay. It's very popular, so I / reserve a table today. I've booked two rooms at the Sandy Beach Hotel, of course. My friends Dave and Connie stay there every summer. They love it. Then, on Sunday we / visit Sheila and Michael. They live in Exeter, on our way home. What do you think?

C
1 I could run
2 We couldn't travel
3 some English people could go
4 we could only stay
5 You couldn't change
6 you could buy

WORD FOCUS 1 mirror 2 fan 3 lamp
4 coffee table 5 rug

D
1 We were able to finish
2 We managed to book
3 I couldn't sleep
4 I managed to buy
5 I was able to buy
6 I couldn't find
7 George managed to get

E
1 managed to
2 couldn't
3 could put
4 were able to
5 managed
6 could sleep
7 could you
8 could
9 could eat

F

JAMES Hello. Could we *see* Jo Corrigan, please?

NURSE I'm sorry, but you can't see her at the moment.

JAMES Really? When my wife was in hospital in January, we were *able* to visit her all the time.

NURSE That's right, but at the moment we don't have enough nurses on the ward.

JAMES I suppose we *could* come back later, Kay.

NURSE Could *you* come back in an hour, perhaps?

KAY But is she OK after the operation?

NURSE Oh yes. She *couldn't* eat her dinner last night, but she *managed* to have some breakfast this morning.

JAMES Don't worry, Kay. We could *have* a coffee in the hospital café. Thank you, nurse. We'll come back later.

15 *Should*

A
1 should have a holiday.
2 should talk to Uncle Jim.
3 shouldn't work all the time.
4 should all go to France for a couple of weeks.
5 shouldn't decide today.

B
1 you should think about food
2 you shouldn't eat take-aways
3 You should go to your local shops
4 you shouldn't study
5 you should make a timetable
6 you should go for a walk
7 You shouldn't go out every night
8 you should call me

C

SCOTT Hi, Eve. It's seven o'clock. Are you still at work?

EVE You / ring me at the office, Scott. I can't talk right now. *shouldn't*

SCOTT Have you got a headache again?

EVE Yes. It started this afternoon. I get a headache most days.

SCOTT Then you / see a doctor. *should*

EVE I know. I'll go next week.

SCOTT Good. Anyway, it's my birthday on Saturday. We / have a party. What do you think? *should*

EVE I'm not sure, Scott. I'm so busy at work at the moment.

SCOTT But you / work at the weekend! Life is too short. *shouldn't*

EVE Perhaps you're right. But if we have a party, we / cook anything. I'm too tired. *shouldn't*

SCOTT That's fine. We / ring Max. He could bring some great cold food from his shop. *should*

EVE OK, but we / invite too many people. It's too much work. *shouldn't*

SCOTT I understand. Don't worry, we'll have a quiet party!

WORD FOCUS **1** chest of drawers **2** wardrobe
3 sofa **4** armchair

D
1 should we buy an armchair
2 Should we try it?
3 Should we get it?
4 Should I ask that assistant?
5 Should we go to another shop?
6 Should I look on the internet instead?
7 do you think we should buy a wardrobe
8 should we get a coffee table

E
1 should I	5 should take
2 I visit	6 should go
3 shouldn't try	7 don't think
4 think you	8 you should

F

RACHEL You know that Despina wants to stay longer in Manchester, don't you, Sean?

SEAN Yes. I think it's a good idea for her. She / look for a room or a small flat.

RACHEL Yes, but she doesn't know the city very well, so / we help her? (*Despina arrives home.*)

DESPINA Hi Rachel, Sean! I've found a great photography course at the university, but my mother wants me to return to Greece. What / I do?

RACHEL How long is the course, Despina?

DESPINA Six months. Do you think I / find a different course in Athens?

RACHEL No, but I think you / speak to your mother today or tomorrow.

SEAN You / tell her that your course is only six months long, Despina, and that you'll go home for Christmas!

16 *Must* and *have to*

A **1** e   **2** b   **3** a   **4** d

B
1 I must speak	4 I have to meet
2 he has to sell	5 we must have
3 we must do	6 I have to go

C

FRAN Hi there, Tim! Nice to see you! How's life? Are you still painting?

TIM Yes, but I find a job this week, because I don't have any money. What about you? Are you OK? *I've got to find* 0

FRAN I'm OK, but my mother is ill, so I return to America. *I've got to return* 1

TIM Oh, I'm sorry. I hope she gets better.

FRAN I'm sure she will, but she listen to her doctor. She won't stay in bed! *She's got to listen* 2

TIM If you like, I'll give you one of my paintings to take to her.

FRAN That's kind, Tim, but you sell your paintings, if you want to make money! *you've got to sell* 3

TIM I know. Anyway, how are your brother and his wife? I haven't seen them recently.

FRAN They're fine, thanks. They've just bought a big, new house in the south of London, and now they find some furniture for it. *they've got to find* 4

TIM Do they want a big painting for their living room?

FRAN That's a good idea. I'll talk to them. But I go now. I'm going to buy my plane ticket this morning. *I've got to go* 5

D
1 don't have to	5 don't have to
2 don't have to	6 mustn't
3 mustn't	7 mustn't
4 don't have to	8 don't have to

E
1 Do we have to get the ticket at Waterloo?
2 Do we have to change in Paris?
3 Do we have to choose our date of return tomorrow?
4 Does he have to pay the full price?
5 Do I have to bring my own food?
6 Do we have to arrive early for our train?
7 Do we have to take our passports?

F
1 mustn't forget	5 have to take
2 have to feed	6 mustn't use
3 must eat	7 must ring
4 don't have to water	

17 The imperative

A
1 Give me your coat and gloves.
2 give her my best wishes.
3 Have a seat by the fire.
4 Help yourself to sugar and milk.
5 Look outside at the weather.
6 Try my fruitcake with your coffee.
7 Tell me all your news.

B
1 Give my love to your parents.
2 Give me a ring when you get there.
3 Have a good journey!
4 Enjoy your holiday!
5 Don't forget to email me.
6 Look after yourself.
7 Drive carefully.

C
1 spend a couple
2 turn right at
3 eat all
4 make yourself
5 see the famous
6 forget our
7 have a swim
8 relax in
9 enjoy it

D
1 Wait
2 tell
3 don't cross
4 turn
5 Don't go
6 follow
7 don't touch
8 enjoy

E
1 stay
2 be
3 Decide
4 Work
5 spend
6 go out
7 lose
8 have

F
1 Put your
2 Have a
3 Look at
4 Don't eat
5 But use
6 Don't go
7 help yourself
8 but ask
9 give Sally
10 be careful
11 don't burn
12 don't eat
13 put it
14 have some

18 *Have got* and *have, make, do,* and *get*

A
1 I've
2 she's
3 's got
4 hasn't
5 haven't
6 got
7 've got

B
1 Have you got a headache?
2 Have you got any friends at this college?
3 I haven't got any friends here
4 He's got lots of DVDs
5 My parents have got a farm there
6 Have you got any brothers or sisters?

C
I'm *having* a sandwich, because I'm bored. Can I come over? Sunday morning is always the same in my house. Mum *has* a bath. Dad *has* a walk. Sonia and Diana *have* breakfast together. Then Dad comes home and *has* a shower. Next, Mum and Dad *have* a cup of tea together. Then Dad reads the papers. Then Mum, Dad, Sonia and me *have* lunch together. Diana doesn't *have* lunch with us because she goes to the gym. Anyway, what are you doing at the moment? Are you *having* breakfast? Do you want to go for a swim or something?

D
1 Are you having fun
2 My sister is having a bad time
3 She's having a walk
4 She's having a game
5 He's having a swim

E
1 do
2 does
3 makes
4 making
5 does
6 made
7 made
8 doing

F
1 make do
2 do make
3 ✓
4 ✓
5 made got
6 ✓
7 made did
8 got did
9 ✓
10 do get

G
1 's got
2 getting
3 doing
4 doing
5 making
6 've got
7 gets
8 has
9 makes
10 getting

19 Verb + infinitive

A
1 needs to write
2 planning to do
3 decided to change
4 hoping to open
5 planning to create
6 wants to open
7 need to find
8 wanted to look
9 hoping to see

B **Tuesday:**

I'm learning *to dance* at the moment, and I went to my evening class. I tried *to hold* my partner's hand, but we were dancing too fast and we both fell over! Maggie took a photo on her phone. (hold, dance)

Wednesday:

I started *to cook* some spaghetti at home for my sister, but then the phone rang and it was Claire from New York, and I forgot *to watch* the spaghetti, and it burnt. Oh dear! I made a real mess. (cook, watch)

Thursday:

I remembered *to meet* Susie and Maisie in town for coffee, but I forgot the name of the café, so I spent twenty minutes looking for them. I managed *to text* Maisie in the end, though. (text, meet)

Friday:

I tried *to finish* an important essay for college on Friday morning, but my neighbour, Ross, is learning *to play* the drums and it was impossible to work, so I took a photo of him instead, and then I went to the college library. (finish, play)

C
1	to drive	3	to marry	5	to help
2	to answer	4	to say		

D
1 It's impossible to finish
2 It's easy to use the photocopier, and
3 It's hard to say that you've
4 It's interesting to visit other
5 It's crazy to go to
6 It's wrong to send an email if

E
1 I'm happy to be
2 I'm very pleased to meet
3 I'm surprised to see
4 we were sad to hear
5 he was afraid to
6 we're glad to welcome

F
1	pleased to hear	7	promise to visit
2	decided	8	I was surprised to hear
3	want	9	I'm afraid to buy
4	offered to	10	My parents have refused to give
5	difficult to	11	I hope to hear
6	trying		

20 Articles and nouns

A
1	an	4	a	7	an
2	a	5	a	8	a
3	an	6	an	9	an

B

ANNE Great! It's *a* big site, isn't it? How many people are there?

GREG Well, there are *a* hundred and eighty tents, so we have around six hundred people, I suppose. There's *a* small supermarket, and someone comes once *a* day to sell fresh fish.

SUE That's nice. Can we wash our clothes here?

GREG Sure. There's *a* washing machine in every shower house. It costs *a* euro *an* hour to use.

ANNE Is that *a* farm next to the site?

GREG That's right. You can buy apples there for two euros *a* kilo. We've got *a* little cinema as well. There's *a* film three times a week. Are you both students?

SUE I'm *a* student, but Anne is *an* actor.

GREG Really? Well, I'll show you where to go. Come on!

C
1	✔	5	a the	9	✔
2	the a	6	the an	10	✔
3	the a	7	a the	11	a the
4	✔	8	a the	12	a the

D
1	women	3	cities	5	watches
2	People	4	feet	6	lives

E
1	loaves	4	sandwiches	7	potatoes
2	pounds	5	fish	8	tomatoes
3	pence	6	pieces		

21 *There is, there are; this, that, these, and those*

A
1 there's a bus stop
2 there's another bus
3 is there a supermarket
4 there was a shop
5 there are four or five good supermarkets
6 is there a laundrette
7 is there anything
8 there isn't anything
9 there are two lectures

B Hi Glenn,

How are you? Are you looking forward to Christmas? I know that / are lots of things to do, but it's fun, isn't it? We had our Christmas lunch at work today, and / were thirty five of us in a very small Italian restaurant! Then I went shopping, but I didn't buy many presents, because / were thousands of people on Oxford Street. Anyway, / are only six days left until Christmas now. The kids will be excited this weekend. Perhaps I'll take them to the cinema – / are one or two new Christmas films at the moment. Do you want to bring your two boys if we go to something? Let me know. Bye for now!

WORD FOCUS   **1** omelette   **2** chillies   **3** sauce
4 herbs   **5** garlic

C
1 there's	**5** There are	**9** There are
2 There's	**6** Is there	**10** there isn't
3 There were	**7** there's	
4 there aren't	**8** Are there	

D
1 this	**3** that	**5** that
2 those	**4** these	

E
1 those	**7** those	**13** those
2 that	**8** That	**14** this
3 those	**9** those	**15** this
4 this	**10** This	**16** this
5 These	**11** this	
6 that	**12** that	

F
1 this	**5** there	**9** That
2 There	**6** that	**10** There
3 this	**7** There	
4 that	**8** This	

22 Countable and uncountable nouns

A
1 piece	**3** cup; spoonfuls
2 packet	**4** slices

B
1 traffic	**3** advice	**5** petrol
2 rain	**4** ice	**6** luggage

C
1 a	**7** toast	**13** homework
2 any	**8** –	**14** –
3 the	**9** pieces	**15** snow
4 A	**10** coffees	**16** the
5 bread	**11** some	
6 any	**12** some	

D
1 many	**3** much	**5** much
2 much	**4** many	**6** many

E
1 many	**4** much	**7** a lot of
2 a lot of	**5** much	
3 a lot of	**6** many	

F
1 a	**6** some	**11** many
2 a lot of	**7** some	**12** a lot of
3 some	**8** The	**13** a
4 any	**9** a	**14** some
5 much	**10** some	

23 Pronouns and possessives

A
1 he	**4** him	**7** she
2 her	**5** She	**8** her
3 them	**6** We	**9** They

B
1 It's	**5** It's	**9** it
2 it's	**6** it	**10** It's
3 it	**7** us	**11** it
4 you	**8** me	**12** It's

C Ladies and gentlemen, can I ask / to sit down for a moment, please? I'd like to talk to / for a minute before you go. Thank you. I hope that / will agree with me that we've had an interesting day. When / look at paintings carefully, you understand more about the people around you, don't you ? And as you relax at home tomorrow, perhaps / will think again about some of the beautiful paintings you've studied today. After all, paintings tell you stories about yourselves, your friends and your families. I want to ask you, before / go, to look at one final painting, one of my favourites. What do / think about when / see it? Look at this successful man. Look at the flowers. What do / see? I won't give you the answers. I don't have the answers, anyway. But isn't it true that when you get older, / understand that some things are important, and some things aren't important? Thank / for coming.

D
1 her	**5** my	**9** your
2 Her	**6** their	**10** your
3 your	**7** our	
4 your	**8** his	

E
1 my	**5** your	**9** his
2 yours	**6** my	**10** hers
3 mine	**7** yours	**11** your
4 my	**8** mine	

F

Hi Nora,

Tom left this morning but her *his* books are still here! I'll text him tomorrow. I asked Emily for hers *her* key to the flat. But I'm not sure if the blue cups in the kitchen are ours *our* cups or theirs – you forget these things when he *you* live with people for a long time, don't you? By the way, your Mum rang this morning. She's going to visit we *us* at the weekend. Is it sunny in Mumbai? I don't know what time he *it* is in India, but I'm going to bed here! Bye!

Hi Brian,

Thanks for your message. Its *It's* Monday morning in Mumbai. I've just washed the *my* hair, and I'm looking out of the window. There's a small bird in the hotel garden, and it's singing an Indian song! Anyway, I'm travelling to Delhi later today. It's about two hours by plane. The name of mine *my* hotel in Delhi is The Metropolitan. I hope things are OK now at the flat. Did you text Tom? I think some of those books are my *mine*, actually. And the blue cups are our *ours*! Your sister gave them to us. And is my mother arriving on Friday or Saturday? Bye for now!

24 Possessives (2)

A
1	Sabino's shoes	5	men's toilets
2	Lucas's coat	6	Thomas's cup
3	your sister's sandwich	7	children's coats
4	boys' football		

WORD FOCUS **A** newsagent's **B** greengrocer's **C** baker's **D** optician's **E** butcher's **F** chemist's **G** florist's

B
1	baker's	3	chemist's	5	butcher's
2	newsagent's	4	optician's		

C
Turkey*'s* Prime Minister arrives in Uganda at the beginning of the Africa Trade Talks
After today*'s* meeting, Shell*'s* Chief Executive refuses to answer questions from journalists. Film star says that the Government*'s* idea for a new airport is wrong
A small plane lands on the top of a mountain in Peru to help three Australian tourists
No tickets left for next month*'s* concerts by the Philadelphia Orchestra at New York*'s* Carnegie Hall

D
1	friends of mine	4	flatmate of hers
2	friend of my Dad's	5	colleague of Paul's
3	schoolfriend of ours	6	a good idea of mine

WORD FOCUS **1** a pearl necklace **2** a diamond ring **3** a gold bracelet **4** an earring **5** a gold ring

E
1	✓	6	✓
2	yesterday's evening news	7	✓
3	guests' coats	8	next month's big sale
4	✓	9	London's number one
5	friend of mine		

F

MANDY Hi, Toby! How are you? How are things going?

TOBY Well, Mandy. There's not much happening really. My brother *brother's* wife, Shelly, is going to have her fifth baby in June. The friend's other four are girls, so she's hoping for a boy. Then, my best friend *friend's* son has decided to go and live in India. He wants to make carpets, I think. And then, do you remember my sisters? Kate and Mirabelle? They have a florist *florist's* in Birmingham. Well, Kate *Kate's* boss won two million pounds in last week *week's* lottery, and she gave Kate a hundred thousand pounds, and now Kate and Mirabelle are going to travel around the world, and my dad is going to buy my sister *sisters'* shop. What about you? Any news?

MANDY No, my life is really boring at the moment. I've just spent half an hour at the dentist *dentist's*. That's not very interesting, is it? And I've just been to the shoe shop as well and changed a pair of Freddie *Freddie's* shoes, because they were too small. And then Carly, a friend of mine, is going to Spain on holiday next week. I think that's all. No, wait a moment. Do you remember my parent *parents'* house in Cornwall?

TOBY Yes?

MANDY Well, I've got a photo of it. Would you like to see it?

25 Adjectives

A(i) Hi Milly, I can come round to your house in the evening, but I'm shopping during the day. to. I'm looking for a <u>white</u> jacket to wear to wear with my <u>blue</u> and <u>green</u> dress at Julie's wedding. I also want two <u>square</u> Japanese plates, some <u>red</u> roses, a <u>small</u>, <u>round</u> lamp, and a <u>short</u> <u>yellow</u> skirt for my holiday. It's a <u>long</u> list, isn't it? I'd better go! See you later, Kate.

(ii) Colour adjectives: white blue green red yellow
Size adjectives: small short long
Shape adjectives: square round

WORD FOCUS **1** high **2** wide **3** huge **4** fat **5** thin **6** tall **7** short

B
1	blue and red	4	huge house	7	yellow dress
2	tall	5	high	8	green table
3	long blonde	6	tiny black and		

C Wouldn't you like to live in a nice town with two beautiful small parks and a huge round lake? In our new town the trees are tall, and the streets are wide. Make a journey to Springville. We'll give you a big welcome when you arrive.

D 1 ~~Scottish wonderful~~ wonderful Scottish
2 ~~old horrible~~ horrible old
3 ~~fantastic little~~ ✓
4 ~~Portuguese great~~ great Portuguese

E 1 tall Welsh
2 beautiful old silk
3 narrow wooden
4 fantastic, red and green, Turkish
5 wide silver

F
1	seems	4	look	7	tastes	
2	sounds	5	feels			
3	smells	6	looks			

26 Comparative and superlative adjectives

A
1	cheaper	6	thinner
2	heavier	7	more powerful
3	lighter	8	faster
4	wider	9	more expensive
5	bigger	10	better

B
1	more famous	7	smaller
2	noisier	8	more beautiful
3	wetter	9	friendlier
4	older	10	richer
5	busier	11	cleaner
6	than	12	more interesting

C 1 He's worse than
2 He's fatter
3 Mr Samson's / Mr Samson is nicer and funnier
4 he's more intelligent
5 Is it more difficult than
6 I think I'm luckier
7 am I prettier than
8 You're sillier than
9 You're hungrier than
10 it's colder

D
1	best	6	most expensive
2	biggest	7	most peaceful
3	most beautiful	8	nicest
4	warmest	9	most famous
5	sunniest		

E
1	friendlier	4	ever	7	expensive
2	than	5	most	8	the
3	nearer	6	of	9	in

F
1	strongest	6	youngest
2	better	7	best
3	tallest	8	older
4	weaker	9	worst
5	more difficult	10	best

27 Adverbs of manner

A
1	quietly	4	carefully	7	slowly
2	correctly	5	properly	8	easily
3	heavily	6	noisily		

B
1	correctly	3	slowly	5	quietly
2	loudly	4	politely	6	beautifully

C … We walked *quickly* into the town centre, and I took them to the market. We had a really good time there. Then we walked *slowly* to the cathedral. But there was one problem in the cathedral. One of the tourists asked a question *loudly*, and a tall woman said something *angrily*. But it was OK in the end. We had a good visit. Unfortunately, it rained *heavily* on the way back to the bus station, but most of the group had umbrellas!

D … She plays the piano very *well*, too. I'm not very good at music, as you know, but I can cook quite *well*, and I can paint *well*, so I'm lucky, aren't I? Anyway, do you want to meet later today? I don't really want to go to Sammy's party this evening. I didn't sleep very *well* last night, so I feel tired today. We could go to that new Japanese restaurant on Dean Street. Greg says that it's doing *well*. Hope to hear from you later.

E
1	fast	4	early	7	early
2	hard	5	fast		
3	hard	6	late		

F
BEN	There's a skiing holiday here for two in Switzerland for £50, if we leave *early* in the morning.
BEN	Yes, it snowed *hard* last week in Austria and Switzerland.
CANDY	Can we pack *quickly* enough? It's nine o'clock already.
BEN	I think so. But there is one problem. I ski very *badly*, I'm afraid.
CANDY	Oh. Well, there will be a ski school. I'm sure you'll learn *fast*.
CANDY	You have to move *correctly*. That's the important thing.
BEN	And you have to turn *slowly*, don't you?

28 Adverbs of degree

A
1. My new colleague Simon is very friendly
2. I was late for a really important meeting
3. I really need another coffee
4. She was very angry
5. I really love weekends
6. it's got to be very cheap
7. I really hope that you find one

B
1. I was fairly lucky
2. I got a flat quite quickly
3. He's pretty funny
4. I quite like the food here
5. the bus service is quite good
6. Our teachers are fairly young
7. and it's pretty cold here
8. but they were quite expensive

C
1. Sure. August would be quite/very good, I think.
2. No, that's late, Charlie. It's a summer car, I know, but consumers buy cars fairly/really early.
3. Alright, but that's pretty/very soon. We need to finish the TV ad.
4. I saw the idea for the advert yesterday, Charlie. It's quite/very serious, isn't it?
5. Sure, they'll remember it, Charlie. It's fairly/very beautiful.
6. But it's also really/pretty sad. My question is: do we want a sad ad?
7. But we've got Sam Taylor in the ad. He's quite/really famous!
8. George is right. Charlie, I'd like you and George to work together on this. Is that OK? I think you could be fairly/very special together. What do you think?

D
1	quite	5	pretty	9	pretty
2	really	6	quite	10	really
3	fairly	7	Quite		
4	quite	8	really		

E
1	✓	4	very really	7	fairly quite
2	✓	5	✓	8	very really
3	pretty quite	6	✓	9	✓

F

MAN: First of all, it's quite a friendly place, in fact. For example, there are quite a lot of cafés where people go with colleagues for coffee, lunch etc. That's very nice.

WOMAN: And I suppose you see quite a lot of famous people. The headquarters building of the BBC is fairly close to Oxford Circus.

MAN: Yes, but I'm more interested in the shops. They're quite expensive, but can get any new CD or DVD immediately!

WOMAN: So are there any problems here?

MAN: Yes. The underground is really busy in the morning, but if you drive to work, it's pretty hard to find a parking space! Sometimes I arrive very early at work, but it's still fairly busy.

WOMAN: Well, thanks very much for your time.

29 Prepositions

A
1	at	3	in	5	on
2	on	4	on	6	in

B
1	at the office	4	at the newsagent's
2	at the airport	5	in bed
3	at the dentist's		

C
1	under	4	on	7	in
2	in	5	in		
3	above	6	at		

D

Hi Alex,

Can we meet today? I'm flying to Mumbai on Friday, and I'd like to talk to you about the trip. Who did you meet when you went there ~~on~~ in May last year? My trip to Mumbai is quite short. I'll be back on Thursday ~~in~~ next week. I'm trying to fix some meetings ~~at~~ in the moment, but I need your help! Anyway, I'm in a meeting ~~on~~ this morning until from ten till eleven, but we could meet ~~on~~ at lunch, if you like. I'm going to visit our Bristol office ~~in~~ this afternoon, so could we have an early lunch at ~~in~~ twelve o' clock perhaps? If that's not possible, maybe we could meet ~~on~~ in the evening? I hope to hear from you soon.

E
1	in	6	at	11	At
2	in	7	in	12	In
3	at	8	on	13	under
4	till	9	At	14	above
5	behind	10	in	15	at

F
1	on	5	in	9	on
2	in	6	under	10	on
3	until	7	at	11	this
4	at	8	from	12	at

30 Conjunctions

A   Hi Linda,

I've just got back from Scotland. It was fun, / it was also very tiring! It rained every day, of course, / the mountains were beautiful. We camped near in the Highlands near Inverness. The kids loved the campsite, / it was pretty cold at night! We bought most of our food at the campsite shop. It took a long time to get our meals ready in the evening, / they tasted delicious. After dinner the kids played games, and I read my book. I'm sure we'll return to the campsite one day, / next time we'll go in August, not April!

Best wishes, Maggie

B

1	or a cup	3	or a TV	5	or read a
2	or any sugar	4	or a quiz		

C   Our kids need to eat healthy food, *but* we know they often prefer burgers, pizzas *and* chips. Experts say that we should all – kids *and* adults – eat five portions of fruit *or* vegetables every day, if we can. This may be a good idea, *but* what do we do when our kids say 'no'? That's the question. You can give your kid a piece of fruit – a banana or an apple *or* a pear – to take to school, *but* you won't be there at lunchtime! Last week I put an apple in my son's lunch box every day, *and* he took it to school, *but* then he brought it home again, *and* said, 'I wasn't hungry, Mum.' If you've got any good ideas, write to me *or* email me, and we'll put your letter in the magazine.

D

1	and	5	but
2	but	6	and
3	or	7	and
4	and	8	and

E

1	so	3	because	5	Because
2	so	4	so	6	so

F
1   I'm going to a wedding.
2   I could work on Sunday afternoon.
3   her mother is ill.
4   I need to work in the library on Thursday.
5   you could leave early then.
6   I'm sure we'll sell lots of them.
7   we'll close the shop for tonight.

G

1	and	5	but	9	because
2	so	6	and	10	and
3	but	7	so		
4	because	8	or		

Answer key Over to you

01 *Be*: Present simple

I'm Daniel and I'm from Frankfurt. I'm 30 years old and I'm a doctor. What's your job? My sister is younger than me and she's a teacher. Our parents are from Munich. Munich is in the south of Germany. Their house is a lovely old building and they are happy to live there. It's a beautiful day here today in Frankfurt, but it's cold. Is it sunny where you are?

Best wishes,

Daniel

02 Present simple

1	speak	3	go	5	love
2	play	4	eat	6	don't like

My friend Carlos comes from Burgos in the north of Spain. He speaks Spanish and English. He goes to the gym every week, and he buys two or three new CDs at the weekends. He sometimes goes skiing in the Pyrenees. He likes pizzas and pop concerts, but he doesn't like homework.

03 Present continuous

MIKE	Dina? It's Mike here. What are you doing?
DINA	I'm sitting in the garden. What about you?
MIKE	I'm listening to a CD. Is Dan in?
DINA	No, he's spending the weekend in Scotland.
MIKE	How is he, anyway?
DINA	He's OK, but he's working too hard. How are you?
MIKE	Not bad, thanks. I'm enjoying life at college. And you?
DINA	Fine. I'm learning French again, but it isn't easy.

04 Present simple and present continuous

Hi Mark!
I come from Bangkok. I live with my parents, and I teach English in a local school. I play basketball and tennis at the weekends, and I cook Thai food for my friends every week. My parents are visiting my grandmother in the north of Thailand at the moment, so I'm looking after myself. I'm learning to drive this year. I like reading and I love swimming in the sea, but I don't like English grammar!
Best wishes, Bo

05 Present simple and present continuous questions

- When does Buckingham Palace open in the morning?
- Have you got any information about the Tower of London?
- Where is the Globe Theatre, please?
- Does the British Museum open every day?
- Have you got a map of the City of London?
- Does the underground go to Hampton Court Palace?

06 Past simple

1   I got up early on Saturday morning, but I didn't do very much. In the afternoon, I went into town. I met a couple of friends, and we did some shopping. We didn't buy very much, but we had a good time. In the evening, I saw a film at our local cinema. Afterwards, we had a pizza and I took a taxi home. On Sunday morning, I played football in the park. In the afternoon, I did some work for college, and then I watched TV for a few hours.

In 2005, I visited my brother in America. First, I flew to Seattle. Then my brother and I travelled together to California. We spent a week in Los Angeles. Then we drove to the Grand Canyon. It was fantastic! We camped for a few days in the Rocky Mountains. Afterwards, we flew from Denver to New York, and we met some friends there. They showed us the Statue of Liberty and Macey's and Central Park and all those things. Finally, I took the plane back to London, and my brother returned to Seattle.

2   Where were you born?
Did you write stories at school?
Did you go to university?
What did you study?
What did you do after university?
When did you write you first book?

Was your first book successful?

07 Past continuous

Tuesday 24 July:
I went to work by bus. While I was walking along Oxford Street on the way to the office, I met a colleague, Bill, and we had breakfast together. I was working hard on the computer all morning, so at lunchtime I went for a walk in Regent's Park. It was a sunny day. People were sitting on the grass. In the afternoon, I went to two long meetings. I was talking to Bill at the end of the second meeting when my brother rang. He said he was in London for two days on business. We had a meal together in the evening.

08 Present perfect

- I've had four cups of coffee.
- I've been to the supermarket.
- I've spoken to my brother on the phone.

- I've never been to Morocco.
- I've never played golf.
- I haven't swum in the Red Sea.

- Roger Federer has won Wimbledon again.
- It has rained every day.
- The new Prime Minister has answered questions in Parliament.

- Have you ever made a film in London?
- Have you ever met Brad Pitt?
- Have you ever kissed Julia Roberts?

09 Past simple and present perfect

Dear Sir/Madam,

I'm interested in becoming a Saturday assistant at 'Coffee Time'. I've never worked in a coffee shop, but I was a waiter in a restaurant in Italy last summer, and I cleaned tables, too. I also worked in a clothes shop two years ago on Oxford Street in London. I've studied English for six years, and I've lived in London for three months. I started my English course two months ago at the Shakespeare School of English, and I've made good progress. Last week I passed my class test with 80%. I enjoy talking and listening to customers.

I look forward to hearing from you.

Yours faithfully,

10 The future with *going to*

Hi Christine,

Thanks for your message. My weekend is quite busy. On Saturday morning, I'm going to go into town. I want to buy some new CDs. I'm going to meet Steve at lunchtime, and we're going to play tennis in the afternoon. I'm not going to go out on Saturday night, but I'm going to take the train to Brighton on Sunday morning. My girlfriend and I are going to spend the day by the sea. It's going to be a good weekend! Are you going to work on Saturday as usual? Are you going to see Mike on Saturday evening? Email me again soon!

Dave

11 The future with *will* and *shall*

MATT	Di? It's Mike here. Shall we go out tonight?
DI	Sure. We had a meal last week, so shall we go to the cinema this time?
MATT	OK. What film shall we see?
DI	Well, I think the new film with Kiefer Sutherland will be good.
MATT	Great. When does the film start?
DI	I don't know. I'll phone the cinema, and call you back.
MATT	Good. Do you think the cinema will be busy?
DI	Perhaps. Shall I book tickets on the phone?
MATT	I think that's a good idea.
DI	OK. I'll talk to you again in a moment.
MATT	Fine. Bye!

12 Questions

WHAT	What sort of books do you like?
WHAT	What do you do on Saturday nights?
WHAT	What sort of job do you do?
HOW	How often do you play sports?
HOW	How far do you travel to work?
HOW	How many books do you read every month?
WHERE	Where are you going this morning?
WHERE	Where do you do your shopping?
WHERE	Where do you go on holiday?
WHEN	When do you normally get up?
WHEN	When do you finish work?
WHEN	When do you go on holiday?

13 *Can*

Dear Mr Spurling,

I would like to apply for the post of Student Assistant. I can swim and I can play football, tennis and basketball. I can also sing one or two English songs. I can't dance, but I can play the guitar. I often go for long walks with friends in the countryside, and I can tell the names of many flowers and trees. I can also drive, and I can cook simple meals. Unfortunately, I can't work for you in the last week of July, because I need to finish a university project. Can I start on 1 August? I can work an extra week after the end of the camp, if you need me.

Yours sincerely,

John Smith

14 *Could, was able to, managed to*

1 • Could I have an alarm call at seven in the morning, please?
 • Could I have some chicken sandwiches in my room, please?
 • Could I check my email, please?
 • Could I reserve a table for three for tomorrow night, please?
 • Could I have a swim in the pool, please?
 • Could you call me a taxi, please?

2 See B in unit 14.

15 *Should*

See the second email in exercise E.

16 *Must* and *have to*

1 • You must see the famous sights in London, for example, Buckingham Palace and Big Ben.
 • You must visit one or two of the hitorical English cities like Bath, Oxford and York.
 • You must spend a few days in Scotland, because it's a beautiful country.

2 • I have to get up at seven in the morning to go to work, but I don't have to work late – I normally finish at five.
 • I have to take my mother's dog for a walk every day.
 • I don't have to do any work in the garden, because we live in a flat!
 • I have to cook dinner on Friday evenings, but I don't have to wash up.

17 The imperative

 • Visit the big museums - they're normally free.
 • Take a boat trip on the Thames. You'll get some great views of London!
 • Don't take taxis everywhere, because they're expensive.
 • Try to find a budget hotel on the internet before you arrive.
 • Enjoy the parks. Often you can walk through them on your way to a gallery or the shops.
 • Don't forget to buy a travel card. You'll save money on the tubes and buses.

18 *Have got* and *have*; *make, do,* and *get*

1 • I've got a new computer.
 • I've got four Metallica CDs.
 • I've got two brothers.
 • I've got an aunt in Scotland.
 • I've got black hair.
 • My dad's got a big nose.

2 • My brother sometimes does the washing-up.
 • We have breakfast at 7 a.m.
 • I often get an English newspaper.
 • My dad is making dinner.
 • Steve is having a good time on holiday.
 • Maria is doing very well at college.

19 Verb + infinitive

Saturday 15 November:
I tried to go to the gym on Monday, but I got up too late. I'll try to go on Monday and Wednesday next week. On Tuesday, I bought a book on South America. I'm planning to visit Brazil in the summer. On Wednesday, Sara offered to buy me dinner. (I helped her in her garden last week.) I went to a Portuguese class on Thursday, but it's difficult to learn a new language in the evening, when you're tired. On Friday, I was surprised to get an email from my American friend, Stu. He's coming to England next month.

20 Articles and nouns

1 See exercise B

2 We went to Borough Market yesterday. There were a lot of people there. Josie bought two brown loaves. Then I bought some sandwiches because we were hungry, and Josie bought two pieces of haddock at the fishmonger's. The woman was very friendly. Finally, I bought some potatoes and tomatoes at the greengrocer's. It was a good trip. In the evening we had fish and chips with a tomato salad.

21 *There is, there are, this, that, these* and *those*

Hi Matt,
Do you want to do something this evening? There's a new swimming pool in the town centre. We could go there for an hour. Do you remember that afternoon at the old pool? The water was so cold. I hope this new pool is better. Or we could go to the Café Mozart. There were a lot of people there last night. It was fun. Give me a ring later. Are there any things that you want to do? Bye for now.
Sally

22 Countable and uncountable nouns

'Hi Sarah! This is Paul here. Thanks for going to the supermarket. We need some milk, and we need two loaves of bread. Also, we haven't got any apples or oranges, and we haven't got any rice. And we need some chicken for the weekend, and we haven't got any pasta! I think that's everything. See you later.'

23 Pronouns and possessives

Hi Dave,

How are you? It's raining here in Rome. I'm writing this email on my new laptop. I hope you get it! Gina, one of my best friends, is going to London next week. It's her first trip to England. Can I give her your phone number? Hers is 07896 456321. By the way, have you seen a pair of brown gloves? If you have, they're mine! I'm sure I left them in your house in December. Bye for now!

Silvano

24 Possessives (2)

Hi Phoebe,

I hope you're well. An old schoolfriend of mine is visiting me this next week. We're going to borrow my sister's car and drive to a colleague's flat by the sea. I think it will be nice. Then, next month my brother and I are flying to my parents' house in France. They bought it last year. My brother's new girlfriend is coming, too.

Anyway, that's all for now. I hope to hear your news soon!

25 Adjectives

Dear Donna,

I'm staying in a great little hotel in Portugal. The sun feels fantastic after the rain in Manchester. There's a friendly Spanish couple in the room next to me. We had a nice meal together yesterday evening. You would love it here – you can buy silver and gold jewellery at the market on Tuesdays and Fridays.

See you soon!

Frances

26 Comparative and superlative adjectives

1   Bath is my home town. It's close to Bristol. Bristol is a much bigger, noisier city, but the centre of Bath is older and prettier. Hundreds of tourists visit Bath in the summer.

2   The Lake District is one of the most beautiful parts of the UK. It's the best place for nice, long walks near lakes and mountains. August is the busiest time, so it's better to visit in June, for example, or September. The prettiest little town is Ambleside, in my opinion. It's close to Lake Windermere, the biggest of the lakes.

27 Adverbs of manner

1   •   I can swim well.
    •   I can play the piano well.
    •   I cook quite well.
    •   I write essays quite well.
    •   I don't speak Spanish very well.
    •   I can't sing or dance very well.

2   •   My brother works very hard for his company.
    •   My friend Mike eats noisily.
    •   My uncle talks very quietly.
    •   My teacher speaks very clearly.

28 Adverbs of degree

See exercise E for an example.

29 Prepositions

Hi Tony,

Could we meet soon? I can't meet today. I'm the only person in the office. Dave is in hospital, and Brenda is at home, because her son is ill. Pete is in New York at a conference. Sally is at college. She studies business management one day every week. So could we meet tomorrow? I'm free in the afternoon. Shall we meet at three o'clock? I hope to hear from you soon.

30 Conjunctions

Dear Ms Brown,

I would like to apply for the post of assistant for your Summer School. I'm twenty two years old, and I live in Spain. I'm looking for an interesting and useful summer job before I start work for a travel company in September. I will finish university in June this year. I am studying languages (French, English and Italian) because I want to work in different countries during my career. I have a driving licence, and I can use computers. I haven't done many jobs, but I have worked for a travel agent's in Madrid as part of my university course. I've been to Britain many times, so I believe I can help your students with their trips. I am happy, of course, to send you my CV or references from my university.

Best wishes,

Carmen Nieto

Index